BETTER
COLLEGE
READING

BETTER COLLEGE READING

Marvin S. Zuckerman and Gerald F. Wojcik

Los Angeles Valley College

HarperCollins*Publishers*

Sponsoring Editor: Phillip Leininger
Project Editor: Eleanor Castellano
Designer: Ben Kann
Production: Delia Tedoff
Compositor: TriStar Graphics
Printer and Binder: R. R. Donnelley & Sons Company
Art Studio: Vantage Art, Inc.

BETTER COLLEGE READING

Library of Congress Cataloging in Publication Data

Zuckerman, Marvin S.
  Better college reading.

  Includes index.
  1. College readers.   I. Wojcik, Gerald F.   II. Title.
PE1417.Z82   1984   428.6   83-18385
ISBN 0-06-047394-0

Contents

Contents

Alternate Contents

(Arranged by Rhetorical Type*)

---

* The selection listed first and in boldface contains the best example(s) of the type.

SUMMARY

EXAMPLES/DETAILS

All articles contain numerous examples and details.

Preface

Better College Reading aims to intrigue and improve. It intrigues by gathering in one place thirty relatively short articles—culled from scores of mass media sources—on lively, interesting subjects, ranging from how movie stunt men work, to the awakening of prejudice in children, to police decoys, to the importance of the name one bears, to man-hunters in Australia, to the difficulties facing an ambitious *Chicana,* to honesty, robotics, and speed reading (to name just nine).

It improves by arranging the articles according to length and difficulty and by providing exercises and scorekeeping devices designed to challenge the student to enlarge his/her vocabulary and to increase his/her reading-speed and comprehension.

The selections in *Better College Reading* also provide good models for students struggling to write beginning short compositions in the various modes traditionally used in beginning writing classes (e.g.,description, narration, classification and division, comparison and contrast—see "Alternate Contents"). Each article is followed not only by objective questions but by suggestions for writing and questions designed to stimulate thought and discussion.

The thirty articles range in length from 350 to 2500 words, each succeeding article a little longer than the one preceding it. The exercises grow in length and difficulty to match the length and difficulty of the articles: the exercises for Selections 11 through 20 are longer and more difficult than those for Selections 1 through 10; and those from 21 through 30 are longer and more difficult than those for 11 through 20.

The articles include words ranging from the somewhat familiar *decoy* and *baffled* to the relatively abstruse *androgynous, odyssey,* and *anachronism.* The vocabulary exercises following each article present some of the more difficult words in the context of their sentences. The student should look these words up in the dictionary and, after selecting the appropriate definition from the several to be found for any given word, write it in the blank provided. This will help the student understand the article better and help fix those words in his/her memory. The student should also add to the list other unlisted words from the article that are unfamiliar to him/her. (The midlength–to–longer articles should have several of these.) An index of all the vocabulary words presented in all thirty articles is provided at the end of the book.

The other exercises—the true/false, completion, and multiple choice questions—are meant to test (a) basic understanding of what has been read and (b) retention of significant detail.

Since they test *overall* comprehension of the main idea of a selection, as well as its author's underlying aim, the final "theme" and "purpose" questions are more heavily weighted.

The "Overall Reading Score" chart at the end of each selection represents a useful innovation. The chart eliminates cumbersome reckoning of reading rates or looking up of words–per–minute in the back of the book. The student has only to keep track of how long it took to read the selection: the left-hand column will then automatically show his/her reading rate and whether it is "average" or "above average," and so forth. Then, by connecting with any straightedge the place on the left-hand reading-rate column with the place on the right-hand comprehension-and-retention column, the chart will automatically average and translate both scores into an overall "reading success" placement. The back of the book provides three simple graphs for the student to chart his/her progress from chapter to chapter.

Better College Reading was designed with the specific needs of beginning and/or remedial students in mind. An anthology with selections by Thoreau, Orwell, Thurber, and E. B. White will not do for such students. These students need something else; namely, short, journalistic pieces, well written and current, but not too topical. The pieces are not so difficult as to dishearten the students, nor yet so easy as to leave them unchallenged.

The subjects of the pieces chosen touch the lives and feelings of contemporary college students. They are arranged according to their degree of challenge—according to their level of vocabulary, complexity of thought, syntactical sophistication, and length. The result is a reader that is growth-producing, one that constantly probes the student's ability to understand, continually stretching his/her capacity to read a little faster, comprehend a little more, read articles just a little longer, with just a few more "vocabulary words," and a bit more complexity.

We would like to thank, first of all, our students at Los Angeles Valley College for giving us insight into what kind of a reader they (and others like them) needed. Thanks go to our families for their patience with our temperaments and time away to "do the book"; special thanks to Ingrid Horowitz for an intelligent, fast, and reliable typing and critiquing job; thanks to Ann Rayner Harootyan for help with the graphs; thanks to Margarita Vasquez and Julie Avery for cutting and pasting and other such essential chores; and finally, thanks to Marie Enders and George Gath for first believing in the book.

We have worked hard to put together a book that will help students grow and learn. We dedicate *Better College Reading* to them.

Marvin S. Zuckerman

Gerald F. Wojcik

Selection 1

Sipping Fermented Sap Sends Butterflies, Birds on a Binge

WASHINGTON (UPI)—Drunken butterflies? Potted parrots? Hung over hummingbirds?

Not a pretty thought, but according to *Smithsonian Magazine,* intoxication among butterflies is fairly common. As it is among hummingbirds, bees, fruit bats and woodpeckers. Not to mention chickadees, parrots, ruffed grouse and cedar waxwings.

A report on whistle-wetting among man's feathered friends, and a few furry ones as well, is contained in a recent issue of the Smithsonian Institution publication.

"The facts are that virtually any plant material containing sugar—fruits, berries, sap, nectar—can under certain circumstances ferment into tolerably high-proof booze, and creatures of all kinds occasionally get a big kick out of their close encounters with it," writes the author, John V. Dennis.

"In Australia, parrots imbibe the rich nectar of eucalyptus flowers till they fall out of the trees," he writes. "Robins and cedar waxwings, gobbling up old apples, will flutter wildly, fall and lie on their backs with legs kicking."

And what of fruit bats after a night of sipping fermented coconut milk?

One observer quoted by Dennis has them "returning home in the early morning in a state of extreme and riotous intoxication, or in being found the next day at the foot of the trees, sleeping off the effects of their midnight debauch."

Dennis came across an account in the magazine *Bird-Lore* of birds, insects and small mammals drinking fermented tree sap from holes drilled by woodpeckers.

"Hummingbirds that had been imbibing too freely were performing strange aerial acrobatics and seemed totally demoralized," he relates.

Source: Los Angeles Times, July 5, 1979. Reprinted by permission of United Press International.

Anyone who has ever seen a sober hummingbird probably can readily imagine what the inebriated stunt flying might be like.

Do birds that have one too many fermented berries suffer hangovers or delirium tremens? Dennis says there is no clear-cut evidence on that point. There is, however, no doubt that an avian toot can spell trouble.

"Birds that have overindulged fly into plate-glass windows, often with fatal results, or, fluttering on the ground, fall prey to teetotaling cats," he reports.

And bees, "which lead otherwise exemplary lives, occasionally get so drunk that they fall stupefied from the flowers on which they feed and are then decapitated by predatory wasps."

No. of Words: 350

Reading Time: _____

Selection 1

*Sipping Fermented Sap Sends Butterflies,
Birds on a Binge*

VOCABULARY BUILDING

*Below are several words used in this article. They are presented in the
context of the sentences or phrases in which they occur. If you are unsure
of their meanings and cannot define them from the context, look them up
in the dictionary. Spaces are provided for additional unfamiliar words
from the article to add to your vocabulary.*

1. "One observer . . . has them 'returning home . . . in a state of extreme
   and *riotous intoxication,* or in being found the next day . . . sleeping
   off the effects of their midnight *debauch.*'"

   riotous: *funny people, something very funny*

   intoxication: *make drunk, poison by alcohol*

   debauch: *wild party, cant remember what happened*

2. "'Hummingbirds that had been *imbibing* too freely were performing
   strange *aerial* acrobatics and seemed totally *demoralized.*'"

   imbibing: *drinking*

   aerial: *antenna, like air, high up*

   demoralized: *corrupt, weaken morals, out of control*

3. "Anyone who has ever seen a sober hummingbird probably can readily imagine what the *inebriated* stunt flying might be like."

   inebriated: _____

4. "And bees, 'which lead otherwise *exemplary* lives, occasionally get so
   drunk that they fall *stupefied* from the flowers . . . and are then *decapitated* by *predatory* wasps.'"

   exemplary: *model, sample, good example*

   stupefied: *shock, stuped, made stuped
   from someone else*

3

decapitated: *cut off head*

predatory: *exploding others, hunter*

5. _____ : _____

6. _____ : _____

7. _____ : _____

8. _____ : _____

9. _____ : _____

10. _____ : _____

RETENTION AND COMPREHENSION

A. True/False (1 point each)

1. Intoxication among butterflies is very rare.

    1. T _____ F _____

2. Bees, when drunk, will decapitate predatory wasps.

    2. T _____ F _____

B. Completion (3 points each)

3. Any plant material containing sugar can, under certain circumstances, _____ into tolerably high-proof booze.

    3. _____

4. Birds that have overindulged can fly into _____.

    4. _____

C. Multiple Choice (2 points each)

5. Parrots imbibe the rich nectar of (a) old apples, (b) coconut milk, (c) eucalyptus flowers, (d) fermented tree sap.

    5. _____

6. There is no clear-cut evidence that birds who overindulge (a) have hangovers, (b) fall prey to teetotaling cats, (c) perform strange aerial acrobatics, (d) fly into plate glass windows.

    6. _____

7. Fruit bats sip (a) the blood of birds that have eaten fruit, (b) fermented coconut milk, (c) fermented tree sap, (d) fermented apple juice.

    7. _____

8. The information in this article first appeared in a report in (a) the *New York Times,* (b) *Our Fine-Feathered Friends,* (c) *Sunset Magazine,* (d) *Smithsonian Magazine.*

8. _____

D. Thematic *(5 points)*

9. Which statement *best* expresses the theme (*main* idea) of the article?
   (*a*) Birds and insects sometimes get drunk.
   (*b*) Birds and insects often act stupefied.
   (*c*) Avian toots can spell trouble.
   (*d*) Birds and insects also enjoy imbibing alcohol.

9. _____

E. Purpose *(4 points)*

10. The author's *chief* purpose is
   (*a*) to persuade people that drinking too much alcohol is bad for all creatures, be they man, bird, or insect.
   (*b*) to warn us of the effects of fermented fruits and berries on birds and insects.
   (*c*) to inform us that birds and insects occasionally get drunk.
   (*d*) to inform us that virtually any plant with sugar can turn into booze.

10. _____

Total Retention and Comprehension Score: _____

QUESTIONS FOR DISCUSSION (MEANING AND TECHNIQUE)

1. From the very first paragraph the reader knows this subject is going to be treated in a light-hearted way. How?

2. Look up "alliteration" in the dictionary. Does paragraph 1 use it? Where? Why? Are there other examples of alliteration in this article?

3. Can you point out certain words and phrases that make you smile or laugh. Why do they?

4. Aside from the funny words and phrases, what is funny about the whole article, if anything?

5. Are the birds and insects being compared to people (without the writer actually saying so)? How?

6. Do you believe this article to be factual? What makes you think so?

7. Go to the periodicals room of your library and find and read a copy of the *Smithsonian Magazine*. Then lead a class discussion on something you read in it.

SUGGESTIONS FOR WRITING

1. Write a paragraph in which you convey factual information about fishing, surfing, tennis, jogging, pets, or anything you like, in a humorous way.

2. This article is a summary of an article in the *Smithsonian Magazine*. Write a humorous summary of an article you find in the *Smithsonian, National Geographic, Mechanix Illustrated*, or in any other newspaper or magazine containing nonfiction articles.

Overall Reading Performance

Your overall reading performance is a combination of how fast you read and how much you comprehend and retain. The chart below allows you to find out quickly your "overall reading performance."

First enter your "reading time" and your "retention and comprehension" score in the two blanks at the bottom of the page. Then simply lay a straightedge of any kind (the edge of a sheet of paper or a pencil will do) across the chart, placing the left side of the straightedge at the appropriate point on the "Reading Rate" scale, and the right side at the appropriate point on the "Retention and Comprehension" scale. The point at which the paper or pencil intersects the scale in the middle of the page will indicate your overall performance.

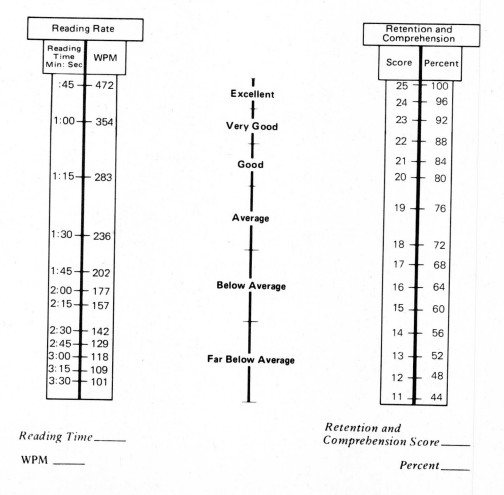

Reading Rate	
Reading Time Min: Sec	WPM
:45	472
1:00	354
1:15	283
1:30	236
1:45	202
2:00	177
2:15	157
2:30	142
2:45	129
3:00	118
3:15	109
3:30	101

Excellent

Very Good

Good

Average

Below Average

Far Below Average

Retention and Comprehension	
Score	Percent
25	100
24	96
23	92
22	88
21	84
20	80
19	76
18	72
17	68
16	64
15	60
14	56
13	52
12	48
11	44

*Reading Time*_____

WPM _____

*Retention and Comprehension Score*_____

*Percent*_____

Selection 2

Aussie Tracker Always Gets His Man

BRISBANE, Australia—Australian Aborigines have tracking skills which verge on the supernatural. Across hundreds of miles of shifting sand and baked mallee desert, the black trackers follow minute signs that exist only for them.

These are skills passed down for generations and emanating from what Aborigines call the Dreamtime—an undefined period long before European settlement, when the real world and the spirit world were as one and men were at peace with their gods.

Now there is little peace for the Aboriginal people—and even less peace for any rustler or outback criminal unlucky to have a black tracker breathing down his neck.

And among the handful of trackers working with police in various states, one name causes most sleeplessness among lawbreakers: Nardoo Burns. Of 500 tracking jobs he has handled for Queensland police in the far north of Australia, the big sergeant has never once failed to find his man.

Apart from anything else, Burns is the only tracker who can pursue his quarry underwater. Not literally, but as his father taught him: by painstakingly touching small pebbles and muddy sections at the bottom of rivers for signs of disturbance by man or horse.

Over 14 years Burns, who says no man has ever put him on his back and shakes hands with the vigor of a cement mixer, has roamed thousands of miles on the trail of robbers, rustlers, rapists and killers. And if Nardoo is tracking he will succeed, even if it takes six months.

Such was the case on a recent job that took him alone over 800 miles of semidesert in search of a gang and 300 head of stolen beef. Burns began with a cold trail, lived on lizards and roots—anything—and stuck to the trail of the thieves as firmly as the infamous north Queensland burrs stuck to him.

Source: Los Angeles Times, Nov. 15, 1979. Reprinted from Australian Illustrated Features.

The thieves ran through a range of tricks to throw Nardoo off the scent but knew they had failed one evening when they noticed him sitting calmly on the gate of a makeshift corral watching them.

"I didn't want them to panic," Burns explained. "Thought I better sit there a while and let them get used to the sight of me . . ."

Most of the gang he brought in himself and he laughed when they threatened dire revenge after prison.

"Everyone says that," he said. "But so far they're all just talking."

No. of Words: 395

Reading Time: _____

Selection 2

Aussie Tracker Always Gets His Man

VOCABULARY BUILDING

Below are several words used in this article. They are presented in the context of the sentences or phrases in which they occur. If you are unsure of their meanings and cannot define them from the context, look them up in the dictionary. Spaces are provided for additional unfamiliar words from the article to add to your vocabulary.

1. "...Burns is the only tracker who can pursue his *quarry* under-water."

   quarry: *prey place where rock is excavated.*

2. "...by *painstakingly* touching small pebbles...at the bottom of rivers for signs of disturbance..."

   painstakingly: *doing something carefully that is very painful*

3. "...and he laughed when they threatened *dire* revenge..."

   dire: *deadly, evil, weeked, terabable*

4. _____ : _____

5. _____ : _____

6. _____ : _____

RETENTION AND COMPREHENSION

A. True/False (1 point each)

1. Nardoo Burns is not the only tracker working with the Australian police.

   1. T _____ F _____

2. Burns has never failed to find any person he was tracking.

   2. T _____ F _____

B. Completion (3 points each)

3. Australian aborigines believe in a prehistoric

   3. _____

11

peaceful period of mixed reality and spirituality
called _____.

4. In his fourteen years of service, Burns has handled
about _____500_____ tracking jobs.

4. _____

C. Multiple Choice (2 points each)

5. From the article the reader can tell that Queensland is largely (a) a tropical jungle, (b) a vast
swamp, (c) an arid desert, (d) a grassy plain.

5. _____

6. Burns holds the rank of (a) captain, (b) sergeant,
(c) private, (d) scout.

6. _____

7. In a recent case Burns traveled 800 miles to capture (a) a killer, (b) a rapist, (c) a gang of robbers,
(d) a gang of cattle rustlers.

7. _____

8. During that chase, Burns lived on (a) dehydrated
foods, (b) roots and lizards, (c) airplane food
drops, (d) dried biscuits and water.

8. _____

D. Thematic (5 points)

9. Which statement *best* expresses the theme (*main*
idea) of the article?
(a) Nardoo Burns is a successful tracker because
he uses supernatural powers.
(b) Burns' aboriginal background helps make him
the best tracker in Australia.
(c) Burns is not afraid of revenge from the criminals he has helped capture.
(d) All the Australian aborigines are outstanding
trackers.

9. _____

E. Purpose (4 points)

10. The author's *chief* purpose is
(a) to show that aborigines are tough, honest, determined trackers.
(b) to indicate that criminals in Australia are pur-
sued until they are captured.
(c) to convince the reader that crime does not pay
in northern Australia.

10. _____

(d) to show that primitive hunting and survival skills contribute to Burns' success.

Total Retention and Comprehension Score: _____

QUESTIONS FOR DISCUSSION (MEANING AND TECHNIQUE)

1. Why does the writer refer to the tracking skills of early Australian aborigines and the Dreamtime in the opening paragraphs?

2. What do you know about Nardoo Burns? What does the writer *not* tell you about him? Why?

3. The phrase "to throw Nardoo off the scent" is *figurative* language because it tells us something indirectly. What other *figurative* phrases appear in the article?

4. Why did the writer select the story about rustlers to tell us about Burns? Should he have given us more actual accounts of Burns' skills?

5. Burns is quoted at the end of the article. How does this help us to understand him better?

6. Why would the Queensland police continue to use trackers when airplanes and helicopters are available?

SUGGESTIONS FOR WRITING

1. Few jobs today are as unusual, exciting, and dangerous as Burns' work. If you know someone who has a dangerous job or has worked at one in the past, write about the job and the person in a paper.

2. Using Nardoo Burns as the main character, write a plot for a movie or an hour-length television program.

3. Both Nardoo Burns and Bobby Hurst in Selection 7 are involved in the apprehension of criminals. Write a composition showing how their jobs are alike and/or different.

Overall Reading Performance

Your overall reading performance is a combination of how fast you read and how much you comprehend and retain. The chart below allows you to find out quickly your "overall reading performance."

First enter your "reading time" and your "retention and comprehension" score in the two blanks at the bottom of the page. Then simply lay a straightedge of any kind (the edge of a sheet of paper or a pencil will do) across the chart, placing the left side of the straightedge at the appropriate point on the "Reading Rate" scale, and the right side at the appropriate point on the "Retention and Comprehension" scale. The point at which the paper or pencil intersects the scale in the middle of the page will indicate your overall performance.

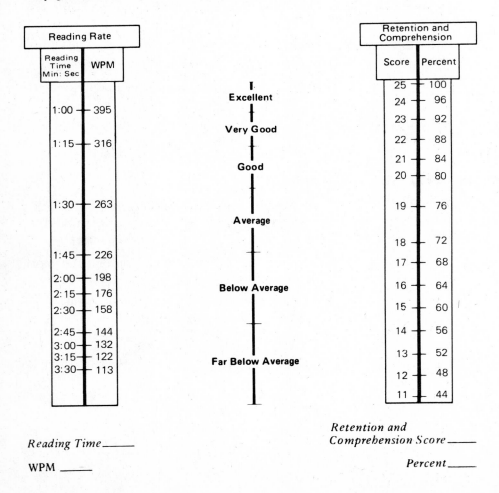

Reading Rate	
Reading Time Min: Sec	WPM
1:00	395
1:15	316
1:30	263
1:45	226
2:00	198
2:15	176
2:30	158
2:45	144
3:00	132
3:15	122
3:30	113

Excellent

Very Good

Good

Average

Below Average

Far Below Average

Retention and Comprehension	
Score	Percent
25	100
24	96
23	92
22	88
21	84
20	80
19	76
18	72
17	68
16	64
15	60
14	56
13	52
12	48
11	44

*Reading Time*_____

WPM _____

*Retention and Comprehension Score*_____

*Percent*_____

Selection 3

Family Food Waste per Year at Least $150, Researcher Says

BOISE, Idaho (AP)—University of Arizona researcher Dr. William L. Rathji says that after a study based on looking into garbage cans, he concludes that the average family wastes at least $150 per year in food.

"Homemakers go out of their way to save pennies at the store and then don't realize that waste of edible foods adds up much more at home," said Dr. William L. Rathji, an anthropologist.

He was one of about 100 food experts who met in Boise for a conference on food waste and ways to prevent it.

American families throw out between 8 and 20% of edible food at a cost of $4.5 billion per year, he said. That's almost as much as the federal government spends every year for food stamps and child nutrition programs.

He based his estimates on an annual garbage collection study by Arizona students, measuring food wasted in the Tucson area. He conceded it was rather presumptuous to make national estimates based on Tucson-area studies.

"But . . . there's no other data available," he said, in proposing more research on the subject.

In somewhat of a paradox, food items which are costly and in short supply tend to be wasted more, he found. During the 1973 meat shortage, meat waste increased to 9%, compared with 3% in 1974 and 1975.

Sugar and sugar products waste jumped to 19% in 1975, when sugar prices doubled from the previous year.

Rathji theorizes that high prices force consumers to experiment, sometimes buying in large quantities. In the case of meat, sometimes low-priced cuts or unappetizing varieties are purchased. Consumers then tend to waste more.

"My own theory, and it still is a theory, is that the more variety in food bought, the more wasted," he said.

Source: Los Angeles Times, Nov. 4, 1976. Reprinted by permission of Associated Press.

"Regular bread is wasted at about a 10% rate, but specialty breads and rolls are wasted at a 20% rate.

"If people are eating the same thing every day, they learn how to manage it. But if you're trying to pull something out of the Captain Rochelle cookbook every night, there's bound to be some waste," he said.

Another finding is that lower-income families in the Tucson area waste less food than middle and upper-income families. And the study found that dog food, which accounts for 8% of a shopping cart, is rarely wasted.

Fresh produce and frozen items are more likely to be wasted, Rathji said.

The study also showed people with the most knowledge of safe, edible food waste the least. Much food is tossed out, he said, because a homemaker suspects it is spoiled when it is not.

No. of Words: 430

Reading Time: _____

Selection 3

Family Food Waste per Year at Least $150, Researcher Says

VOCABULARY BUILDING

Below are several words used in this article. They are presented in the context of the sentences or phrases in which they occur. If you are unsure of their meanings and cannot define them from the context, look them up in the dictionary. Spaces are provided for additional unfamiliar words from the article to add to your vocabulary.

1. "Homemakers . . . don't realize that waste of *edible* foods adds up . . ."

   edible: _you can eat it (eateble)_

2. ". . . Dr. William L. Rathji, an *anthropologist*."

   anthropologist: _Specialist of human culture_

3. "He conceded it was rather *presumptuous* to make national estimates on Tucson-area studies."

   presumptuous: _you dont know the answer (we dont know for shure)_

4. "In somewhat of a *paradox,* food items which are costly and in short supply tend to be wasted more . . ."

   paradox: _a opposit happened that you expect_

5. _____ : _____

6. _____ : _____

7. _____ : _____

RETENTION AND COMPREHENSION

A. True/False *(1 point each)*

1. Inexpensive foods tend to be wasted more than expensive foods.

   1. T _____ F _____

2. Large quantities of food are tossed out   2. T _____ F _____
   because a homemaker suspects it is
   spoiled when it is not.

B. Completion (*3 points each*)

3. The two kinds of foods most likely to be wasted are   3. _____
   fresh produce and _____.

4. The average family wastes at least $_____   4. _____
   worth of food per year.

C. Multiple Choice (*2 points each*)

5. Dr. Rathji is (a) a home economist, (b) a financial   5. _____
   economist, (c) an anthropologist, (d) an agrono-
   mist.

6. American families throw out between (a) 5–8%,   6. _____
   (b) 8–10%, (c) 8–20%, (d) 20–28% of edible food.

7. Dr. Rathji's estimates are based on (a) observing   7. _____
   the food-purchasing habits of Americans, (b) ques-
   tioning housewives, (c) measuring food in trash,
   (d) knowledge of American eating habits.

8. When sugar prices doubled, waste of sugar (a)   8. _____
   went down, (b) went up, (c) stayed the same, (d)
   was cut in half.

D. Thematic (*5 points*)

9. Which statement *best* expresses the theme (*main   9. _____
   idea*) of the article?
   (*a*) American housewives are not good homemak-
       ers.
   (*b*) Upper-income families are more wasteful than
       lower-income ones.
   (*c*) For several reasons, American families throw
       away almost as much food as they consume.
   (*d*) Americans waste a great deal of food.

E. Purpose (*4 points*)

10. The author's *chief* purpose is   10. _____
    (*a*) to report on the results of some research show-

ing how much food the American consumer wastes.

(b) to persuade Americans that "waste not, want not" is still a good principle to follow.

(c) to convince consumers that eating regular bread, low-priced cuts of meat, and fresh produce will result in less food waste.

(d) to inform us that American families throw out enough food to pay for the government's food stamp and child nutrition programs.

Total Retention and Comprehension Score: _____

QUESTIONS FOR DISCUSSION (MEANING AND TECHNIQUE)

1. Why does the writer quote Dr. Rathji in the article?

2. Is "looking into garbage cans" an unusual way to conduct a scientific study? Are Dr. Rathji's findings based on a large enough sample?

3. What would happen to the percentages of food waste if restaurants were included in the survey? Why?

4. Do you think this kind of research is worthwhile? Why or why not?

5. What is meant by "trying to pull something out of the Captain Rochelle cookbook every night"?

6. How has Dr. Rathji grouped the food that was measured?

7. Why is dog food rarely wasted?

8. Do you agree with all of the findings in the survey? Why or why not?

9. Would a federal program to teach poor people how to decrease food waste be a good idea? Why or why not?

SUGGESTIONS FOR WRITING

1. How do the eating habits of Americans compare to those of other nationalities? Write a composition showing the similarities and differences in American eating habits and those of another people (or person) with which you are familiar. You could compare such things as staples, delicacies, holiday dishes, methods of preparation, or meal times.

2. Describe the best, or worst, restaurant you have ever eaten in. Include comments about the food and the people who worked there.

3. Anthropologists and archaeologists are sometimes described as "people who like to look through ancient trash dumps." In a composition show that there is a certain amount of truth in that description of their work.

4. "Institutional" food (meals served in school cafeterias, on military bases, and in hospitals) does not have a good reputation. Compare the food served in "institutions" in which you have eaten. Be specific. Before you start, decide whether your paper will be humorous or serious.

5. Spend a day analyzing your own family's food consumption and waste. Then write a composition about the food you or your family waste and how. Be specific.

Selection 3

Overall Reading Performance

Your overall reading performance is a combination of how fast you read and how much you comprehend and retain. The chart below allows you to find out quickly your "overall reading performance."

First enter your "reading time" and your "retention and comprehension" score in the two blanks at the bottom of the page. Then simply lay a straightedge of any kind (the edge of a sheet of paper or a pencil will do) across the chart, placing the left side of the straightedge at the appropriate point on the "Reading Rate" scale, and the right side at the appropriate point on the "Retention and Comprehension" scale. The point at which the paper or pencil intersects the scale in the middle of the page will indicate your overall performance.

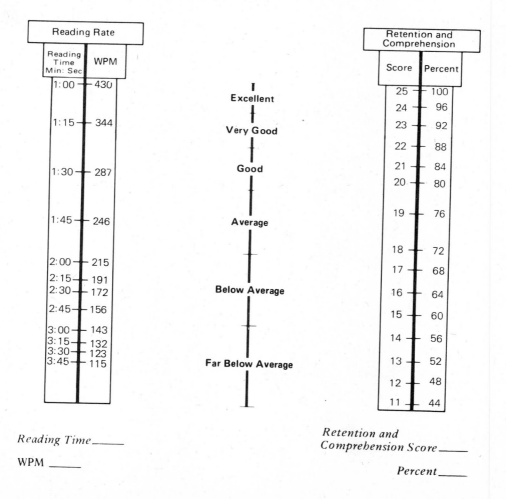

Reading Time_____

WPM _____

Retention and
Comprehension Score_____

Percent_____

Selection 4
WW II Deserter Out of Hiding

SHADY POINT, Okla. (UPI)—Pvt. D. B. Benson lived a life of quiet desperation for 36 years, never marrying, never holding a job, flitting like a shadow through the back reaches of the Kiamichi Mountains of Oklahoma. Few even knew he existed.

For all those years, Benson, 57, lived in fear he would be shot as a deserter from the old Army Air Corps. Tuesday his flight from the military ended.

Absent without official live

Benson, who went AWOL from the old Army Air Corps in 1943, said, "I just learned how to live" in the mountains. He lived a lonely existence for his more than three decades on the run.

cheap girls

"Fast cars, jet airplanes, and fast girls" were Benson's biggest surprises upon emerging for the last time from the Kiamichi Mountain area of southeastern Oklahoma.

He said he would take a house in some town and would not return to the mountain wilderness to live.

Benson never married and never held a full-time job because of a constant fear that Social Security records would be traced to his military background.

Benson apparently had been in touch with his parents, now in their 90s, since he went AWOL from Amarillo Air Force Base in June 1943. He signed preliminary discharge papers July 3, clearing the way for his Tuesday discharge.

The ex-soldier, dressed in jeans and wearing a green baseball cap, stood outside his sister's home and talked with reporters for the first time late Tuesday after Air Force officials gave him an other than honorable discharge from the armed forces.

Neither his sister nor any of his relatives, except his parents, had seen him in more than 30 years, and most believed he was dead.

He said he wished he had come out of the woods earlier but he feared the Air Force would have him court-martialed, executed or force him to complete his tour of duty.

you're arested under the army court

Source: *Evening Outlook*, Aug. 1, 1979. Reprinted by permission of United Press International.

Will and Marva Stacy, Benson's nephew and his wife, who convinced the private to come out of hiding, said the fugitive was told by a sergeant that he would not be any good at war and told him to go home and wait for his discharge.

Benson left his post at an Amarillo air base and disappeared.

Mrs. Stacy said it was more than a year before he realized he had done something illegal.

"He was hard to convince of the fact that he would not be shot," Will Stacy said.

In a prepared statement, Stacy said Benson had been living in a variety of makeshift shelters but all were on private land. Locations of the shelters were not revealed.

Roy Gentry, a professional trapper for 42 years, said he is not sure how Benson survived the harsh winters and said he is surprised he never ran across the ex-soldier during trapping expeditions.

"I'd like to know how he did it. I could probably learn something from him." Gentry said.

No. of Words: 482

Reading Time: _____

Selection 4

WW II Deserter Out of Hiding

VOCABULARY BUILDING

Below are several words used in this article. They are presented in the context of the sentences or phrases in which they occur. If you are unsure of their meanings and cannot define them from the context, look them up in the dictionary. Spaces are provided for additional unfamiliar words from the article to add to your vocabulary.

1. "Pvt. D. B. Benson lived a life of quiet *desperation* for 36 years . . ."

desperation: *hoplessnes*

2. "He signed *preliminary* discharge papers . . ."

preliminary: *the first step in the proces*

3. ". . . Benson had been living in a variety of *makeshift* shelters . . ."

makeshift: *temporary*

4. _____ : _____

5. _____ : _____

RETENTION AND COMPREHENSION

A. True/False *(1 point each)*

1. D. B. Benson went AWOL from the Army Air Corps in June of 1943.

1. T _____ F _____

2. Benson was aided during his desertion by his wife.

2. T _____ F _____

B. Completion *(3 points each)*

3. Benson hid from the authorities in the mountains of southeastern_____.

3. _____

4. For over thirty years the only relatives who came in
   contact with Benson were his_____ .

   4. _____

C. Multiple Choice *(2 points each)*

5. According to the article, Benson got most of his
   food (a) by hunting, (b) by stealing, (c) by beg-
   ging from farmers, (d) not mentioned.

   5. _____

6. Benson was persuaded to come out of hiding by
   (a) his nephew and his wife, (b) a professional
   trapper, (c) government officials, (d) his sister.

   6. _____

7. Benson's relatives said that an Air Corps sergeant
   told Benson that he would not be any good at war
   and (a) to apply for a discharge, (b) to desert, (c)
   to go home and wait for his discharge, (d) to report
   to the base commander for reassignment.

   7. _____

8. Benson's biggest surprises after he came out of
   hiding were (a) transistor radios and color TV; (b)
   fast cars, jet airplanes, and "fast" girls; (c) computers; (d) styles of clothing.

   8. _____

D. Thematic *(5 points)*

9. Which statement *best* expresses the theme (*main*
   idea) of the article?
   (a) Benson could not have deserted for thirty-six
       years without help from relatives and friends.
   (b) The Air Corps sergeant was responsible for
       Benson's desertion.
   (c) A man's lack of understanding and fear of pun-
       ishment caused him to live most of his life as
       an outcast.
   (d) Large governmental agencies can destroy a
       person's life by failing to make allowances for
       individual differences.

   9. _____

E. Purpose *(4 points)*

10. The author's *chief* purpose is
    (a) to reveal how criminals can avoid the authori-
        ties for long periods.

    10. _____

(b) to show the clever things Benson did to survive.

(c) to report on an unusual case of desertion from the armed forces.

(d) to persuade the reader that Benson made a mistake by not giving up sooner.

Total Retention and Comprehension Score: _____

QUESTIONS FOR DISCUSSION (MEANING AND TECHNIQUE)

1. How does the writer try to get the reader's sympathy for Benson early in the article?

2. Benson received "an other than honorable discharge" from the armed forces. What does that mean? What other kinds of discharges are there?

3. Who do you think was responsible for Benson's long flight—the Air Corps sergeant, Benson himself, others? Why?

4. Should Benson have gone to prison for his desertion? Why or why not?

5. What is the purpose of the statement by the trapper, Roy Gentry, that he's not sure how Benson survived the harsh winters and that he's surprised he never ran across the soldier?

6. Benson never had a "full-time" job and his shelters were on unrevealed "private land." Are there other statements that suggest there is more to the story? What are they? What do they suggest?

SUGGESTIONS FOR WRITING

1. Write a composition that offers possible alternatives for draftees who want to serve their country, but not as combatants in the armed forces.

2. Imagine that a close friend or relative is an escapee (from a prison, a hospital, the army, etc.) and contacts you for help. In a short essay discuss what you think you would do and why.

3. Have you or someone you know ever changed your attitude about some matter, such as cheating on tests, cutting classes, returning found or stolen property, etc.? Describe the change. Explain the reasons for the change, if you can.

4. Write an argument for or against allowing women members of the armed forces to fight in combat.

Selection 4

Overall Reading Performance

Your overall reading performance is a combination of how fast you read and how much you comprehend and retain. The chart below allows you to find out quickly your "overall reading performance."

First enter your "reading time" and your "retention and comprehension" score in the two blanks at the bottom of the page. Then simply lay a straightedge of any kind (the edge of a sheet of paper or a pencil will do) across the chart, placing the left side of the straightedge at the appropriate point on the "Reading Rate" scale, and the right side at the appropriate point on the "Retention and Comprehension" scale. The point at which the paper or pencil intersects the scale in the middle of the page will indicate your overall performance.

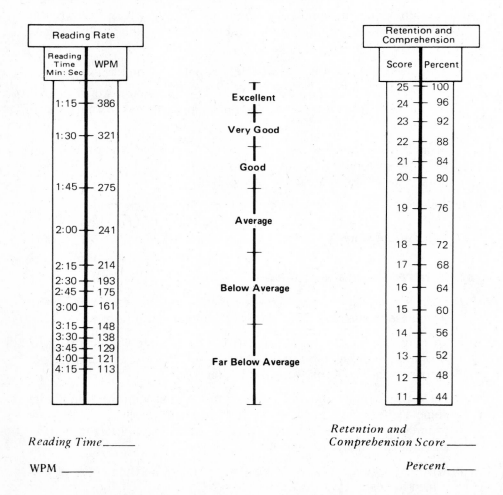

Reading Time _____

WPM _____

Retention and Comprehension Score _____

Percent _____

Selection 5

Too Many Bosses Spoil the Job

Industry should get rid of half its bosses, says behavioral psychologist Alfred J. Marrow.

"Adults are quite capable of handling their lives outside their homes, at their jobs," Marrow said in an interview. They need fewer supervisors and managers, not more.

As president of the American Board of Professional Psychology and former Commissioner of Human Rights of New York City, he's heard the complaint from working people over and over again: too many bosses.

If a shirt manufacturer's customers are returning merchandise because the collars are crooked, he said, the people who make the shirts are more likely than management to identify the problem quickly if they get together to talk about it.

But if the boss comes on as an adversary, bawling them out for bad work and threatening to or actually firing some, the remaining workers will probably react angrily and work will suffer.

Spread the Boredom

He recalled an insurance company in Hartford, Conn., that got about 50,000 pieces of mail every morning. One person was assigned to slit the envelopes, starting at 6 a.m. When a meeting was called to discuss the frequent turnover of employees in that job, one worker suggested that the starting hour be changed to 7:30, and the one person to a team of four or five.

The solution worked, Marrow said, because one person was no longer stuck with a boring and lonely job for four to five hours. The work got done in one hour, and the people who did it were then given more varied and interesting clerical duties the remainder of the day.

That's called "job enrichment." More American companies are turning

Source: Los Angeles Times, Aug. 8, 1977. Reprinted by permission of United Press International.

to it because surveys show it's No. 1 on employees' lists of importance: "Not wages, not hours. They are fifth, sixth, seventh," Marrow said.

Job enrichment and employee participation gain the support of top organizations because they are good for production and reduce staff turnover, he said. For employees who have not yet discovered they can actually influence management, he suggests:

If you have a problem or objectives that will be good for the company, first discuss them with your coworkers.

Loners Are Losers

"Get together as many people as you want, but don't coerce any to join you. This is not what a guidance committee is for.

"If you have six in ten who are willing to speak to the boss, you're likely to be successful. Tell the others, 'We won't involve you, but you're welcome to join us later if you want to.'"

Marrow said it is best for all who share the same views and objectives to be present when the presentation is made.

"A spokesperson almost always gets back to a one-to-one basis again," and loners are losers, he said. You have to give each person a sense of involvement, although a group that grows beyond 25 persons puts many in a passive position, which isn't good.

One big corporation solved that problem by calling meetings of 20 persons each, for a total of 400 meetings of one hour each over about three months. Marrow said it cost the company about 8,000 production hours and $40,000 in time lost, but if it resulted in 1% improvement in company production, it saved the company more than $1 million in costs.

At the beginning of this century, two industrial engineers recommended job simplification to increase production.

"It took us 50 years to find out that doesn't work," Marrow said. "Most stress in peoples' lives comes from their jobs. Problem-solving and job enrichment are preventive medicine. They eliminate stress. People in jobs are just beginning to realize that (a good) salary isn't enough to pay for heartbreak on the job."

No. of Words: 607

Reading Time: _____

Selection 5

Too Many Bosses Spoil the Job

VOCABULARY BUILDING

Below are several words used in this article. They are presented in the context of the sentences or phrases in which they occur. If you are unsure of their meanings and cannot define them from the context, look them up in the dictionary. Spaces are provided for additional unfamiliar words from the article to add to your vocabulary.

1. "... if the boss comes on as an *adversary* bawling them out ..."

   adversary: *an anamy*

2. "... but don't *coerce* any to join you."

   coerce: *to force (make somebody to do somthing)*

3. "Industry should get rid of half its bosses, says *behavioral psychologist* Alfred J. Marrow."

   behavioral: *how to act (act badly)*

   psychologist: *study of the mind*

4. _____ : _____

5. _____ : _____

6. _____ : _____

RETENTION AND COMPREHENSION

A. True/False *(1 point each)*

1. Wages and hours are more important to employees than "job enrichment."

   1. T _____ F _____

2. Most stress in people's lives comes from their jobs.

   2. T _____ F _____

B. Completion (3 points each)

3. Marrow said that it took industry _____ _____ years to find out the truth about job simplification.

3. _____

4. Although one big corporation spent $40,000 on "job enrichment" meetings, the result was a saving of more than $_____ in costs.

4. _____

C. Multiple Choice (2 points each)

5. If customers are returning shirts because of crooked collars, the people most likely to identify the cause of the problem are (a) the salesmen, (b) the supervisors, (c) top management, (d) the people who make the shirts.

5. _____

6. A worker who has an idea that will be good for the company should (a) speak first to the boss about it, (b) speak first to his coworkers about it, (c) wait for the right moment to speak to the boss about it, (d) speak to the boss's boss about it.

6. _____

7. A group puts too many people in a passive position if it grows beyond (a) six people, (b) ten people, (c) twenty people, (d) twenty-five people.

7. _____

8. Problem solving and job enrichment are preventive medicine because they (a) reduce stress, (b) impose penalties for absenteeism, (c) result in better health insurance benefits, (d) prevent too many bosses from interfering in the work process.

8. _____

D. Thematic (5 points)

9. Which statement *best* expresses the theme (*main* idea) of the article?
   (a) Bosses create stress.
   (b) Workers don't need bosses.
   (c) Workers should participate more in decision making.
   (d) Workers know better than bosses.

9. _____

E. Purpose (4 points)

10. The author's *chief* purpose is

10. _____

(a) to inform us that people are dissatisfied with their wages and hours.

(b) to explain that "job enrichment" creates job satisfaction and improves production.

(c) to suggest that bosses hinder production more than they help it.

(d) to persuade us to carry out greater "job simplification."

Total Retention and Comprehension Score: _____

QUESTIONS FOR DISCUSSION (MEANING AND TECHNIQUE)

1. Is the first sentence a good way to begin this article? Why or why not?

2. According to the article, what steps should a worker take to solve a problem or to offer a suggestion to help the company?

3. Give examples of "job simplification" from your work or from watching fast-food outlets, assembly lines, department store sales. Explain what Marrow, the psychologist, means in the sentence, "It took us 50 years to find out that doesn't work." Do you agree? Why or why not?

4. Why does the writer *not* name the companies mentioned in the article?

5. Discuss Marrow's findings from the employer's viewpoint.

6. Has the writer shown any bias in the article? If so, where?

7. Does this article make a case for unions and labor organizations? Explain.

SUGGESTIONS FOR WRITING

1. Write a paper showing the way problems or suggestions are treated at your place of work. Could they be handled differently to the benefit of workers and the company? Explain how by giving an example.

2. If you have experienced "job enrichment," write a paper describing what happened and how it affected you and your work.

3. Describe your experiences in trying to solve a job problem or improving productivity at work. What was the result?

4. Write a paper that presents the problems of supervising employees

and increasing productivity from a boss's viewpoint. Use first-hand experience and refer to the material in the article, if at all possible.

5. What would be the ideal job for you? Write a paper describing it. It should be meaningful, productive work, not something silly or unrealistic. If such a job does not exist, make one up for yourself. Include your training, wages, duties, coworkers, location, and other aspects of this job.

6. If you have a labor organization at work (or are familiar with one), write an argument for or against joining it. Support your attitude with examples, statistics, anecdotes, and other specific information.

Overall Reading Performance

Your overall reading performance is a combination of how fast you read and how much you comprehend and retain. The chart below allows you to find out quickly your "overall reading performance."

First enter your "reading time" and your "retention and comprehension" score in the two blanks at the bottom of the page. Then simply lay a straightedge of any kind (the edge of a sheet of paper or a pencil will do) across the chart, placing the left side of the straightedge at the appropriate point on the "Reading Rate" scale, and the right side at the appropriate point on the "Retention and Comprehension" scale. The point at which the paper or pencil intersects the scale in the middle of the page will indicate your overall performance.

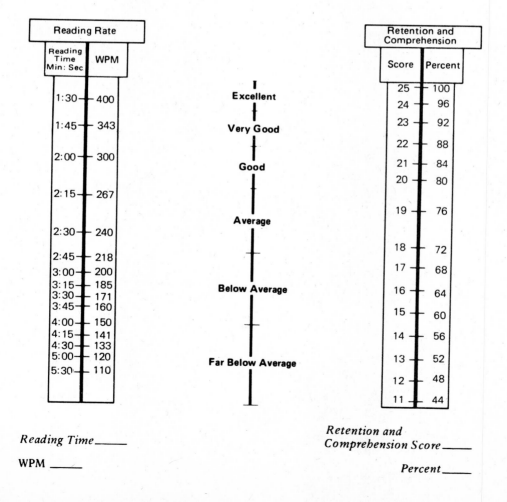

Reading Time_____

WPM _____

Retention and
Comprehension Score_____

Percent_____

Selection 6

My *Pony,* My *Saddle,* My *Corral,* My *Prejudice*

DAVID WATSON

When I was 11, I lived in a small town in Kentucky. Everyone in our town was judged according to his social position and material possessions. Our leading citizens considered themselves aristocrats in the venerable Southern tradition. Despite my youth, I knew that being accepted depended on my being "somebody."

My father was the town veterinarian and was a part owner of the most successful horse clinic in the state. My friends—and, more important, their parents—knew that horse trainers and owners brought their animals from five states to be treated by my father. And so I benefited socially by being "Dr. Watson's son."

My family lived on a two-acre parcel of land in a new house that wasn't part of a suburban development. My father had simply bought the land and built the house that my mother had always wanted. Since it was the first all-electric house in town, I gained added prestige. I was now "Dr. Watson's son living in Dr. Watson's new house."

Because of my father's generosity, my sister and I were the first children in town to own ponies. My father built the barn for them himself. He fenced a corral for riding, and gave us new red, black and silver saddles, bridles and reins.

So, when I was 11, I was "Dr. Watson's son living in Dr. Watson's new house and owning his own pony." I was sure that I was *somebody,* definitely superior to the average child in town.

For this reason, I was shocked to open the front door one day to find Billy and Charles, two neighbor children, standing on my front porch.

"Are you and Debbie going to ride your ponies today?" Billy asked me.

"No," I said, as rudely as possible.

"Well, then, Charles and I are going to ride them this afternoon."

Source: Los Angeles Times, Dec. 13, 1978. Reprinted by permission.

I couldn't believe their audacity. "Oh, no, you're not. Those are *my* ponies, and no one rides them unless I say so!"

Charles' rejoinder astounded me. "We already asked your father at the clinic, and he said we could ride your ponies whenever we wanted as long as you and Debbie weren't riding them. He said we could, even if you said no."

I vividly remember those words, because I swore then that I would hate my father forever for letting those "colored" boys ride my ponies.

Watching from the back window, I saw Billy and Charles catch *my* pony, cinch up *my* saddle and ride through *my* corral. The precedent was set. In the days and weeks that followed, Billy and Charles even brought along friends to share in the fun. Sometimes they rode all day.

It wasn't long before my friends and their parents found out that Dr. Watson let "coloreds" ride his children's ponies. The snide comments from people in town were eroding my air of superiority.

But my father didn't seem to care what the neighbors said. My mother ignored my complaints, and my sister was too young to understand. As for the ponies, they didn't seem to care who rode them.

At first I told my friends that my father had hired Billy and Charles to exercise the ponies, but that explanation wore thin. Finally I, too, learned to ignore the gibes.

When I was 12, my sister invited a friend to our house to spend the night. My sister's friend was Billy's younger sister, Allyson. By that time it seemed the most natural thing in the world for Allyson to be in our house. I had forgotten the prejudices of my 11th year.

But the community's attitude hadn't changed. The comments about Dr. Watson's visitors became crueler, more vicious. Now Debbie and I were just "Dr. Watson's children who have colored kids over."

So we told our parents that it might be better if Allyson never came over again. We both liked her, but we disliked the abuse of our friends more.

Six months later, my mother gave up her dream house, and my father sold his interest in the horse clinic. Then we packed up and moved to California, leaving the ponies behind. I didn't really understand—then— why my parents told our new neighbors in Porterville that they had moved the family west for the children's sake.

No. of Words: 710

Reading Time: _____

Selection 6

My *Pony,* My *Saddle,* My *Corral,* My *Prejudice*

VOCABULARY BUILDING

*Below are several words used in this article. They are presented in the
context of the sentences or phrases in which they occur. If you are unsure
of their meanings and cannot define them from the context, look them up
in the dictionary. Spaces are provided for additional unfamiliar words
from the article to add to your vocabulary.*

1. "My father was the town *veterinarian* . . ."

   veterinarian: _animal flu medicine_

2. "My family lived . . . in a new house that wasn't part of a *suburban*
   development."

   suburban: _small city that is out side of the big city_

3. "I couldn't believe their *audacity.*"

   audacity: _fearlessness_

4. "Charles' *rejoinder astounded* me."

   rejoinder: _____

   astounded: _____

5. "The *snide* comments from people in town were *eroding* my air of
   superiority."

   snide: _____

   eroding: _____

6. _____ : _____

7. _____ : _____

8. _____ : _____

Benge – a situation if you drink or eat too much.

39

RETENTION AND COMPREHENSION

A. True/False *(1 point each)*

1. When the author was 11 years old, he overcame his prejudice.

      1. T _____ F _____

2. The author's father rebuilt an old house just the way his mother wanted it.

      2. T _____ F _____

B. Completion *(3 points each)*

3. When the author was 11, he lived in a small town in _____.

      3. _____

4. As a boy, the author benefited socially by being "_____."

      4. _____

C. Multiple Choice *(2 points each)*

5. The author's father was the town (a) doctor, (b) teacher, (c) veterinarian, (d) lawyer.

      5. _____

6. Billy and Charles were (a) distant cousins, (b) neighbor children, (c) patients at Dr. Watson's clinic, (d) the author's ponies.

      6. _____

7. Dr. Watson had (a) hired Billy and Charles to exercise the ponies, (b) ordered the author to take care of Billy and Charles, (c) told Billy and Charles they could ride the ponies, (d) told Billy and Charles no "coloreds" could ride his ponies.

      7. _____

8. The author and his sister told their parents that (a) they didn't like Allyson, (b) they didn't want Allyson coming over anymore, (c) they disliked black children, (d) they didn't care what the neighbors thought.

      8. _____

D. Thematic *(5 points)*

9. Which statement *best* expresses the theme (*main* idea) of the article?
   (a) If there is widespread prejudice in a community, even unprejudiced people feel pressured to conform.

      9. _____

(b) If you are forced to share your possessions, you will learn to "love thy neighbor."
(c) Prejudice is something children learn from their parents.
(d) There is less prejudice in Porterville than in Kentucky.

E. Purpose (4 points)

10. The author's *chief* purpose is   10. _____
    (a) to give us a glimpse inside a small boy's mind.
    (b) to show how a boy's prestige is determined in large part by his father's position in town.
    (c) to emphasize how important it is to let children decide whether to allow others to borrow their most precious possessions.
    (d) to show how community attitudes can exert enormous pressure on people.

Total Retention and Comprehension Score: _____

QUESTIONS FOR DISCUSSION (MEANING AND TECHNIQUE)

1. Were the boy's parents right to move away from Kentucky "for the children's sake"? What do you imagine might have happened if they had stayed?

2. Why did the boy telling the story feel no prejudice in his twelfth year, although he had felt it in his eleventh? What does this tell us in general about prejudice or relations between people?

3. Although the boy's father is never directly described, what image do you have of him? What kind of man do you think he is? What are his values? His attitudes towards people and prejudice?—towards children and their upbringing?

4. Explain the reason for the boy's attitude the first time the neighbor children come to ride his pony? Do you think he was justified? Why or why not?

5. Was the father right to let the neighbor children ride his children's ponies?

6. The person who wrote this article is an adult. From the way the article is written, how do you think he feels now about his childhood experi-

ence? Was it a good one? Do you think he's now a prejudiced person? Does he seem to think his father did the right thing or not?

7. Do you think the family ever encountered attitudes in Porterville similar to the ones they had left behind in Kentucky or not? Discuss this possibility.

8. What was it that bothered the children most about the neighbor children coming over? Were they right to be bothered?

9. How is the story introduced? Why is the "background" for the story important?

10. Are you completely free of prejudice? Why or why not? Is anyone? Why or why not?

SUGGESTIONS FOR WRITING

1. Write a personal narrative, like this one, about an experience from which you learned something about life, yourself, other people, society, etc.

2. This article could be considered an "illustration" essay. It uses an episode by one person to illustrate an idea: all of us can be prejudiced, prejudice can be overcome, and societal pressures can sometimes be almost impossible to resist. Write an illustration essay in which you illustrate your thesis (idea) with a story.

3. Write this story from the point of view of one of the neighbor boys (Billy or Charles) who come to ride the ponies; or from the point of view of Allyson, the neighbor girl who comes to stay over; or from the father's point of view, or the mother's; or from the point of view of one of the townspeople.

4. Did something similar ever happen to you, either an experience having to do with prejudice or an experience which you didn't understand properly at the time but do now? Write about it.

5. Write an essay defining "prejudice" or its opposite. What is "prejudice?" Give examples from life.

6. Write an essay in defense of prejudice, after first explaining what you mean by it.

Selection 6

Overall Reading Performance

Your overall reading performance is a combination of how fast you read and how much you comprehend and retain. The chart below allows you to find out quickly your "overall reading performance."

First enter your "reading time" and your "retention and comprehension" score in the two blanks at the bottom of the page. Then simply lay a straightedge of any kind (the edge of a sheet of paper or a pencil will do) across the chart, placing the left side of the straightedge at the appropriate point on the "Reading Rate" scale, and the right side at the appropriate point on the "Retention and Comprehension" scale. The point at which the paper or pencil intersects the scale in the middle of the page will indicate your overall performance.

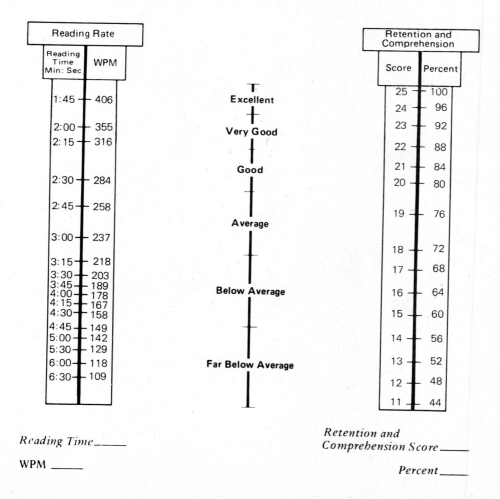

Reading Time_____

WPM _____

Retention and
Comprehension Score_____

Percent____

Selection 7

'Easy Mark' Traps Robbers, Killers

CHRIS ROBERTS

PHILADELPHIA—The old immigrant, his bowed frame leaning into a raw spring wind, headed down the street, a link of kielbasa and a soiled shirt tucked in his valise.

A lean young man, maybe 17, eyed him from the doorway of a hock-shop. Across the street an unshaven man, a big man with a big gun, waited, frozen behind a bush on a trash-strewn railroad embankment.

"Critter in white sneaks," whispered the big man as the teen-ager stepped into the sunlight. "Looks like he's on."

The old man started across the street, bent in half now by the wind. The young man followed, his sneakers straightening out the crooked path of the old man.

Then suddenly the man with the gun was running—up the embankment and over the tracks, to the top of steps leading out of a pedestrian tunnel. Crouching, he was ready to spring.

But it didn't go down that day.

The "old man" emerged from the tunnel. "Something spooked him," he said to the man with the gun. Then he pounded his fist—a mighty smack. "Damn it!" he said. He straightened up and there, for every thug in the world to see, stood this town's most famous decoy cop.

For 10 years, Bobby Hurst has cruised the shady side of the street, some days dressed like the immigrant, others like a granny, a business executive, an insurance salesman, a cabbie, a nun, a bus driver, a sailor, a watermelon vendor, a bum.

Anything to get robbed and mugged.

And always he is shepherded by big men with big guns, undercover police with .357 magnums and walkie-talkies, moving in at the last second to arrest the thugs and sometimes to save Hurst's life.

He's been slashed with knives and straight-edge razors 38 times, cut badly enough eight times to be hospitalized. He's been shot at 10 times, hit four, had gun barrels stuck in his ear.

Source: Los Angeles Times, May 18, 1980. Reprinted by permission of Associated Press.

45

He's been beaten senseless, attacked with machetes, scissors, meat cleavers, swords, baseball bats, chair legs, a ball and chain, knocked unconscious with a frozen mackerel wrapped in a newspaper.

"Somebody's got to do it," he says. "Somebody's got to get the doers off the streets." So on he walks, a father of four, playing the streets like a rodeo clown, luring society's crazed misfits.

At age 41, Hurst has mastered deception. The other night, a beat patrolman shooed him off a corner, not realizing the drunken loiterer was a fellow cop.

Hurst has been awarded 20 merit citations, three more for bravery. Four years ago he received the department's highest tribute, the citation for valor.

He has a gentle face. Pale blue eyes, an auburn beard sprinkled with white, a soft voice. He's 5-foot-10, 160 pounds. He has shot and killed "perhaps 10 people" with the snub-nosed revolver he straps to his ankle. "I don't keep score," he says.

Hurst says there are two kinds of street thieves: "The dipper goes into your pocket and takes what's there. He doesn't like violence.

"Then there's the shark or the critter. . . . He will rob you, hurt you, rape you, kill you. That's the shark—that's the one we're after."

At last count, Hurst, a former Green Beret, had been "hit" 274 times, hospitalized 36.

He says to get a conviction, "You're going to have to take your banging. You anticipate you're going to take a beating." Often he does, and the results are a prosecutor's delight.

Hurst provides these statistics: 90% of those arrested plead guilty; of those who stood trial in the past 10 years, only three have been acquitted.

For that Hurst has had his hair set on fire, a .25-caliber automatic stuck in his ear, a German Luger shoved down his throat and chains wrapped around his neck.

Once he was held up by a man with a cucumber.

"This guy came up from behind and said, 'Don't move, my man, or I'll blow you all over the street.'

"It felt like a finger in my back, but in this business I have to assume that fingers are loaded. So I opened my key (the hidden microphone) and I said, 'Hey, friend, you don't need that gun.'

"And he said, 'Take the money out nice and easy and hand it back.' So I reached in and gave him the money and he said, 'Now start walking and don't turn around. I'll blow you baby, I'll cap you right here.'

"Then the troops came down and there underneath the pile was the cucumber. And the guy said, 'Well, I didn't have anything else.'"

No. of Words: 764

Reading Time: _____

46

Selection 7

'Easy Mark' Traps Robbers, Killers

VOCABULARY BUILDING

Below are several words used in this article. They are presented in the context of the sentences or phrases in which they occur. If you are unsure of their meanings and cannot define them from the context, look them up in the dictionary. Spaces are provided for additional unfamiliar words from the article to add to your vocabulary.

1. "He straightened up and there, for every thug . . . to see, stood this town's most famous *decoy* cop." *[handwritten: bad guy, thief]*

   decoy: *a person or thing that looks like something that it is not. (under cover)*

2. "And always he is *shepherded* by big men with big guns . . ."

   shepherded: *person who takes care of sheep*

3. "He's been beaten senseless, attacked with *machetes,* scissors, meat cleavers . . ." *[handwritten: to splash a pork]*

   machetes: *big hairy knife*

4. _____ : _____

5. _____ : _____

6. _____ : _____

RETENTION AND COMPREHENSION

A. True/False *(1 point each)*

1. Bobby Hurst's street disguises are selected for him by his superiors.

   1. T _____ F _____

2. Hurst has had to kill only one person during his assignment as a decoy.

   2. T _____ F _____

B. Completion *(3 points each)*

3. Hurst divides street thieves into two types: the dip-
   pers and the _____.

4. For protection he carries a hidden microphone and
   a _____.

3. _____

4. _____

C. Multiple Choice *(2 points each)*

5. According to the article, Hurst has not disguised
   himself as a (a) cabbie, (b) sailor, (c) street clean-
   er, (d) nun.

6. One time, he was knocked unconscious with a frozen (a) liver sausage, (b) mackerel, (c) chicken,
   (d) apple pie.

7. Another time, Hurst was held up by a man using a
   "gun" which was really a (a) fountain pen, (b)
   lead pipe, (c) paintbrush, (d) cucumber.

8. He is so successful that (a) 90% of those criminals
   arrested plead guilty, (b) he has been cited for
   bravery three times, (c) he has been asked to train
   other decoys, (d) he has earned the rank of detec-
   tive.

5. _____

6. _____

7. _____

8. _____

D. Thematic *(5 points)*

9. Which statement *best* expresses the theme (*main*
   idea) of the article?
   (a) Any person who acts as a police decoy must
   take a lot of physical punishment.
   (b) Philadelphia's use of police decoys is the best
   way to decrease street crime in any large city.
   (c) Hurst's success as a decoy results from his ability to play the role of an easy victim for street
   criminals.
   (d) Without the support of undercover police,
   Hurst's job would be even more dangerous.

9. _____

E. Purpose *(4 points)*

10. The author's *chief* purpose is
    (a) to reveal how brutally street criminals treat
    their victims.

10. _____

(b) to report on the recent increase of crime in the United States.

(c) to inform us of how one man has taken it upon himself to catch criminals.

(d) to show that one way of fighting crime is effective because of the skills and bravery of one policeman.

Total Retention and Comprehension Score: _____

QUESTIONS FOR DISCUSSION (MEANING AND TECHNIQUE)

1. In this article the writer uses many descriptive words and phrases such as "unshaven man," "white sneaks," and "auburn beard, sprinkled with white." Find other examples of the use of descriptive words and phrases. Why does the writer use them?

2. The writer uses "street" language such as "Looks like he's on" and "But it didn't go down that day." Why? When is the use of slang or "street" talk permitted in student writing?

3. What is meant by "For 10 years, Hurst has cruised the shady side of the street . . ."? Find other phrases that are *figurative,* that mean more than they "say."

4. Is there an element of humor in this article? If so, what kind of humor is it?

5. Why does the writer tell us that Hurst has four children, has a gentle face, and is an ex-Green Beret?

6. What is the difference between a "dipper" and a "shark"?

SUGGESTIONS FOR WRITING

1. Would you like to work as a decoy? Write a composition explaining why or why not?

2. Compare the article on Nardoo Burns in Selection 2 and this one on Bobby Hurst. What are the similarities and differences in the way each man is presented? What is the resulting view in each treatment?

3. Imagine that crime in your area has been almost eliminated. Write a paper discussing what the effects on your life would be.

4. Some people object to the use of "decoys" to catch criminals. Find out the meaning of the word "entrapment" and write an essay which

favors or opposes the use of undercover law officers posing as dope dealers, prostitutes, or possible victims to catch criminals.

5. In this essay the writer uses some examples of the special language or *jargon* of street criminals. If you are familiar with the jargon of a group (musicians, computer programmers, athletes), list some of the words it uses. Explain their meanings, usage, and origins, if possible. Then write a composition using a particular jargon.

Overall Reading Performance

Your overall reading performance is a combination of how fast you read and how much you comprehend and retain. The chart below allows you to find out quickly your "overall reading performance."

First enter your "reading time" and your "retention and comprehension" score in the two blanks at the bottom of the page. Then simply lay a straightedge of any kind (the edge of a sheet of paper or a pencil will do) across the chart, placing the left side of the straightedge at the appropriate point on the "Reading Rate" scale, and the right side at the appropriate point on the "Retention and Comprehension" scale. The point at which the paper or pencil intersects the scale in the middle of the page will indicate your overall performance.

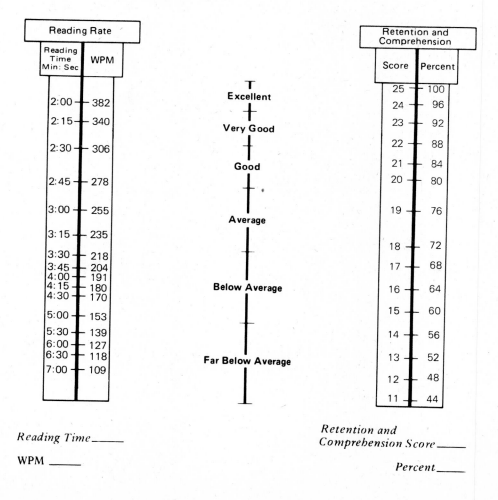

Reading Time _____

WPM _____

Retention and
Comprehension Score _____

Percent _____

Selection 8

Did Indians Trick Settlers?

CHARLES HILLINGER

name of a deserte

ON THE OLD MOJAVE WAGON ROAD—Pioneers called the steep, rock-ribbed desert peak Rocky Ridge.

A better name may well have been Mt. Bamboozled.

All through the 1850s, soldiers, trappers, prospectors and early settlers struggled to make it up the long, tortuous grade. *like hunters* *person who looks for gold*

"Indian guides led the wagon trains straight to the mountain," explains Dennis Casebier, a physicist who has been studying and writing about the Old Mojave Wagon Road for 15 years.

Then the wagons had to be unloaded for the final climb over the 3,900-foot-high peak.

"Early journals," adds Casebier, "tell how all the men in a party would assist the mules in pulling each unloaded wagon to the crest, how they lugged the wagon supplies on their backs."

But the travelers were being deceived by the Indians, for less than a mile away was a pass, an easy way through the mountains. *to lie*

Finally, in 1859, a party led by Samuel A. Bishop (for whom Bishop, Calif., is named) found the easy way around Rocky Ridge—without any help from the Indians.

It certainly wasn't ignorance of the desert that caused the Indian guides to put the wagon trains on the more difficult mountain route.

"The Indians knew the Mojave Desert like the back of their hands," says Casebier. "It was their home for centuries.

"But the Indians left no written records. So we just have to go on speculation, that the Indians could well have been slipping it to the pioneers, perhaps because of deep-seated animosity. Or perhaps it was a trick or a joke they were pulling." *making you the victom of a joke.* *hate from the bottom of your heart.* *unkind*

Much of Casebier's research on the old wagon road is carried out at the Library of Congress and the National Archives in Washington, D.C. His work as a physicist takes him to Washington several weeks each year.

He has pored over military records—hundreds of troops used the *study* road—and read travelers' journals describing the laborious trek over the mountain, mentioning the presence of Indian guides and commenting on how there surely had to be an easier way.

When he retraced every foot of the old wagon road, he found the route over Rocky Ridge. In the vicinity, he discovered musket balls, buttons, a metal barrel strap, square nails, a mule shoe and a hand-forged metal fitting from a wagon.

Elsewhere along the old wagon road can be found potsherds, arrow points and other Indian implements, as well as rings of rocks marking the location of Indian shelters.

The Old Mojave Wagon Road began at the Colorado River north of Needles and extended westward nearly 300 miles to Barstow, Victorville, over the Cajon Pass and through San Gabriel to the present day Los Angeles Harbor.

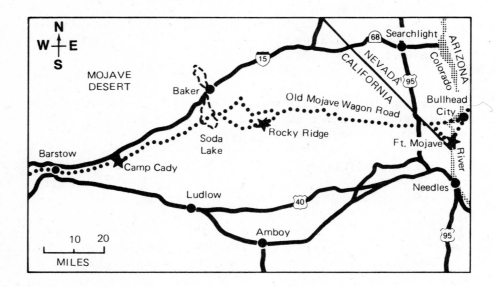

The section of the road that particularly interests Casebier runs for 130 miles from the Colorado River to old Camp Cady, 20 miles east of Barstow.

The old road, its wagon ruts easily discernible, can still be identified as it winds through remote, seldom traveled areas of the Mojave Desert, miles from any paved highway or habitation.

Practically all 130 miles of the road are on U.S. Bureau of Land Management land, so Casebier has been trying to get the agency to preserve and develop the road as a historic hiking trail.

"It is one of the major historical resources on the Mojave Desert," he says. "There are ruins here of old forts, a wealth of Indian petroglyphs,

before the history
first comers

prehistoric and pioneer campsites at watering spots and marvelous scenic *good to look* country the entire length of the old trail."

The wagon road closely follows a trail used for centuries by a nation of Indians living along the Colorado River. They called themselves Hamahabs. Pioneers called them Mahabs and later Mohaves.

The first non-Indian to use the trail was Franciscan priest Francisco Garces, who accompanied a group of Mohave Indians from the Colorado River to the coast at the same time Ben Franklin and Thomas Jefferson were writing the Declaration of Independence in Philadelphia.

Jedediah Strong Smith in 1826 used the trail to become the first American to reach California overland.

Kit Carson also used it, as did many who played important roles in early California, men like Edward F. Beale, Amiel Weeks Whipple and Winfield Scott Hancock.
male of

The great American camel experiment was conducted on the Old Mojave Road during the late 1850s when 100 dromedaries imported from the Middle East were tested for their usefulness, endurance and economy as a beast of burden in the West. *coming to a conclusion*

The experiment was deemed a failure. The camels were released in the desert wilds and until recent times, sightings in remote corners of the Mojave of wild camels were reported.

The old road was finally abandoned in 1883 when the railroad was pushed through the desert and a new road followed the tracks.

Casebier, 42, has produced seven books about the road. He writes, edits, sets the type and operates his own publishing house—headquartered in his Norco home—called Tales of The Mojave Road Publishing Co.

No. of Words: ___840___

Reading Time: _____

55

Selection 8

Did Indians Trick Settlers?

VOCABULARY BUILDING

*Below are several words used in this article. They are presented in the
context of the sentences or phrases in which they occur. If you are unsure
of their meanings and cannot define them from the context, look them up
in the dictionary. Spaces are provided for additional unfamiliar words
from the article to add to your vocabulary.*

1. "... early settlers struggled to make it up the long *tortuous* grade." *the angle of*

    tortuous: twisting, turning, difficulte.

2. "... along the old wagon road can be found *potsherds,* arrow points,
    and other Indian implements ..." *shard - a broken pice of eny-*
    thing sharp

    potsherds: broken seramic poots

3. "'There are ruins here of old forts, a wealth of Indian *petroglyphs,* ...
    and pioneer campsites ...'"

    petroglyphs: drawings on rocks

4. "The old road, its wagon ruts easily *discernible,* can still be identi-
    fied ..." track, mark

    discernible: eassy to see, feel or understand

5. "A better name may well have been Mt. *Bamboozled.*"

    bamboozled: bing cheeted

6. _____ : _____

7. _____ : _____

8. _____ : _____

RETENTION AND COMPREHENSION

A. True/False *(1 point each)*

1. The first non-Indian to use the Old Mojave Wagon Road trail was Jedediah Smith.

    1. T _____   F _____

2. Much of Dennis Casebier's research on the history of the Old Mojave Road is based on interviews with Indians of the area.

    2. T _____   F _____

B. Completion *(3 points each)*

3. The Old Mojave Road extended from the Colorado River almost _____ miles to the Los Angeles Harbor.

    3. _____

4. Casebier has been studying and writing about the old road for about _____ years.

    4. _____

C. Multiple Choice *(2 points each)*

5. Casebier speculates that the Indian guides failed to tell travelers about the easy pass through the mountains because (a) the pass was too far away from the original trail, (b) the Indians didn't know about the pass, (c) the Indians were playing a joke on the settlers, (d) the pass was on Mojave Indian sacred ground.

    5. _____

6. The travelers lessened the mules' loads up Rocky Ridge by (a) making the Indians carry the supplies, (b) carrying the supplies themselves, (c) throwing away unnecessary items along the trail, (d) using camels to help pull the wagons.

    6. _____

7. Casebier would like the government to preserve the Old Mojave Wagon Road for use as (a) a historic hiking trail, (b) a western theme amusement park, (c) a national park site, (d) an archaeological dig.

    7. _____

8. The attempt to use camels as beasts of burden in the Mojave in the late 1850s was deemed a failure because (a) the railroad was more efficient, (b) the camels were unused to their new environment, (c)

    8. _____

the project was too expensive, (d) no reason was given in the article.

D. *Thematic (5 points)*

9. Which statement *best* expresses the theme (*main* idea) of the article?
   (a) The Old Mojave Wagon Road is one of the major historical resources in the Mojave Desert.
   (b) Indians of the area were not reliable guides for the early settlers.
   (c) The attempt to use camels in the Mojave Desert proved unsuccessful.
   (d) Many famous early settlers, like Kit Carson, used the old trail to reach California.

9. _____ *a*

E. *Purpose (4 points)*

10. The author's *chief* purpose is
    (a) to make clear that the Indians were aware of the easier route because they had lived in the desert for centuries.
    (b) to show that the Old Mojave Wagon Road played an interesting and important part in the development of California.
    (c) to explain that if not for the Old Mojave Wagon Road, settling in California would have taken a much longer time.
    (d) to make the point that the Mojave Indians should have informed the travelers of the easier trail.

10. _____

Total Retention and Comprehension Score: _____

QUESTIONS FOR DISCUSSION (MEANING AND TECHNIQUE)

1. How does the writer of the article, Hillinger, give interest and importance to the history of the Old Mojave Wagon Road?

2. How many major elements does this article have? Which is best developed? Which is least developed? How are they tied together?

3. Is "Did Indians Trick Settlers?" the best title for the article? Why do you suppose the writer chose it? Can you suggest other titles?

4. What is the degree of Dennis Casebier's interest in the Wagon Road? Find passages in the article which help you to appreciate that interest.

5. Should the government take steps to preserve and develop the Wagon Road? To what extent should it be developed? Give reasons.

6. Ben Franklin and Thomas Jefferson are mentioned in the article. Why?

7. In your opinion why did the Indians not tell the settlers about the easier route?

SUGGESTIONS FOR WRITING

1. If you have recently visited a historical site, describe it and explain why it is important. What impression did it leave on you? Try to convince the reader to visit it.

2. Describe a strong interest you may have had in something or somebody—a sport, a famous person (rock star, actor), a hobby (horses, stamps). How did you behave? Feel?

3. In the library find the journal of an early explorer, pioneer, soldier, settler, or traveler. Using information from the journal, write a summary of a battle or a discovery or an amusing incident. Or compare living conditions as shown in the journal to your own experiences as a traveler, hiker, or camper.

4. Look up one of the historical figures mentioned in the article and write a report on that person's life and accomplishments. Get your information from more than one source.

Selection 8

Overall Reading Performance

Your overall reading performance is a combination of how fast you read and how much you comprehend and retain. The chart below allows you to find out quickly your "overall reading performance."

First enter your "reading time" and your "retention and comprehension" score in the two blanks at the bottom of the page. Then simply lay a straightedge of any kind (the edge of a sheet of paper or a pencil will do) across the chart, placing the left side of the straightedge at the appropriate point on the "Reading Rate" scale, and the right side at the appropriate point on the "Retention and Comprehension" scale. The point at which the paper or pencil intersects the scale in the middle of the page will indicate your overall performance.

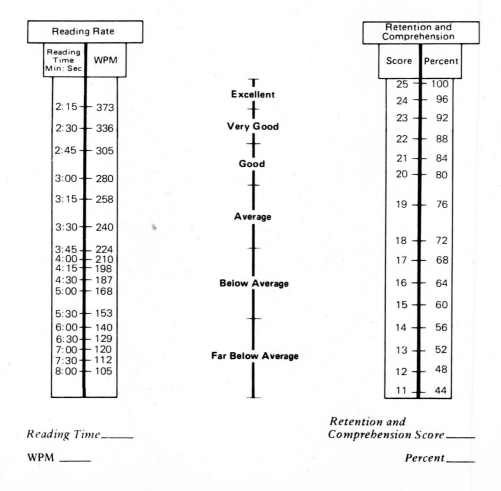

Reading Rate	
Reading Time Min: Sec	WPM
2:15	373
2:30	336
2:45	305
3:00	280
3:15	258
3:30	240
3:45	224
4:00	210
4:15	198
4:30	187
5:00	168
5:30	153
6:00	140
6:30	129
7:00	120
7:30	112
8:00	105

Excellent

Very Good

Good

Average

Below Average

Far Below Average

Retention and Comprehension	
Score	Percent
25	100
24	96
23	92
22	88
21	84
20	80
19	76
18	72
17	68
16	64
15	60
14	56
13	52
12	48
11	44

Reading Time _____

WPM _____

Retention and Comprehension Score _____

Percent _____

Selection 9

Love in the Afternoon—in a Crowded Prison Hall

SARA KING

Each time I visit my man in prison, I relive the joy of reunion—and the anguish of separation.

We meet at the big glass door at the entrance to the small visitors' hall at Lompoc Federal Correctional Institution. We look at each other silently, then turn and walk into a room jammed with hundreds of molded fiberglass chairs lined up side by side. Finding a place in the crowded hall, we sit down, appalled that we're actually in a prison. Even now, after four months of such clocked, supervised, regulated visits, we still can't get used to the frustrations.

Yet, as John presses me gently to his heart, I feel warm and tender, and tears well up inside me, as they do each weekend. I have seven hours to spend with the man I love—all too brief a time for sharing a lifetime of emotion: love and longing, sympathy and tenderness, resentment and anger.

The guard's voice jars us: "Please keep the chairs in order!"

We can't keep from laughing, for we're struck by the absurdity of the scene: 60 couples, some with families, packed in a single room—each trying, somehow, to create an atmosphere of intimacy. And what's demanded by the single guard who's assigned to oversee us? *Chairs in a straight line.*

Nevertheless, John and I abide by the rules, holding each other as close as we can—without moving our chairs—and the loneliness of the past week gradually subsides.

We break our silent communion with small talk much like the kind we shared at home for the past three years. Like: *Should we have the van repaired, or sell it?*

Then we speak of our separate needs and fears. He feels defeated—by confinement, by prison life, by the 20 months left to serve on a two-year sentence for a drug-related charge that we think should never have come

Source: Los Angeles Times, Nov. 5, 1976. Reprinted by permission.

[handwritten note: Is nothing she is going out with others?]

to trial. He feels deeply insecure, too, doubting my fidelity and hating himself for doubting me. He wants support and reassurance.

But what about me? *Doesn't he understand that this has been an ordeal for me, too?* My whole life fell apart when he went to prison: Our wedding plans were canceled; I had to quit school, sell everything, find a job and move in with relatives.

Prison has become my second full-time occupation. Each weekend I spend 10 hours traveling. Always I must save money—money for my motel room in Lompoc, money for his collect phone calls to supplement the letters we write, money for his supplies at the prison commissary. *[handwritten note: store]*

Worst of all, there's the almost unbearable burden of conducting my home life alone. At least in prison he has no decisions to make, no meals to worry about, no rent. So I, too, need reassurance and emotional support.

Suddenly we're arguing over who should write more often. Then we realize we have only a few more hours together, and this helps us find in each other the sympathy we both seek. This cycle of misunderstanding, resentment, resolution repeats itself throughout the day's visit.

We're not alone in trying to withstand the emotional stress of prison visits. All around the crowded room couples are weeping, arguing, embracing.

A woman I see every time I come here is chatting with her husband as she diapers one of her three children. I admire the strength of this woman who, despite obvious hardship, manages to keep herself and the children neat and reasonably cheerful for these difficult weekly journeys.

Near the window a man is trying to be the strong, affectionate mate his wife must have always wanted. Rubbing her neck gently, he wipes the tears from her cheek—but he too is crying.

Sexual tension pervades the room. The rules permit kissing and embracing within the bounds of good taste. But many couples, either through months of practice or with the complicity of the other couples, succeed in fooling the guard and carrying out a variety of sexual activities. The risk, however, is great, for, if caught, the inmate is sent to solitary confinement.

Most prisoners and visitors are troubled by the behavior code. Interpretation and enforcement is left to the guards, and they tend to be unpredictable. While some guards are understanding, others seem bent on turning visits into punitive exercises, especially for racially mixed couples.

Even worse, these rules overlook the enormous importance of private visits—for prisoners and their loved ones alike. Despite hopeful talk in the visitors' hall, there are no signs that the federal system is about to implement a family-visitation program like the one California adopted in 1969 for its prison system.

For the prisoner, private visits would aid rehabilitation by providing a small measure of continuity in his life and a sense of what freedom really means. For loved ones, they would mean hope and encouragement in the seemingly endless ordeal of waiting.

But, until such visits come to pass, John and I will have to carry on as best we can, locked in longing for the end of his prison sentence. It's a term of loneliness and despair to which, whether he realized it or not, the judge also sentenced *me*.

No. of Words: ___850___

Reading Time: _____

Selection 9

Love in the Afternoon—in a Crowded Prison Hall

VOCABULARY BUILDING

Below are several words used in this article. They are presented in the context of the sentences or phrases in which they occur. If you are unsure of their meanings and cannot define them from the context, look them up in the dictionary. Spaces are provided for additional unfamiliar words from the article to add to your vocabulary.

1. "I relive the joy of reunion—and the *anguish* of separation."

   anguish: _bad fillings, pain on your fillings/hart also pisical_

2. "He feels deeply insecure, too, doubting my *fidelity* . . ."

   fidelity: _trust someone with sexuality_

3. ". . . many couples . . . with the *complicity* of the other couples, succeed in fooling the guard . . ."

   complicity: _being a partner in the crime, cooperaiting in the crime_

4. ". . . others [guards] seem bent on turning visits into *punitive* exercises . . ."

   punitive: _punishment_

5. _____:_____

6. _____:_____

7. _____:_____

8. _____:_____

RETENTION AND COMPREHENSION

A. True/False (1 point each)

1. The author has been visiting her friend in prison every weekend for over four months.

   1. T _____ F _____

2. According to the article, the federal prison system has a visitation program
which is the same as the visitation program in the state of California prison system.

2. T _____ F _____

B. *Completion* (*3 points each*)

3. The prisoner is allowed to spend _____ hours
with visitors.

3. _____

4. The author's friend is serving a two-year sentence
for a _____ conviction.

4. _____

C. *Multiple Choice* (*2 points each*)

5. At Lompoc prison prisoners are (a) allowed to
bring visitors into their cells, (b) can take visitors
to any area which is not restricted, (c) must remain
in the visitor's hall with other prisoners and visitors, (d) can meet with friends and relatives in a
special room reserved for small groups.

5. _____

6. When her man was convicted, the author had to (a)
sell a van for living expenses, (b) move to Lompoc
to be near the prisoner, (c) give up her job, (d)
quit school.

6. _____

7. The author states that her man feels so defeated by
being in prison that he (a) fails to understand her
own ordeal, (b) cannot make necessary decisions,
(c) argues with her during most of the visit, (d)
cannot show any affection for her.

7. _____

8. The author suggests that the prison guards are (a)
unnecessarily cruel to both prisoners and visitors,
(b) understanding of the couple's situation, (c)
unpredictable in the way each one enforces the
behavior code, (d) too concerned with keeping
the chairs in order.

8. _____

D. *Thematic* (*5 points*)

9. Which statement *best* expresses the theme (*main*
idea) of the article?

9. _____

(a) Judges are too harsh in giving prison terms to married couples.
(b) Prison confinement, in a sense, also punishes guiltless relatives and friends as well as the prisoner.
(c) Our entire prison system is unsympathetic to the social needs of prisoners' families.
(d) The visitation facility at Lompoc Prison is too outdated and small to accommodate prisoners and visitors comfortably.

E. Purpose (4 points)

10. The author's *chief* purpose is
    (a) to make us realize how mean the guards are during the family visitations with their emphasis on the "rules."
    (b) to persuade us that her man was wrongfully imprisoned for two years on a drug-related charge that should never have come to trial.
    (c) to inform us of the inequities of the California family visitation program compared to the federal one.
    (d) to make us understand what she and her man (and others like them) go through every week and to persuade us that privacy during these weekly visits is important.

10. _____

Total Retention and Comprehension Score: _____

QUESTIONS FOR DISCUSSION (MEANING AND TECHNIQUE)

1. Should prisoners be allowed private visits with their loved ones or not? Would it aid in rehabilitation, as the author claims, or not? What are the arguments for and against?

2. Why do you suppose guards are particularly hard on racially mixed couples?

3. Why do you think the guards insist on having the chairs "in a straight line"? Should they?

4. In what way has the judge sentenced the author of the article as well as her loved one?

5. How and why do you think people like the author's loved one wind up in prison? Are they bad people?

6. Do you think most prisoners have such devoted loved ones on the outside, or do you think this is an exceptional case?

SUGGESTIONS FOR WRITING

1. Write a letter to a real or imagined loved one in prison.

2. Imagine yourself in prison. Describe a visit you've just had with your loved one or with your children, or with both.

3. Imagine yourself in prison. Write a letter to your loved one(s). You could do one, several, none, or all of the following: describe how you landed in jail, describe the conditions, express your longing for freedom and/or your loved ones, describe what you'll do on your first day of freedom.

4. Write an argument for or against capital punishment, private visitations, better (or worse) prison conditions, rehabilitation.

5. Write an essay on why you feel society is (or is not) responsible for criminals.

Selection 9

Overall Reading Performance

Your overall reading performance is a combination of how fast you read and how much you comprehend and retain. The chart below allows you to find out quickly your "overall reading performance."

First enter your "reading time" and your "retention and comprehension" score in the two blanks at the bottom of the page. Then simply lay a straightedge of any kind (the edge of a sheet of paper or a pencil will do) across the chart, placing the left side of the straightedge at the appropriate point on the "Reading Rate" scale, and the right side at the appropriate point on the "Retention and Comprehension" scale. The point at which the paper or pencil intersects the scale in the middle of the page will indicate your overall performance.

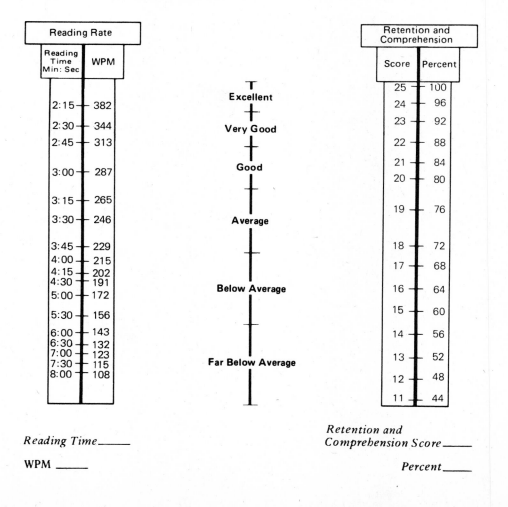

Reading Time_____

WPM _____

Retention and
Comprehension Score_____

Percent_____

Selection 10

Kudzu Vines Creeping into Heart of Dixie

NICHOLAS C. CHRISS

ALONG HIGHWAY 78, Miss.—This is the home of the dreaded kudzu vine, which grows a foot a day, has been rumored to overtake slow-moving Southerners, and covers acres of Dixie every summer with its thick tangle of green leaves and fragrant purple flowers.

Some of the most spectacular kudzu displays may be seen along this two-lane blacktop road in northeast Mississippi.

Few people from other parts of the country have ever heard of it or seen it, but the kudzu vine is renowned in the South. It multiplies so fast there is a saying about it: "When you plant kudzu, drop it and run."

The kudzu has been around almost a century, but Southerners have never been able to establish a good relationship with the vine. It continues to perpetuate itself, popping up everywhere in Dixie.

Dr. Jack Tinga, of the University of Georgia experiment stations, probably the world's leading expert on the kudzu, said he got a call from Hollywood not long ago. "They wanted to do a horror movie about the kudzu vines," he said.

"It can sure enough cause some problems," said Pete Johnson at Ye Old Liquor Store in Olive Branch on Highway 78, deep in kudzu vine country.

Like many Southerners, Johnson has learned to be wary of the kudzu, for he has seen it cross highways, slither into homes, inundate barns.

It is difficult to think of any worth the cursed kudzu contributes to mankind, except that it probably has done more to beautify the Southern countryside than Mrs. Lyndon B. Johnson and the Highway Beautification Act.

The kudzu, as travelers along Highway 78 can see, has covered abandoned privies and billboards, trash heaps, rusted cars, eroded creek banks and hotels and motels that failed.

The *Atlanta Constitution* once carried an editorial urging the federal

Source: Los Angeles Times, Sept. 1, 1977. Reprinted by permission.

government to put the unemployed to work digging up the kudzu before it took over the world.

But like it or not, the kudzu is as much a part of Dixie as grits and mules. It is as much a part of the atmosphere along Highway 78 as yams, speeding lumber mill trucks, carp for 39 cents a pound and country songs such as "Don't Mess With the U.S. Male."

"It was planted here years ago to stop erosion, but it's done took over now," said Sam Moses at the North Mississippi U.S. Soil Conservation Station near here.

That was a time when the U.S. Agricultural Stabilization and Conservation Service thought the kudzu vine might be the salvation of the South. The kudzu was supposed to rejuvenate the once-rich Southern earth from which the topsoil had disappeared. The long kudzu roots would provide nitrogen.

The young men of the Civilian Conservation Corps were put to work in the 1930s along thousands of miles of roads planting vines on creek banks and in gullies.

But the kudzu did nothing to help the South rise again. In fact, so much of it was planted some people thought that kudzu would be king, not cotton.

Then everyone discovered something terrible: once the kudzu got going, it was hard to stop. And where the kudzu grew, nothing else grew. It so effectively covered vegetation, trees included, that it blocked out all the sunshine and much of the vegetation underneath died.

Still, Tinga of the University of Georgia sees some good in the vine: not long ago he suggested that kudzu be planted in barrels and placed on rooftops. The proliferating vines would completely cover the buildings and thereby reduce air conditioning costs, he said.

Don't laugh. That was one of the original uses of the kudzu—poor tenant farmers grew it to cover their shanty homes and help them keep cool.

Tinga may be one of the few friends the kudzu has left in the world. He also has recommended using the vine as a kind of reserve food supply for livestock.

"If you have 100 acres of land, you take 10 acres of it, plant kudzu and put a fence around it so it will not escape. When a drought comes along and you don't have a grazing pasture, you turn your livestock in to the 10 acres of kudzu," Tinga said.

But in these times of highly mechanized and expensive farming, not many farmers can set aside 10 acres for kudzu.

The kudzu vine came to the United States from Japan in 1876 when it was used as part of an ornamental plant exhibition in Philadelphia. Somehow it ended up down South, where it thrived in the heat and humidity.

Today it is seen mainly in the poorer areas of the South where the roadbeds are unkempt, covering acres of neglected land. Some of the most spectacular displays are at the junction of Highways 78 and 30 at New Albany, Miss., near the approach to the Tippa River bridge, at Hickory Flats, and on the outskirts of Byhalia and Chulehoma.

It is in these areas, Tinga said, that the kudzu "holds the world together," preventing more erosion on creekbanks and neglected acreage, and binding together old barns, privies and shacks that might long ago have disintegrated.

One of the worst things about fighting the kudzu is that it takes a very powerful herbicide to get rid of it. One or two applications simply won't do it.

"You've got to hit it more than a couple times," Tinga said, "otherwise it'll gallop right on." The roots go down seven to eight feet.

No. of Words: 915

Reading Time: _____

Selection 10

Kudzu Vines Creeping into Heart of Dixie

VOCABULARY BUILDING

Below are several words used in this article. They are presented in the context of the sentences or phrases in which they occur. If you are unsure of their meanings and cannot define them from the context, look them up in the dictionary. Spaces are provided for additional unfamiliar words from the article to add to your vocabulary.

1. ". . . . but the kudzu vine is *renowned* in the South."

    renowned: *well known, famouse.*

2. "It continues to *perpetuate* itself, popping up everywhere in Dixie."

    perpetuate: *to keep growing*

3. "Johnson has learned to be *wary* of the kudzu, for he has seen it cross highways, *slither* into houses, *inundate* barns."

    wary: *becareful*

    slither: *slite, (lik a snake)*

    inundate: *cour over*

4. "The kudzu was supposed to *rejuvenate* the once-rich Southern earth."

    rejuvenate: *young*

5. "'It was planted here years ago to stop *erosion*.'"

    erosion: *the active reoty, to wash away*

6. _____ : _____

7. _____ : _____

8. _____ : _____

9. _____ : _____

10. _____ : _____

RETENTION AND COMPREHENSION

A. True/False *(1 point each)*

1. The kudzu vine came to the United States from China.

   1. T _____ F _____

2. The kudzu vine grows mainly in the wealthier areas of the South.

   2. T _____ F _____

B. Completion *(3 points each)*

3. Dr. Tinga recommends that if a farmer has 100 acres of land, he should plant_____ acres of it with kudzu.

   3. _____

4. So much kudzu was planted, people thought kudzu would be_____, not cotton.

   4. _____

C. Multiple Choice *(2 points each)*

5. Dr. Tinga received a call asking him (a) to recommend an effective herbicide, (b) to explain some beneficial uses for the kudzu vine, (c) to help with a horror movie on the kudzu vine, (d) to give his opinion about planting the kudzu vine on rooftops.

   5. _____

6. The kudzu vine grows at the rate of (a) 2 feet a day, (b) ½ foot a day, (c) 1 inch a day, (d) 1 foot a day.

   6. _____

7. The kudzu vine has been growing in the South about (a) 200 years, (b) 100 years, (c) 50 years, (d) 30 years.

   7. _____

8. The young men of the Civilian Conservation Corps were put to work (a) uprooting thousands of miles of kudzu vine, (b) planting kudzu vines on rooftops to reduce air conditioning costs, (c) planting kudzu as a kind of reserve food supply for livestock, (d) planting many kudzu vines on creek banks and in gullies.

   8. _____

D. Thematic *(5 points)*

9. Which statement *best* expresses the theme (*main idea*) of the article?

   9. _____

   (a) The southern kudzu vine grows fast, is hard to kill, and covers everything in its path.

(b) Although the kudzu vine is disliked, it reminds many people of the old South.

(c) The kudzu vine has many good uses to which it could be put.

(d) The kudzu was planted to stop erosion, but now it "holds the world together."

E. Purpose (4 points)

10. The author's *chief* purpose is

    10. _____

(a) to make us laugh at the problem of the kudzu vine in the South.

(b) to awaken us to a wasted resource in our own backyard.

(c) to report, with some humor, on an unusual, picturesque, and somewhat troublesome plant very common in parts of the South.

(d) to report, with some humor, on the history of a plant common in the South, and some recommended uses for it.

Total Retention and Comprehension Score: _____

QUESTIONS FOR DISCUSSION (MEANING AND TECHNIQUE)

1. How does the writer achieve humor in the very first paragraph?

2. What was the Civilian Conservation Corps in the thirties? Why was it created? Was it a good idea? Would reviving it now be a good idea?

3. Why was the kudzu vine planted in the first place? Is it performing that function at all?

4. Is the kudzu vine associated with any social/economic class? What statements in the selection support your answer?

5. Why is Dr. Tinga of the University of Georgia considered a "friend" of the kudzu?

6. What do you think of some of the suggested uses for the kudzu? Can you think of any others?

7. What are some of the specifics and details given in the article to make it more vivid?

8. What do the quotes add to the article?

9. Would the article benefit from a different conclusion?

SUGGESTIONS FOR WRITING

1. If you think the conclusion of this article is unsatisfactory, write one you think more suitable.

2. Describe in a somewhat humorous way your own battle with a weed (or weeds).

3. Write a composition describing something you or someone else did with good intentions but that ended up with all kinds of unforeseen, unfortunate consequences.

4. Write a proposal for doing away with the kudzu and explain why it should be eradicated (you can be only half serious).

5. Write a proposal for planting the kudzu in other parts of the country and explain why and how it should be done, its benefits, etc. (you can be only half serious).

6. Perhaps you have personally some connection or recollection of kudzu; if so, write about it.

7. Write an imaginary interview with Dr. Tinga about the history, uses, and abuses of kudzu. Write it in the form of questions and answers.

Selection 10

Overall Reading Performance

Your overall reading performance is a combination of how fast you read and how much you comprehend and retain. The chart below allows you to find out quickly your "overall reading performance."

First enter your "reading time" and your "retention and comprehension" score in the two blanks at the bottom of the page. Then simply lay a straightedge of any kind (the edge of a sheet of paper or a pencil will do) across the chart, placing the left side of the straightedge at the appropriate point on the "Reading Rate" scale, and the right side at the appropriate point on the "Retention and Comprehension" scale. The point at which the paper or pencil intersects the scale in the middle of the page will indicate your overall performance.

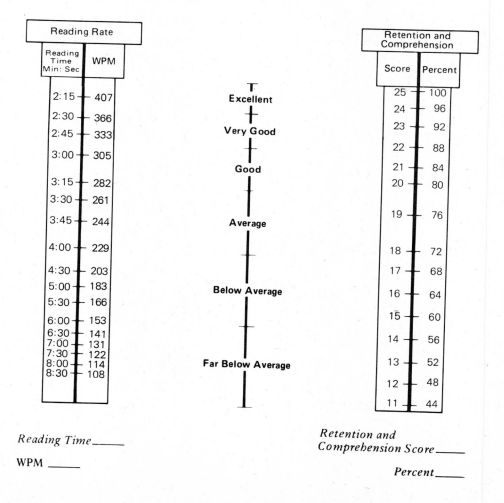

Reading Time_____

WPM _____

Retention and
Comprehension Score_____

Percent_____

Selection 11

It's Never Too Late for Success

CHARLES D. RICE

You and your parents can stop worrying—Pasteur, Edison, Darwin and lots more were far from being geniuses in their teens.

History books seldom mention it, but the truth is that many of our greatest figures were practically "beatniks" when they were teen-agers. They were given to daydreaming, indecision, hebetude (plain dullness), and they showed no promise of being doctor, lawyer or Indian chief.

So, young men and women, if you suffer from the same symptoms, don't despair. The world was built by men and women whose parents worried that they would "never amount to a hill of beans." You don't hear too much about their early failure because parents prefer to cite more inspiring examples.

A Man They Don't Tell You About

If you take piano lessons and your attitude towards practicing is marked by laziness, your parents might justly complain and flaunt before you the famous picture of little Mozart in his ruffled nightshirt, playing the piano at midnight in the attic. But the point is, your parents would not show you a picture of a certain party who never showed a whit of interest in music during his formative years. In fact he never showed talent in any direction whatever. Finally put to studying law, he barely passed his final exams. It was not until he was 22 that he suddenly became fired with a great passion for music, and his name was Peter Ilyitch Tschaikowsky.

In the sciences, there have been hundreds of geniuses who aimed straight at the goal from earliest years, and hundreds who showed no aptitude at all. There were the teen-age Mayo brothers, who actually assisted their father in his crude country operating room. On the other hand, Harvey Cushing, one of the world's greatest brain surgeons, might have become a professional ballplayer if his father hadn't pleaded that he give medicine a try.

Source: Charles D. Rice, United Newspaper Magazine Corp. Reprinted by permission of P. A. R. Inc.

The great Pasteur's parents were in despair because teen-age Louis did nothing but draw pictures and go fishing. Pasteur was 20 years old before he became even faintly interested in science.

Edison Was "Addled"

So it goes. You have the Wright brothers, who were brilliant at engineering in their early teens, and you have Thomas Alva Edison, whose teacher tried to get him out of the class because his brain was "addled." You have the Nobel Prize physicist Enrico Fermi, who at 17 had read enough mathematics to qualify for a doctor's degree. And you have the great Albert Schweitzer, who wavered between music and the church until he was 30. Then he started his medical studies.

Darwin Hated School

Charles Darwin's early life was a mess. He hated school, and his father once shouted: "You care for nothing but shooting dogs and rat-catching, and you will be a disgrace to yourself and all your family!" He was sent to Glasgow to study medicine, but he couldn't stand the sight of blood. He was sent to divinity school and barely managed to graduate. Whereupon he chucked the whole business and shipped to the South Seas on the famous exploring ship *Beagle*. On that voyage, one of history's greatest scientists was born. It was here the he collected the material for the book that would revolutionize biological science—*The Origin of the Species*.

Faulkner Failed in English

Politics offers a familiar example of contrast. Herbert Hoover must have learned administration in the cradle. When he was at school he was drafted as football manager, though he didn't know the game, and the glee club manager, though he couldn't sing a note. Whatever he touched went smoothly, glee club or food for a starving Europe.

But one of his successors in the White House had about as checkered a youth as can be imagined. Turned down by West Point because of poor vision, Harry Truman tried a dozen jobs, including stretches in a drugstore, a bank, a bottling works, and a railroad yard. But he got there just the same.

Great writers are supposed to be born, not made, but here again there are many fascinating exceptions. William Faulkner quit school in the fifth grade and rattled around the country as a house painter and a dishwasher.

Once he tried attending college, but failed in freshman English and quit. He wangled a postmaster's job in a small Mississippi town, and infuriated the populace by getting the mail all mixed up and closing the office whenever he felt like it. Faulkner was 25 before he started the writing career that won him a Nobel prize.

And just to show that girls can be as confusing as boys, take Pearl Buck, who from early youth made it a point to write at least a few lines every day of her life. Then take Edna Ferber, whose sole ambition was to be an actress; she never even thought of writing anything until she was in her 20's and had to take a $3-a-week job on a newspaper to help her family.

How About Those Prodigies?

And added to all the aforementioned paradoxes you have a small army of child prodigies who were graduated from college when they were 15, and are now obscure clerks in accounting departments. And you have a small army of men who were too stupid or indolent to get into or finish college and who are today presidents of the firms that hire the prodigies.

So who's to say what about youth? Any young boy or girl who knows what he wants to do in life is probably the better off for it. But no teen-ager need despair of the future. He has that one special advantage over the greatest man alive—time! If you don't think time counts, look at Grandma Moses. She never sold a painting till she was 80.

No. of Words: 945

Reading Time: _____

Selection 11

It's Never Too Late for Success

VOCABULARY BUILDING

Below are several words used in this article. They are presented in the context of the sentences or phrases in which they occur. If you are unsure of their meanings and cannot define them from the context, look them up in the dictionary. Spaces are provided for additional unfamiliar words from the article to add to your vocabulary.

1. "... parents prefer to *cite* more inspiring examples."

   cite: _____

2. "... your parents might justly complain and *flaunt* before you the famous picture of little Mozart ... playing the piano at midnight ..."

   flaunt: _____

3. "In the sciences, there have been hundreds ... who showed no *aptitude* at all."

   aptitude: _____

4. "He *wangled* a postmaster's job in a small Mississippi town ..."

   wangled: _____

5. "And added to all the aforementioned *paradoxes* you have a small army of child *prodigies* who ... are now obscure clerks ..."

   paradoxes: _____

   prodigies: _____

6. "And you have a small army of men who were too stupid or *indolent* to get into or finish college ..."

   indolent: _____

7. _____ : _____

8. _____ : _____

9. _____ : _____

10. _____ : _____

RETENTION AND COMPREHENSION

A. True/False *(1 point each)*

1. Mozart wasn't interested in music till he was past his teens.

   1. T _____ F _____

2. Truman showed great skill as a leader and organizer all through his youth.

   2. T _____ F _____

3. Cushing might have become a professional ballplayer if he hadn't become a surgeon instead.

   3. T _____ F _____

4. Girls tend to show their talent and know where they're headed earlier than boys.

   4. T _____ F _____

B. Completion *(3 points each)*

5. Tschaikowsky didn't get interested in music till he was_____years old.

   5. _____

6. Edna Ferber, the writer, always wanted to be a(n)_____when she was young.

   6. _____

7. Edison's teacher tried to get him out of the class because his brain was_____.

   7. _____

8. Grandma Moses never sold a painting till she was_____years old.

   8. _____

C. Multiple Choice *(2 points each)*

9. Pasteur, Edison, and Darwin (a) as teenagers, were very interested in their future work, (b) were far from showing genius in their teens, (c) showed early promise, (d) failed in school as boys.

   9. _____

10. The Wright brothers (a) were brilliant at engineering in their early teens, (b) wavered between music and the church, (c) were poor at their engineering studies as teenagers, (d) barely managed to graduate.

   10. _____

11. The writer, Pearl Buck, (a) never wrote a line till

   11. _____

she was 25, (b) had to take a $3-a-week job to help her family, (c) failed English, (d) from early youth wrote a few lines every day of her life.

12. Child prodigies (a) always succeed later in life, (b) always fail later in life, (c) often don't make great careers for themselves later in life, (d) "never amount to a hill of beans."

12. _____

13. At the age of 17, Nobel Prize physicist Enrico Fermi (a) wavered between music and the church, (b) helped his father in his crude country operating room, (c) couldn't stand the sight of blood, (d) had read enough mathematics to qualify for a doctor's degree.

13. _____

D. Thematic (8 points)

14. Which statement *best* expresses the theme (*main idea*) of the article?

14. _____

(*a*) Most adult successes showed signs of failure in their teens.

(*b*) Failure in school often leads to success later in life.

(*c*) Early success in school is not important for success later in life.

(*d*) Some very successful adults were average or seemed like failures when they were teenagers.

E. Purpose (7 points)

15. The author's *chief* purpose is

15. _____

(*a*) to show that most successful adults were failures as teenagers.

(*b*) to show that early schooling is not important for later success.

(*c*) to show that sometimes teenagers who fail or show no signs of great worth or talent turn out to be greatly successful as adults.

(*d*) to give many examples of successful adults who were failures or showed no signs of worth or talent as teenagers.

Total Retention and Comprehension Score: _____

QUESTIONS FOR DISCUSSION (MEANING AND TECHNIQUE)

1. Does this article mean that there's no correlation at all between success as a young person and success as an adult?

2. To be successful as an adult, what is it important to do or be as a young person? Is it the same for everyone?

3. Do you think those who "fail" or are judged "no good" as young people have a better chance or a worse chance of becoming successful adults than those who do well as young people?

4. Since a "young failure" can become an "adult success," are parents wrong to "push" their children to do better? Explain your answer.

SUGGESTIONS FOR WRITING

1. This article can be considered an example of an "inductive essay." It argues that youthful "failures" can become adult successes and supports its argument by citing numerous such instances (e.g., Edison, Truman, Faulkner, etc.). Write an "inductive essay" in which you make a point ("reading novels makes you understand yourself, others, and the whole world better" or "men/women can get you into trouble" or "a college education puts you ahead of others in many ways" or any other point you can think of) and then support your point with many examples—just as the article does.

2. Write an article using people you know as examples of how "bad" kids/people turned out unexpectedly "good."

3. Write an "extended definition" essay defining "success" and/or "failure." What do these words mean? Success or failure according to whom, according to what standards? What is success? What is failure?

4. Write an essay about your own life and its successes and failures.

5. Write an essay explaining what you are doing now to try to assure your future success.

6. Look up the life story of one of the people mentioned in this article and write a summary/report of it.

Overall Reading Performance

Your overall reading performance is a combination of how fast you read and how much you comprehend and retain. The chart below allows you to find out quickly your "overall reading performance."

First enter your "reading time" and your "retention and comprehension" score in the two blanks at the bottom of the page. Then simply lay a straightedge of any kind (the edge of a sheet of paper or a pencil will do) across the chart, placing the left side of the straightedge at the appropriate point on the "Reading Rate" scale, and the right side at the appropriate point on the "Retention and Comprehension" scale. The point at which the paper or pencil intersects the scale in the middle of the page will indicate your overall performance.

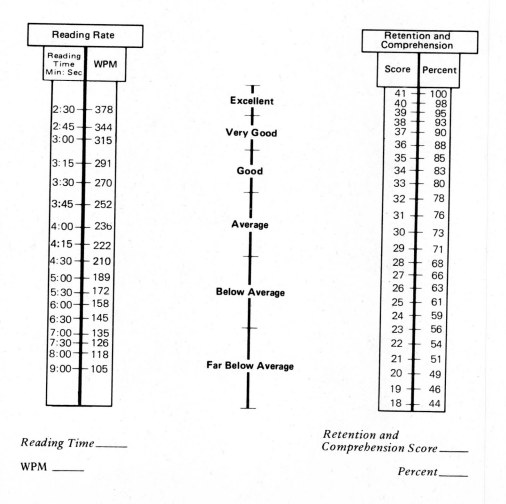

Reading Time _____

WPM _____

Retention and Comprehension Score _____

Percent _____

Selection 12
Is Speed Reading Overrated?

JAMES B. STOREY, DTM

To savor the beauty of good writing,
you must read slowly.

I've heard many exasperated students and professionals express a desire to take a speed reading course so they can increase their knowledge at a faster rate. But the information I've collected over the last few years leads me to believe that "speed reading" may be less useful than most people think.

There *are* techniques that can be taught to help you move your eyes across a page in a more disciplined and efficient manner. When I taught at the University of Oklahoma, I always spent part of the first class period discussing some of these techniques. Primarily, I tried to make students more aware of how the eye tends to wander (usually backwards and upwards) when reading.

There are other bad reading habits that can be broken through instruction, but you don't need a formal course to increase your reading speed. For a couple of dollars, you can buy any one of half a dozen books on speed reading. If you practice the techniques outlined in any one of those books, I'm certain you'll learn to read somewhat faster than you do now. At least you'll discover what you're doing wrong.

Retention

Don't push yourself to read at an extraordinary pace. The claims that you can read and fully comprehend 30,000 or 40,000 words per minute (or even 4000 words per minute) is a gross exaggeration. One researcher proved this in a study in which irrelevant and illogical sentences were added to a passage of writing. The "speed readers" who were tested didn't notice the irrelevant lines—the non-speed readers spotted them immediately.

Source: The Toastmaster, July 1980. Reprinted with permission of *The Toastmaster*, the official publication of Toastmaster International.

And about the 40,000-words-per-minute readers: It was said that President Kennedy read three or four major daily newspapers each morning in just a few minutes. But he probably obtained all the information he needed from the headlines and topic paragraphs. I wish I could have tested him after he completed his daily newspaper reading. I'm willing to bet he would not have known most details revealed in the body of the articles— except for those in stories he read completely. I suspect that's also true of most persons who make claims to great reading speeds.

I've never taken one of the reading courses that promise to increase your reading pace astronomically, but I've spoken at length to many persons who have. Virtually all of them felt the courses had been helpful but, in the long run, didn't make them faster readers.

My secretary used to teach a speed reading course for the personnel department of a large utility company. She told me the follow-up surveys indicated that employees who attended all 12 classes showed no significant long-term improvement in their reading speed. She did add, however, that many company employees took the course to enhance their promotion opportunities, and it may well have served that purpose.

I have also interviewed people who have attended the free introductory sessions offered by some of these courses. Their stories indicate that dubious methods are sometimes used to sell the courses. Here's how: First, you are asked to read a passage from a book with which most persons would be unfamiliar. Your reading speed and comprehension are tested during this exercise. Then, after about an hour of instruction, another reading test is given. But this time the reading is one with which most educated Americans would be familiar—such as *Huckleberry Finn*. Not surprisingly, persons attending these introductory sessions find that their "exit" speed and comprehension are better than their "entry" performance.

I'm not saying the promoters of these courses are unethical. Far from it. They are legitimate business people providing a service which may benefit many people. Whether or not this sales technique is valid is up to you to decide.

Appreciating Beauty

Finally, let's address the question of whether speed reading is even a desirable goal. I am an avid fiction reader. Consciously or unconsciously, readers of fiction appreciate the beauty in good writing. Occasionally I will read a passage or sentence over and over just to let the beauty of its construction soak in. I never fail to be impressed by the opening sentences of Ernest Hemingway's *The Old Man and the Sea,* Vladimir Nabakov's *Laughter in the Dark,* and Herman Melville's *Moby Dick.*

If I was a determined speed reader, I would never have the time to appreciate these beautiful passages. And I'd never have the time to savor the development of a character like Rhett Butler, the Great Gatsby or Captain Ahab. Good writers must be read carefully and thoughtfully to be fully appreciated.

To carry the question of the need for rapid reading a bit further, let's consider the technical or educational material most of us must read for our jobs. If you work in a technical field—and most business and professional people do—you'd better read slowly and carefully. Almost all businesses today are subject to federal regulation to some degree. If you must read the *Federal Register,* the *Code of Federal Regulations,* the *OSHA Handbook* or other technical materials related directly to your job, I'd urge you to take your time. A misreading could be costly or damaging to your firm.

On the other hand, newspapers, news magazines and other publications should be read with some degree of speed. Here's where a general knowledge of speed reading techniques might be useful. Especially since this is the most common type of reading we do.

Anyone can improve their reading efficiency. To do so, you must learn some basic techniques and then consciously apply them. Perhaps an expensive course would help you, but an inexpensive paperback and concentrated practice might provide as much long-term benefit. In any case, you lose nothing by trying the self-help approach.

But before you get too worried about your present reading speed, remember: Most of the publications we read for enjoyment, education or for our jobs should be read slowly and carefully anyway. So maybe we should all worry less about imagined deficiencies in our reading speed.

No. of Words: __1005__

Reading Time: _____

Selection 12

Is Speed Reading Overrated?

VOCABULARY BUILDING

Below are several words used in this article. They are presented in the context of the sentences or phrases in which they occur. If you are unsure of their meanings and cannot define them from the context, look them up in the dictionary. Spaces are provided for additional unfamiliar words from the article to add to your vocabulary.

1. "I've heard many *exasperated* students and professionals express a desire to take a speed reading course so they can increase their knowledge at a faster rate."

   exasperated: _____

2. "I've never taken one of the reading courses that promise to increase your reading pace *astronomically* . . ."

   astronomically: _____

3. "I am an *avid* fiction reader."

   avid: _____

4. "And I'd never have the time to *savor* the development of a character like Rhett Butler, the Great Gatsby, or Captain Ahab."

   savor: _____

5. _____ : _____

6. _____ : _____

7. _____ : _____

RETENTION AND COMPREHENSION

A. True/False (1 point each)

1. In the article the author does not indicate he had any experience teaching.

   1. T _____   F _____

2. He states that the speed-reading course he took did not increase his speed to any great degree.

    2. T _____ F _____

3. He mentions the title *Huckleberry Finn* as a book with which most educated Americans would be familiar.

    3. T _____ F _____

4. He suggests that people interested in improving their reading speeds might try to do so with the aid of an inexpensive how-to paperback before enrolling in a speed-reading course.

    4. T _____ F _____

B. Completion *(3 points each)*

5. The author points out one bad reading habit: how the eye tends to wander, usually backwards and _____ .

    5. _____

6. One person mentioned as a speed reader who supposedly read three or four newspapers each morning was President _____ .

    6. _____

7. The author gives specific examples of federal regulation publications that should be read slowly and carefully. The title of one of those publications is

    _____

    7. _____

8. He doubts that people can read 30,000 or 40,000 words per minute and suggests that even _____ words per minute may be an exaggeration.

    8. _____

C. Multiple Choice *(2 points each)*

9. When speed readers were tested on materials to which irrelevant and illogical sentences were added, they (a) picked out the meaningless sentences quickly, (b) didn't notice the meaningless sentences, (c) were confused by the material, (d) showed a wide range of reading speeds from very slow to very fast.

    9. _____

10. The follow-up surveys taken by the author's secretary suggested that her ex-students had (a) in-

    10. _____

creased their high reading rates; (b) lost an insignificant amount of reading speed; (c) indicated no significant long-term improvement in speed; (d) become, in fact, less confident when reading difficult material.

11. According to the author, some speed-reading course methods may result in questionable fast reading rates because (a) comprehension is considered less important than speed; (b) students skim the material first, resulting in two readings; (c) students select their own speed practice material; (d) postcourse material is easier than precourse material.

11. _____

12. The author feels that learning to speed read good books by great writers (a) is the only way that he can read the best fiction ever written, (b) defeats the purpose of reading to enjoy good writing, (c) is a skill all students must develop, (d) is the main reason why people take speed-reading courses.

12. _____

13. One type of printed material the author thinks can be read quickly is (a) a textbook, (b) a business letter, (c) a news magazine, (d) a phone book.

13. _____

D. Thematic (8 points)

14. Which statement *best* expresses the theme (*main* idea) of the article?
    (a) Speed-reading courses are too expensive and the results are impractical for most people.
    (b) Learning how to read faster is a skill that can be self-taught by practice with readily available, inexpensive materials.
    (c) The technique of speed reading is an asset that may be overblown because it has limited use for most readers.
    (d) Speed readers' claims of high reading rates are probably untrue because no one reads everything at the same rate of speed.

14. _____

E. Purpose (7 points)

15. The author's *chief* purpose is

15. _____

(*a*) to present his view of the values of learning to speed read.

(*b*) to examine the validity of the results proclaimed by speed-reading courses.

(*c*) to persuade the reader that speed reading does not apply to the reading of fiction.

(*d*) to show that, for his purposes, speed reading does not produce a significant amount of improvement.

Total Retention and Comprehension Score: _____

QUESTIONS FOR DISCUSSION (MEANING AND TECHNIQUE)

1. Which sentence best states the theme (main idea) in the article?

2. What is the basis for the writer's opinion? Cite specific paragraphs or sentences.

3. Where is the topic sentence in paragraph 3? Paragraph 6 ("My secretary used to teach . . .")? Paragraph 12 ("To carry the question . . .")?

4. How did President Kennedy get through three or four major newspapers in a few minutes?

5. Using the author's guidelines, explain how you would read *Newsweek, TV Guide,* a rental lease agreement, and a physics text.

6. The author offers several possibilities for the improvement of reading speed. What are they? What other methods can students use to become better readers?

7. Explain the writer's attitude toward speed-reading fiction. Do you think this applies to all fiction?

SUGGESTIONS FOR WRITING

1. Interview a reading teacher on your campus about speed reading. Bring up the writer's views in this article. In a paper compare the views of the writer and the views of the instructor.

2. Will books, periodicals, and newspapers soon become old-fashioned? Write a paper arguing that technology will/will not make the printed page obsolete.

3. Analyze yourself as a reader. What are your strong points? Your weak points? Your reading skills in relation to your academic goals?

Selection 13

Getting More Go From Your Gas

VOCABULARY BUILDING

Below are several words used in this article. They are presented in the context of the sentences or phrases in which they occur. If you are unsure of their meanings and cannot define them from the context, look them up in the dictionary. Spaces are provided for additional unfamiliar words from the article to add to your vocabulary.

1. "Open windows create wind *turbulence* and have the effect of holding back the car."

    turbulence: _____

2. ". . . lubricate better . . . than will a heavier, more *viscous* oil."

    viscous: _____

3. "The 55-m.p.h. speed limit was enacted to help preserve our *dwindling* petroleum reserves."

    dwindling: _____

4. "What about the new *synthetic* oils?"

    synthetic: _____

5. "Their deep cleats *generate* more rolling resistance than conventional tires . . ."

    generate: _____

6. _____ : _____

7. _____ : _____

8. _____ : _____

9. _____ : _____

10. _____ : _____

RETENTION AND COMPREHENSION

A. True/False *(1 point each)*

1. Idling a cold engine for a minute or two before driving uses gas but is good for the engine.

   1. T _____ F _____

2. Varying your speed just 5 miles per hour on the highway can reduce fuel economy by as much as 1.3 miles per gallon.

   2. T _____ F _____

3. Radial tires give greater steering stability than conventional tires but do not increase gas mileage.

   3. T _____ F _____

4. A car equipped with overdrive can improve highway fuel economy by up to 15%.

   4. T _____ F _____

B. Completion *(3 points each)*

5. To save gas, a driver should skip gears to get into economical higher gears at level starts and at _____ starts.

   5. _____

6. A car traveling 70 miles per hour gets only _____ the gas economy of a car going 45 miles per hour.

   6. _____

7. If not adjusted for the seasons, tire pressures can vary by as much as _____ pounds.

   7. _____

8. At highway speeds open windows can lower mileage as much as _____ %.

   8. _____

C. Multiple Choice *(2 points each)*

9. To reach cruising speed from a dead stop rather than from a slow speed takes (a) almost no more gas, (b) almost 50% more gas, (c) up to 20% more gas, (d) almost a half-gallon of gas.

   9. _____

10. When you have a full tank of gas, you should *not* (a) park the car facing downhill, (b) park in the shade, (c) park in the sun, (d) drive with the windows closed.

    10. _____

11. A 20W oil allows better gas mileage, especially in

    11. _____

cold weather, than (a) 40W oil, (b) 20W–50W oil, (c) 10W oil, (d) new synthetic oils.

12. *Not* mentioned as a way to get better gas mileage is (a) increased tire pressure, (b) changing air filters often, (c) decreasing weight in the car, (d) using cruise-control devices.

12. _____

13. The 1978 Federal Highway Administration study showed that a driver who goes 20 miles round trip to work in a standard car can save over $500 a year by (a) using all of the author's suggestions, (b) not using battery-powered accessories, (c) buying a car with a 5-speed transmission, (d) joining a four-person car pool.

13. _____

D. Thematic (8 points)

14. Which statement *best* expresses the theme (*main* idea) of the article?
    (a) Smaller foreign-made cars get better mileage than American-made gas guzzlers.
    (b) In the past American drivers have been wasteful gas users but will have to change now that gas has become expensive.
    (c) Too much gas is wasted because cars are not maintained properly.
    (d) A driver who uses gas-efficient techniques and shares his driving can save gas and money.

14. _____

E. Purpose (7 points)

15. The author's *chief* purpose is
    (a) to tell us that expert drivers use a lot of techniques to save gas.
    (b) to show that drivers will have to expect gasoline to increase in cost as it decreases in availability.
    (c) to make us realize that these fuel-saving techniques should be taught in schools.
    (d) to help the average driver reduce his gas consumption by using accepted gas-efficiency tricks.

15. _____

Total Retention and Comprehension Score: _____

Better College Reading

QUESTIONS FOR DISCUSSION (MEANING AND TECHNIQUE)

1. Does the opening paragraph sound like an "introductory" one? Does the last paragraph read like a "closing" paragraph? Why or why not?

2. Explain what part the section headings have in the article's organization.

3. Analyze the article for its topic sentences. Where are they located in the paragraphs? Can the topic sentences be switched around within the paragraphs with no change or loss of continuity? Does every paragraph have a topic sentence? If not, is it implied? Can you state it?

4. Consider for whom this article was written—the writer's "audience." How well suited is the information for the audience? Is it too technical?

5. Does the writer's choice of words suit the topic? What is the "level of language"? Formal? Too relaxed? Appropriate? Find examples of driving *jargon*.

SUGGESTIONS FOR WRITING

1. Using this article as a guide, write a paper telling the reader how to cut expenses in one area (groceries, travel, clothing, home maintenance, entertainment, energy consumption). Be specific and practical.

2. If you know of an alternative to gasoline as a power source for cars, write about it.

3. Many people have experience or knowledge enough to make them almost "experts" or "authorities" about certain things. Write a paper in which you explain a technical point, an involved process, or a difficult concept so that a reader would have little trouble understanding it. (It may be anything from making homemade beer, to putting up wallpaper, to laying bricks.)

4. If you have ever followed a definite plan to improve yourself (dieting, exercise, education, music lessons), write a composition describing your experiences and the outcome.

5. If you have ever been in a car pool, describe what it was like: you could describe the people in the pool or explain the benefits and/or the disadvantages.

Selection 13

Overall Reading Performance

Your overall reading performance is a combination of how fast you read and how much you comprehend and retain. The chart below allows you to find out quickly your "overall reading performance."

First enter your "reading time" and your "retention and comprehension" score in the two blanks at the bottom of the page. Then simply lay a straightedge of any kind (the edge of a sheet of paper or a pencil will do) across the chart, placing the left side of the straightedge at the appropriate point on the "Reading Rate" scale, and the right side at the appropriate point on the "Retention and Comprehension" scale. The point at which the paper or pencil intersects the scale in the middle of the page will indicate your overall performance.

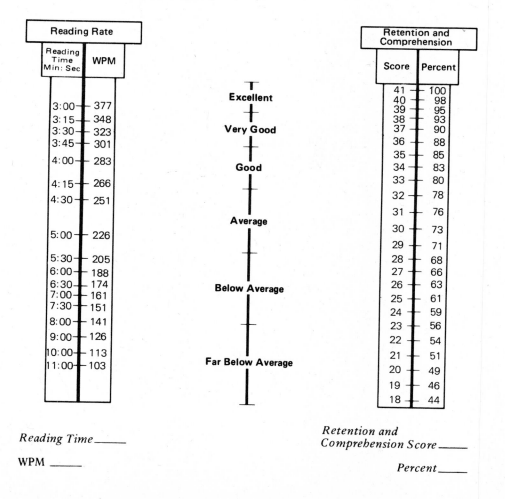

Reading Time_____

WPM _____

Retention and
Comprehension Score_____

Percent_____

Selection 14

A Chicana *Runs a Long, Rough Road*

ROBERTA VELASCO

Any woman who sets out to find her true place in life faces a difficult journey. For a *Chicana* like me, the road has been particularly long and arduous.

It all started in the spring of 1960, when I met Mike. I was a 17-year-old senior at Garfield High School in East Los Angeles. He was 18 and a truck driver for Union Meat Co. We were attracted to each other and enjoyed going to the beach, the movies or Disneyland in Mike's reliable '50 Chevy, or sometimes just doing nothing together. By the end of the summer we were married.

As Mike's bride, I got used to being part of the large Velasco clan. I was happy cooking, cleaning and making a home for my husband, and I felt secure knowing there were uncles, aunts and dozens of young cousins to share our new life. How I looked forward to the lively family parties to celebrate birthdays, marriages and religious holidays! I couldn't imagine a more agreeable existence.

Soon I was pregnant. I joyously accepted the change in my body and my life, and Mike and I were filled with contentment at the thought of a child.

Born Aug. 19, 1961, Sal was a beautiful baby. I basked in the glow of my in-laws' approval, which was double since I had produced not only their first grandchild, but a boy. We named him after Mike's father.

When Sal was just 17 months old, I became pregnant again. For some reason, I was terrified: *No, not a second one so soon.* But I kept my fears—and tears—to myself.

Debbie was a demanding, restless baby, and always crying—so different from Sal. But Mike was pleased that he now had a daughter as well as a son, and I continued to do what was expected of me. Before I knew it, both children were in school.

Ten years of marriage passed, full of housework, helping with homework and family celebrations. But beneath the surface, tension began to develop. The source was Mike's relatives. At first they asked the question only with their eyes. Finally, when Debby was in the second grade, one of them voiced it out loud: *When are you going to have another baby?*

"I won't!" I wanted to shout. "That's not what I want for myself!" But I controlled my rage and managed to avoid answering her.

It's hard to recall exactly when I became dissatisfied with my role as wife, mother, and domestic servant in my own home. I had felt stirrings inside me after both children were in school and tried to stop them by plunging into all sorts of volunteer jobs: room mother, Cub Scout den leader and part-time teacher aide.

But none of these pursuits answered my longing to be someone called *me,* whoever that was. I knew that, to satisfy myself, I would have to be more than just a homemaker. Then, one day in 1974, I made a decision.

"I'm going back to school," I told my husband.

"What about the kids?" was his instant reply.

When I offered a reasonable plan for getting everything done, he began to sense I was serious and forbade me to enroll. Then I told him I'd enter East Los Angeles College the next semester, with or without his approval. A tumultuous week passed in which I poured out to Mike my yearnings, my frustrations, my feelings of resentment and rebellion. In the end, he said he understood—and said yes.

Nervous about my ability to do well after so long an absence from school, I took only one course that first term. But it didn't take long to get over my uneasiness. Two semesters later I was carrying a full load and had made the dean's list.

Not content to just attend classes, I began sampling campus activities. I took a job in a special reading program, counseled other housewives returning to school, helped organize a new women's center, tutored and counseled students, then trained others to do the same.

My appetite for activity—and my energy—grew and grew. I took up long-distance running and joined the ELAC team (and the Amateur Athletic Union) as a 10-miler.

My husband and children were proud of me and, for the first time in a long time, I was happy with myself.

But the Velasco clan disapproved. To them I was a disgraceful mother who had abandoned her poor, helpless family. At first the cousins would corner Mike at parties and accuse me of being unfeminine and even unfaithful. "The wife of a Velasco does not do such things," the young cousins would say, their *machismo* bristling. Whenever I approached such groups, the conversation would turn to a general attack on women's lib.

On one occasion I decided to defend myself. "I'm strong," I said to the men. "I can find fulfillment in my way and allow you to find it in yours. Why do you feel my actions threaten you? It doesn't take courage to deride my husband for letting his wife 'wear the pants in the family'; it takes courage for him to understand my feelings and help me in my struggle to become *me*. All the Velascos in the world won't deprive me of that!"

The estrangement was now official. My own immediate family rallied around me; moreover, Sal and Debbie couldn't understand why everyone wasn't proud of their straight-A, long-distance-running mother. Mike and I explained that many of our people felt that what I was doing went against revered *Mexicano* traditions. We urged the children to be patient with their intolerant cousins.

Still, it was a crisis for all of us, especially for me. I felt emotionally tormented and worn down by the family's unrelenting hostility. On top of this, Sal was about to have his religious confirmation and, despite the pressure of school and antagonism from the Velascos, Mike and I felt we should mark the event with a traditional family party.

When various relatives called to volunteer their help with the cooking, insinuating I was probably "too busy with other things" to give a proper party, I politely declined. I was going to host a successful party—without their help—if it killed me.

Sal and Debbie cheered me on. Thanks to them, my sister and a neighbor, I pulled it off. We prepared a mountain of food: delicious *sopa* and red chili, tortillas and beans, salads, cold cuts and the most elegant hors d'oeuvres that had been served in a decade of Velasco fiestas. More than 30 guests showed up, and the last one didn't leave until 5 a.m.

For me, it was more than a party. It was a celebration of progress in the search for myself. Although I regret the family's antagonism toward me (mainly for my children's sake), I think the journey was worth it for this long-distance runner and her cheering section of three.

No. of Words: <u>1150</u>

Reading Time: _____

Selection 14

A Chicana Runs a Long, Rough Road

VOCABULARY BUILDING

Below are several words used in this article. They are presented in the context of the sentences or phrases in which they occur. If you are unsure of their meanings and cannot define them from the context, look them up in the dictionary. Spaces are provided for additional unfamiliar words from the article to add to your vocabulary.

1. "Any woman . . . faces a difficult journey. For a *Chicana* like me, the road has been particularly long and *arduous*."

   arduous: _____

2. " . . . Sal was a beautiful baby. I *basked* in the glow of my in-law's approval . . ."

   basked: _____

3. "'The wife of a Velasco does not do such things,' the young cousins would say, their *machismo bristling*."

   machismo: _____

   bristling: _____

4. "I felt emotionally tormented and worn down by the family's *unrelenting* hostility."

   unrelenting: _____

5. _____ : _____

6. _____ : _____

7. _____ : _____

8. _____ : _____

RETENTION AND COMPREHENSION

A. True/False *(1 point each)*

1. Roberta and Mike Velasco got married as soon as they graduated from high school.

   1. T _____ F _____

2. After Roberta's second baby, Mike's family urged her not to have any more children.

   2. T _____ F _____

3. At first Mike did not approve of Roberta's plan to enroll in college.

   3. T _____ F _____

4. While going to college, she continued her volunteer work as a room mother and teacher aide.

   4. T _____ F _____

B. Completion *(3 points each)*

5. When they were married, Mike was employed as a _____ .

   5. _____

6. Roberta made her decision to return to school after_____years of marriage.

   6. _____

7. She was helped in preparing for Sal's confirmation party by her children, a neighbor, and her_____ .

   7. _____

8. Mike's cousins accused Roberta of being unfeminine and _____ .

   8. _____

C. Multiple Choice *(2 points each)*

9. While attending classes, Roberta helped organize (a) a tutorial center, (b) a new women's center, (c) a job placement office, (d) a peer counseling program.

   9. _____

10. Roberta became a distance runner to (a) lose weight, (b) irritate her in-laws, (c) try for an athletic scholarship to a four-year university, (d) use her energy in another activity.

    10. _____

11. When confronted by Roberta, Mike's male relative's would attack (a) her participation in athletics, (b) Mike's liberal views, (c) women's lib, (d) her deficiencies as a housewife.

    11. _____

12. Various relatives offered to help Roberta for Sal's party, hinting that she (a) couldn't handle such an important affair, (b) was too busy with other things to give a good party, (c) didn't cook traditional dishes correctly, (d) deserved some friendship after having been snubbed by Mike's family.

12. _____

13. Roberta felt that Sal's confirmation party was also (a) a celebration of progress in her search for self, (b) a victory over the narrow-mindedness of Mike's family, (c) the last step in her complete withdrawal from family activities, (d) an indication to Mike that she was a better hostess than any of the wives in his family.

13. _____

D. Thematic (8 points)

14. Which statement *best* expresses the theme (*main* idea) of the article?
    (a) Roberta realized that married women need other social activities besides those resulting from their marriages.
    (b) Families who stick to old-fashioned traditions create difficulties for newly married couples.
    (c) Roberta's successful efforts to become more than just a good wife and mother outweighed the negative effects on her relatives.
    (d) Roberta's educational experiences will have more influence on the lives of her immediate family than will her relative's attitudes.

14. _____

E. Purpose (7 points)

15. The author's *chief* purpose is
    (a) to show the necessity of a husband's support when a wife tries nontraditional activities.
    (b) to make us realize that many women, if given the chance, can accomplish just as much as men can.
    (c) to show that in order to be happy, some women must take the chance of antagonizing their relatives by doing things considered inappropriate for a housewife.
    (d) to show that, in spite of many obstacles, a minority woman can be mother, housewife and more—but it isn't easy.

15. _____

Total Retention and Comprehension Score: _____

QUESTIONS FOR DISCUSSION (MEANING AND TECHNIQUE)

1. What technique does the writer use to present her "story"? Is it more like the style used in Selection 6 (*My* Pony, *My* Saddle, *My* Corral, *My* Prejudice) or in Selection 12 (Is Speed Reading Overrated)? Why or why not?

2. How do the phrases "cheering section" and "runs a long, rough road" relate to the writer's purpose?

3. Does the writer present herself as a model for other housewives to follow? Is she a rebel? Refer to the article to support your opinion.

4. Why was it so important to put on a successful confirmation party?

5. Does the word *machismo* have a good or bad connotation in the article? In society?

6. Do you feel that there are aspects to the writer's story that have been omitted? What might these be?

7. Which would present a greater threat to the author's relatives: her long-distance running or getting straight A's? Why?

SUGGESTIONS FOR WRITING

1. If you are returning to school after an extended absence, write a paper comparing your experiences to the writer's. How are they the same or different?

2. Write a composition about someone you respect greatly for having attained a goal or having become successful in spite of severe setbacks or handicaps. If you cannot write from personal experience, select someone from history, medicine, the arts, sports, literature, or another area. Tell what their handicap was and how they overcame it.

3. Describe the importance of a family or ethnic tradition in your life. Will you retain and perhaps try to pass it on to the next generation?

4. Discuss the concept of America as a "melting pot." To what degree is or isn't America a melting pot? Support your opinion with evidence.

5. Discuss a problem which has troubled you for at least two or three years. This can be anything from a senile parent to your own extreme shyness.

6. Social groups (family, religious, school, work) can create circumstances like those in which the writer found herself. From your own experiences describe what happened when you or an acquaintance tried to "break out of the mold."

Overall Reading Performance

Your overall reading performance is a combination of how fast you read and how much you comprehend and retain. The chart below allows you to find out quickly your "overall reading performance."

First enter your "reading time" and your "retention and comprehension" score in the two blanks at the bottom of the page. Then simply lay a straightedge of any kind (the edge of a sheet of paper or a pencil will do) across the chart, placing the left side of the straightedge at the appropriate point on the "Reading Rate" scale, and the right side at the appropriate point on the "Retention and Comprehension" scale. The point at which the paper or pencil intersects the scale in the middle of the page will indicate your overall performance.

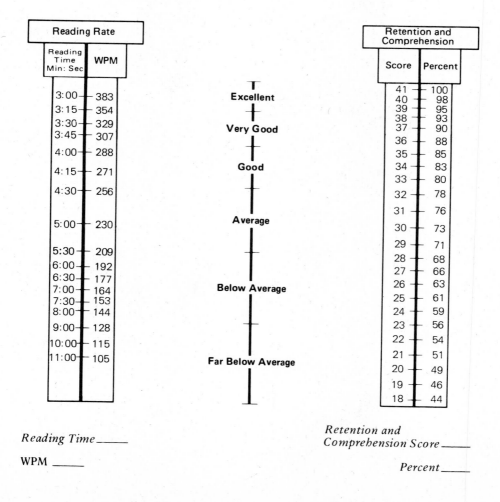

Reading Rate	
Reading Time Min: Sec	WPM
3:00	383
3:15	354
3:30	329
3:45	307
4:00	288
4:15	271
4:30	256
5:00	230
5:30	209
6:00	192
6:30	177
7:00	164
7:30	153
8:00	144
9:00	128
10:00	115
11:00	105

Excellent

Very Good

Good

Average

Below Average

Far Below Average

Retention and Comprehension	
Score	Percent
41	100
40	98
39	95
38	93
37	90
36	88
35	85
34	83
33	80
32	78
31	76
30	73
29	71
28	68
27	66
26	63
25	61
24	59
23	56
22	54
21	51
20	49
19	46
18	44

Reading Time _____

WPM _____

Retention and Comprehension Score _____

Percent _____

Selection 15

Thais Can't Visualize a Life Without Rice

JOHN BURGESS

SUPHANBURI PROVINCE, Thailand—The sun is almost directly over-head; the water is knee deep. In their family's flooded rice paddy, Mawin Chowhuaymok and his two brothers are stooped over a task that can easily be called the foundation on which Asian civilization rests.

They have left their shoes on a dike. Hefting an armload of 20-day-old rice seedlings, each man wades cautiously backward, at each step pushing a seedling's roots into the slippery paddy floor. The plants are spaced about 10 inches apart, just far enough to assure the roots won't choke each other as they grow.

The work looks exhausting, but Mawin, 24, claims it is not. He has planted since childhood and disposes of 50 seedlings per minute with ease. "When a lot of people work together, it can actually be fun," he says without breaking his rhythm.

The bright green seedlings now resemble spring onions. At maturity, they will be golden brown, each standing waist-high and bearing as many as 1,500 grains of rice. The 2.8 acres Mawin's family cultivates will yield more than three tons of rice.

About three-quarters of Thailand's people live in rural communities like Mawin's, and most grow rice as their principal crop. They will harvest about 17 million tons of the grain this year.

Of all the questions village people ask Americans, the most common seems to be: "Is it really true that you don't eat rice?"

In East Asia a meal without rice is not a meal. The grain is food itself, the difference between prosperity and want. Its needs in the field dictate when people work and when they play. It is courted with countless religious rituals.

In Thai, as in many Asian languages, "to eat" translates literally as "to eat rice." When a Thai talks of cooking, he is actually talking of "making

Source: Los Angeles Times, Dec. 17, 1980. Reprinted by permission of *The Washington Post.*

things that go with rice." He can refer to his possessions as his "rice and things."

Many historians credit the rise of East Asia's great civilization to the refinement of rice agriculture. The Khmer Empire, for instance, built a complex grid of irrigation canals that allowed three crops of rice per year in places—thereby freeing people to build temples, debate religion and embark on wars of conquest.

Often wars were directed at capturing neighboring states' most valuable assets—their rice fields and the peasants who tilled them. In old Thailand, fields were often doled out to feudal noblemen whose rank could be determined by how much acreage they controlled.

Botanists classify the simple plant responsible for all of this as a grass. It exists in thousands of varieties. It is grown on the equator in Sumatra or as far north as Hokkaido Island in Japan, roughly the same latitude as New England. It thrives at sea level in flooded paddies or on dry hillsides at 5,000 feet.

In Thailand, the main planting season falls in early summer when the first monsoon rains soften and then flood the country's paddy land.

The farmer's choice of seed depends on how much water enters the field and on labor. If the farmer cannot control flooding depths or has only a few helpers, he usually plants "broadcast" rice—so called because it is sown by casting handfuls of seed directly onto the soil. It can survive varying water depths and needs relatively little tending.

The Chowhuaymok family, however, has diked paddies where flooding can be regulated. It also has the requisite labor—Mawin and his brothers—to raise the more bountiful transplanted varieties of rice.

The seeds are first planted in a carefully tended nursery. These plots' dazzling green hue make them among the most pleasing sights in the Thai countryside. After three weeks the seedlings are meticulously moved by hand to the main paddies.

Transplanting must take place within a very tight time frame. Thus villagers often start their nurseries in sequence, then work cooperatively on each other's fields when the seedlings are ready to be moved. "We help them, they help us," says Mawin. It is one of the few examples of communal labor in the Thai village.

During its first month in the new paddy, the rice needs close tending. Mawin and his brothers will clear away weeds, hunt down rodents and birds and apply insecticide and fertilizer. After that, it is smooth sailing until harvest in October.

Again, the villagers work in each other's fields, with much good-natured banter during the day and drinking and festivities at night. As the last rice is packed into the family bins or sold to visiting merchants, the cycle is completed for the year, though in some villages a second crop is planted.

The harvest rice appears on Thai plates in endless forms. There is the boiled rice Americans know. It also comes as a soup—a favorite for late-night eating in Thailand—snacks made from sun-dried grains, sweets made with coconut juices.

It is soaked and boiled until it becomes noodles. It is fermented into rice wines, which villagers must keep secret from the police.

Byproducts are used too: Husks go to feed pigs or insulate ice blocks being transported in barges. The stalk is left standing in the field, then burned away in the belief that it fertilizes the soil for the next crop.

Rice's role as the staff of life is guarded by religious ceremonies. Each spring Thailand's King Bhumibol Adulyadej plows a ceremonial furrow in Bangkok, using two specially blessed oxen. It is a centuries-old Brahmin rite to symbolically guarantee the fertility of the country's fields.

Villages in northeastern Thailand stage wild festivals that send 20-foot homemade rockets into the clear blue skies of the late dry season. With much drinking and merrymaking on the ground, the heavens are symbolically fertilized by the rockets to make them pregnant with rain.

Transplanting and harvesting often begin with special offerings of food and incense to Mae Phosop, the supernatural Rice Mother. Every villager knows her: she becomes pregnant when the rice flowers bloom and her offspring, the grain, nurture humankind in the same way that a mother's milk, white and pure, nurtures a baby.

The rice she provides has a soul of its own, and the farmer must be careful to safeguard it. Though he or she may sell most of the crop to a merchant, a handful of grain is often carefully returned to the farmer to impregnate the next crop.

Anthropologists have recorded all manner of explanations of rice's place in the cosmic order. Some farmers use today's rice-eating habits as a barometer of morality. In previous epochs, it is said, when the human race was pure, people ate rice by itself with perfect satisfaction. But today vice is on the rise and simple rice is no longer enough. People must use sauces and curries to enhance its flavor.

Some Thais hold that the human body itself is composed of rice, and eating the grain renews the tissues directly. It is the rice diet that distinguishes humankind from the other creatures on earth, in this view.

Farm machines and modern fertilizers have increased yields in Thai paddy fields. But they have not changed the basic cycle of life. Thus, at patriotic moments, Thais still like to quote a stone inscription dated 1292 found at Sukhothai, the capital of the first important Thai state:

"This Sukhothai is good. In the water there are fish. In the fields there is rice."

No. of Words: 1241

Reading Time: _____

Selection 15

Thais Can't Visualize a Life Without Rice

VOCABULARY BUILDING

Below are several words used in this article. They are presented in the context of the sentences or phrases in which they occur. If you are unsure of their meanings and cannot define them from the context, look them up in the dictionary. Spaces are provided for additional unfamiliar words from the article to add to your vocabulary.

1. "It [the rice] is *courted* with countless religious rituals."

   courted: _____

2. "In old Thailand, fields were often *doled* out to feudal noblemen whose rank could be determined by how much acreage they controlled."

   doled: _____

3. "...the main planting season falls in early summer when the first *monsoon* rains soften and then flood the country's paddy land."

   monsoon: _____

4. "In previous *epochs,* it is said, when the human race was pure, people ate rice by itself with perfect satisfaction."

   epochs: _____

5. _____ : _____

6. _____ : _____

7. _____ : _____

8. _____ : _____

RETENTION AND COMPREHENSION

A. True/False *(1 point each)*

1. Rice can be grown only by hand planting small seedlings into the soft soil of a rice paddy.

   1. T _____ F _____

2. At maturity one rice plant can produce as many as 1500 grains of rice.

   2. T _____ F _____

3. Once planted, the rice is not bothered by weeds, rodents, or insects.

   3. T _____ F _____

4. A by-product of rice, the husks are used as feed for pigs.

   4. T _____ F _____

B. Completion *(3 points each)*

5. In the Thai language, "to eat" translates literally as _____.

   5. _____

6. The rice is harvested in the month of _____.

   6. _____

7. One of the Thai ceremonies that has to do with rice planting is the plowing of a small furrow by _____.

   7. _____

8. The shooting off of rockets is a ceremony to assure a plentiful supply of _____.

   8. _____

C. Multiple Choice *(2 points each)*

9. One early improvement in rice cultivation allowed (a) the Thais to have smaller families, (b) three crops of rice per year in some places, (c) the farmers to spend more time on raising domestic animals, (d) the exporting of rice to Japan and Sumatra.

   9. _____

10. When planting rice seedlings, a good worker like Mawin can plant (a) 50 seedlings per minute, (b) 24 seedlings per minute, (c) 10 seedlings per minute, (d) 5,000 seedlings per hour.

    10. _____

11. Not mentioned in the article as one way that Thais prepare rice for food is (a) to boil it, (b) to make it into noodles, (c) to fry it in a rice cake, (d) to sweeten it with coconut juice.

    11. _____

12. Because many Thais believe that rice has a soul of its own, after selling a crop, the farmer keeps a handful of rice (a) to fertilize the next crop, (b) to offer to the supernatural Rice Mother, (c) to retain as a symbol of success, (d) to plant for a second crop.

12. _____

13. Some Thais believe that their rice diet (a) separates the Eastern and Western cultures, (b) keeps their morality high, (c) will be taken up by other peoples as the world's food supply lessens, (d) distinguishes humanity from the other creatures on earth.

13. _____

D. Thematic (8 points)

14. Which statement *best* expresses the theme (*main* idea) of the article?
    (a) Rice-based cultures, like that of the Thais, have not kept pace with modern developments in agriculture and must rely on ceremonies and festivals to produce large rice crops.
    (b) Because successful rice growing requires vast amounts of time and people, the Thais are probably doomed to a low economic standard of living for a long time.
    (c) The Thai cultivation of rice as a nutritious food staple has given rise to other refinements in their culture such as religious and artistic accomplishments.
    (d) The Thais' reliance on rice crops affects their attitudes toward life, family, and religion so much that it is difficult for them to imagine any other way of living.

14. _____

E. Purpose (7 points)

15. The author's *chief* purpose is:
    (a) to help the reader understand the difference between an agricultural society and a manufacturing one, such as that of the United States.
    (b) to make us aware that the dependence on a single necessity has influenced the beliefs and lives of practically an entire nation.

15. _____

(c) to explain why Thailand must continue to rely
on large rice crops to keep the spirit of its people from weakening.

(d) to show how the devotion to one important
goal can unify a country.

Total Retention and Comprehension Score: _____

QUESTIONS FOR DISCUSSION (MEANING AND TECHNIQUE)

1. Why does the writer start this article by focusing on a particular person, Mawin Chowhuaymok? Is that a good technique? Why or why
not?

2. Does the writer display a negative, positive, or relatively "objective"
point of view towards Thai life and custom?

3. Why can't Thais "visualize a life without rice"? What part does rice
play (and what part has it played) in Thai life?

4. Name some of the numerous examples and details given to illustrate
the thesis of this article.

5. Is this article an example of writing about a "cause" and its "effect"?
What is the effect? What is the cause? What can you learn about how to
write a "cause-and-effect" essay from this article?

SUGGESTIONS FOR WRITING

1. Try to think of something in America without which it would be hard
to visualize life (cars, plumbing, gas and electricity, television, ham-
burgers, etc.). Then write a composition containing examples and
details supporting your idea. You may treat the subject humorously or
seriously.

2. Pick an aspect of American life and show how it has "caused" various
"effects" in our way of thinking and behaving.

Overall Reading Performance

Your overall reading performance is a combination of how fast you read and how much you comprehend and retain. The chart below allows you to find out quickly your "overall reading performance."

First enter your "reading time" and your "retention and comprehension" score in the two blanks at the bottom of the page. Then simply lay a straightedge of any kind (the edge of a sheet of paper or a pencil will do) across the chart, placing the left side of the straightedge at the appropriate point on the "Reading Rate" scale, and the right side at the appropriate point on the "Retention and Comprehension" scale. The point at which the paper or pencil intersects the scale in the middle of the page will indicate your overall performance.

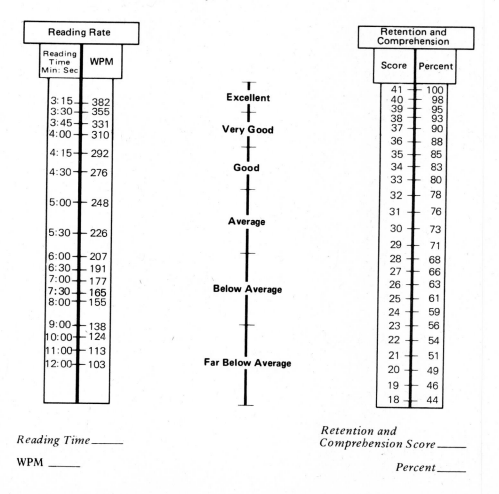

Reading Time_____

WPM _____

Retention and
Comprehension Score_____

Percent_____

Selection 16

Blacks Return to Africa but U.S. Is Home

DAVID LAMB

NAIROBI, Kenya—For more than 20 million Americans, Africa is the distant motherland, beckoning many of her children home with promises of black dignity, cultural affinity, a sense of belonging.

Thousands of black Americans have answered that call and have found everything from joy to disillusionment—but no guarantee of immediate acceptance simply because they are black.

For most, the African experience leaves one overriding impression: Africa may be the homeland, but the United States is home.

"The cultures are very different, and the first thing you learn is how American you are, how much you're a product of your environment and culture," said Cynthia Akuetteh, acting director of the U.S. Peace Corps in Ghana and wife of a Ghanaian.

Most black Americans living in Africa are educated, skilled, middle-class. They are doctors, teachers, diplomats, businessmen, journalists, technical experts, the spouses of Africans.

"I think we're perceived here as Americans first, blacks second," said David French, a Boston doctor who runs a 20-country health program for the World Health Organization in Abidjan, Ivory Coast.

"When I first visited Africa eight or 10 years ago, I had the feeling there was some disdain on the part of Africans toward black Americans. We were suspect, first, because we ended up in the United States in the first place, and second, because we put up with all we did for 300 years.

"Now I get the impression that Africans are asking themselves, 'Where are the most-educated, prosperous, technically trained blacks in the world?' Well, they're in the United States. And the Africans are saying, 'If you've got something to offer, come on over and join us.'"

Those who do are not immune to the frustrations, indifference and apathy of Africa. Time is often an alien concept; individual liberty is frequently the privilege of a chosen few; public services break down with alarming regularity. It often seems that decaying capitals like Kinshasa, Zaire, and Dar es Salaam, Tanzania, are the African cities of tomorrow; the modern, gleaming capitals of Johannesburg and Salisbury are those of yesterday.

Clifford Sharp, a Detroit mechanic who moved to Guinea 11 years ago, said he tells other blacks: "If you want to come to Africa for fun, don't come. If you have a superior attitude, don't come. If you expect to have no problems here, don't come. But if you want to aid the development of the black race, if you care, then come. But you must have pioneer spirit and missionary zeal, because you're certainly going to have some problems getting by day to day."

Sharp, 66, who maintains his U.S. passport and voted for President Carter on an absentee ballot, considers himself not an American but a "returned African." He speaks with pride of being a black man in a black country run by a black president.

"I'd never even seen a black president before I came to Africa," he said. "But just after we arrived in Conakry, we were ushered into President Sekou Toure's chambers. They were beautiful chambers, and he rose to receive my wife and me. A president of a republic stood to receive us!

"He said, 'Bon jour'—we had a translator with us who said that meant 'good day'—and when we left, President Toure rose again and led us to the door and opened it for us. How proud we felt as black people."

Sharp, who is the president's official mechanic and looks after his fleet of cars, has a nodding acquaintance with another American in Guinea, Stokely Carmichael, 37, the 1960s militant. But Sharp says he was never one for politics or revolution, and even though he and Carmichael are both Americans they don't have much in common.

Carmichael, who was recently separated from his wife, South African folk singer Miriam Makeba, came to Guinea in 1968. He has a close relationship with the government—sometimes he writes letters on Toure's presidential stationery—and he still espouses the cause of black revolution. He holds both U.S. and Guinean passports and has the financial resources to travel abroad frequently.

"Since leaving the United States," Carmichael said, "I have realized how stupid and arrogant I was. I actually thought we could change things overnight. This is one thing Africa teaches you—patience."

Most American blacks in Africa believe the United States has made significant steps toward racial equality in recent years. They are struck by the realization that in much of Africa the loss of individual privileges and rights is an accepted way of life. Freedom is a fuzzy concept, to be interpreted by the rulers of the day.

As a black U.S. diplomat put it, "Being here has given my children a whole new appreciation of the United States, a changed perspective they could not have gotten living all their lives in the States."

Ruth Phillips, who runs one of the largest travel agencies in Monrovia, Liberia, has another view of the American experience. She came to Africa 25 years ago as a nurse, is married to the Liberian minister of finance and has taken Liberian citizenship. She has vivid memories of growing up in a black, middle-class neighborhood in Washington, D.C.

"Having had little contact with white people, naturally I assumed they were better because we were always given the worst. But then I went to the Bellevue School of Nursing, and I remember how shocked I was. I was near the top of my class academically, and there were so many white people there who were less prepared than I was.

"I had been so brainwashed, made to feel so inferior, that I didn't realize a black person could be better than a white in anything. That is the cruelest effect of segregation, and it took me a long time to get over the feeling. Even after I came to Africa, the vestiges stayed with me for quite a while."

The call of Africa to black Americans preceded—but was greatly stimulated by—Alex Haley's book, *Roots*, which sold 20 million copies and was translated into 32 languages. Both the call and the book were part of what an American academic here calls the reorientation of American blacks, a shift from self-criticism or self-hatred to being fascinated with and proud of their black origins.

Although some Americans throw up their hands in disgust—"Thank God my granddaddy got aboard that slave ship," one said—others find the African experience moving and emotional, usually more poignant than it would be for a white American traveling for the first time to, say, England.

"You can't help feeling an identification with Africa, even though a lot of blacks, I think, tend to over-romanticize the place," said Larry Still, a Howard University associate professor who teaches journalism at the University of Nairobi on a Fulbright grant.

"The affinity is one of heritage but certainly not life-style. One of the attractions of Kenya is that you can live comfortably here as a foreigner. Sometimes I feel a little embarrassed that we do live so comfortably, and I wonder what Americans' reaction would be if they had to live at the level of the average African.

"Most of my students are very curious about the American black and how he lives in the United States. At least a third of them have applied to study in the States. They're sensitive about our racial struggle, and some of them are surprised to find out there are black mayors, black newspaper reporters, black business leaders.

"They tend to think of American blacks in stereotyped roles, as athletes or entertainers. Partly, I guess, this is because among the Kenya street crowd the only black Americans they've met are slang-talking and hip. I get irritated when someone approaches me as a black American and feels he has to talk slang and jargon to communicate with me."

The Americans who are usually disillusioned with Africa are those who think they will be swallowed up and loved because they are black. But Africans seem to be remarkably unconscious of another's skin. They respond to a person, not a color, and they resent an air of superiority, regardless of its source.

For those black Americans who are here to listen, learn or teach on a basis of partnership—as most black Americans are—Africa does indeed welcome home her children. But few stay in her embrace forever.

No. of Words: 1397

Reading Time: _____

Selection 16

Blacks Return to Africa but U.S. is Home

VOCABULARY BUILDING

Below are several words used in this article. They are presented in the context of the sentences or phrases in which they occur. If you are unsure of their meanings and cannot define them from the context, look them up in the dictionary. Spaces are provided for additional unfamiliar words from the article to add to your vocabulary.

1. "Africa is . . . *beckoning* . . . with promises of black dignity, cultural *affinity*, a sense of belonging."

   beckoning: _____

   affinity: _____

2. "Thousands of black Americans have answered that call and have found everything from joy to *disillusionment* . . ."

   disillusionment: _____

3. ". . . eight or 10 years ago, I had the feeling there was some *disdain* on the part of Africans toward black Americans."

   disdain: _____

4. "Those who do are not immune to the *frustrations, indifference* and *apathy* of Africa."

   frustration: _____

   indifference: _____

   apathy: _____

5. "Time is often an *alien concept* . . ."

   alien: _____

   concept: _____

6. "But you must have pioneer spirit and missionary *zeal* . . ."

   zeal: _____

7. "She has *vivid* memories of growing up . . ."

   vivid: _____

8. ". . . some Americans . . . find the African experience moving and emotional, usually more *poignant* than it would be for a white American traveling for the first time to, say, England."

   poignant: _____

9. ". . . a lot of blacks . . . tend to over-*romanticize* the place . . ."

   romanticize: _____

10. "They tend to think of American blacks in *stereotyped* roles, as athletes or entertainers."

    stereotyped: _____

11. _____ : _____

12. _____ : _____

13. _____ : _____

14. _____ : _____

15. _____ : _____

RETENTION AND COMPREHENSION

A. True/False (1 point each)

1. Most black Americans living in Africa are uneducated.

   1. T _____ F _____

2. Black Americans were not attracted to Africa before the book *Roots* was published.

   2. T _____ F _____

3. Africans are generally unconscious of another person's skin color.

   3. T _____ F _____

4. Africans generally know about black American mayors and business leaders.

   4. T _____ F _____

B. Completion (3 points each)

5. Clifford Sharp, from Detroit, lives in Guinea and is the President's official _____.

   5. _____

6. Stokely Carmichael feels that one thing Africa teaches you is _____.

   6. _____

7. Black Americans in Africa are thought of by Africans as _____ first, blacks second.

7. _____

8. The call of Africa to black Americans was greatly stimulated by _____.

8. _____

C. Multiple Choice (2 points each)

9. When David French, a Boston doctor, first visited Africa years ago, he (a) was welcomed warmly by Africans, (b) was asked to come back because of his medical skills, (c) was looked down on by the Africans, (d) loved the pride and freedom he felt there.

9. _____

10. Many American blacks in Africa now realize (a) how oppressed black people are in America, (b) that much progress has been made toward equality in America recently, (c) how much better things are for people in Africa, (d) how similar life is in America and Africa.

10. _____

11. For most black Americans in Africa, Africa may be the homeland, but America is (a) a home away from home, (b) a bad memory, (c) a good place to be from, (d) home.

11. _____

12. Ruth Phillips, who now lives in Liberia, remembers that when she studied nursing in America she was shocked because (a) she was so severely discriminated against, (b) she was so poorly prepared, (c) she was told she had to drop out, (d) she was one of the best students.

12. _____

13. Most African students think of American blacks (a) as oppressed, (b) as superior, (c) in stereotyped roles, (d) as inferior.

13. _____

D. Thematic (8 points)

14. Which statement *best* expresses the theme (*main* idea) of the article?
    (*a*) Black Americans who go to Africa should understand that they won't be lovingly welcomed just because they're black.
    (*b*) Black Americans who go to Africa will never look at things exactly the same way again.

14. _____

139

    (c) Black Americans who go to Africa realize for the first time how good things are in America.

    (d) Black Americans who go to Africa find that the cultural differences are too great and frequently return.

E. Purpose *(7 points)*

15. The author's *chief* purpose is   15. _____
   (a) to convince black Americans that conditions are better for black people in Africa.
   (b) to stimulate further growth of the "Back-to-Africa" movement.
   (c) to publicize the admirable progress black Americans have made in Africa.
   (d) to inform readers of some of the realities of life for black Americans who do go back to Africa.

Total Retention and Comprehension Score: _____

QUESTIONS FOR DISCUSSION (MEANING AND TECHNIQUE)

1. For what reasons do some black Americans feel a desire to go to Africa?

2. Does the writer base this article on his own observations and opinions? If not, then on whose? Who are some of the people whose outlook and experience he presents? Is this an interesting or convincing way to inform us on the subject? What are some alternative ways? Would they have worked as well or not? Why?

3. Do other American ethnic groups experience a similar urge, desire, or curiosity about their "roots"? How? Why?

4. Are you a member of an American minority-ethnic group? Do you understand/empathize with the feelings of black Americans who want to return (either temporarily or permanently) to their motherland? Explain your answer.

5. Which black Americans would be most apt, according to one source, to be disillusioned in Africa? Why? Which would not? Why?

6. What are some different ways Africans view black Americans? According to one source, have their attitudes toward black Americans changed? How? Why?

7. What is the attitude of Clifford Sharp, official mechanic to the president of Guinea, toward Stokely Carmichael, the 1960s American militant? Can you understand why? Do you agree with him?

8. Have Stokely Charmichael's attitudes changed? How? Why? Do you agree with him? Why or why not?

9. A black U.S. diplomat says, "Being here [in Africa] has given my children a whole new appreciation of the United States, a changed perspective they could not have gotten living all their lives in the United States." What do you think he means? Explain what that "appreciation" might be, what that "changed perspective" might be. Changed in what way?

10. A former black nurse from America tells what she thinks is the "cruelest effect" of segregation. What does she think it is? Do you agree or disagree? Why?

11. How or why did Alex Haley's book *Roots* stimulate "the call of Africa to black Americans"?

12. Do you agree with the statement "Africa may be homeland, but the United States is home"? What does it mean?

13. How does the writer introduce and conclude this article? Are they effective ways to begin and end? Does the introduction interest you? How? Does it announce the subject? How? Does the conclusion echo any idea(s) from the introduction? Is that a good way to end? Why or why not?

14. How many black Americans living in Africa did the writer interview or mention? Are they a good cross section? Was this a good way to explore the subject?

15. Why did Mr. Sharp (the president's mechanic) feel so strongly about meeting President Seku Toure? What did it mean to him?

SUGGESTIONS FOR WRITING

1. This article is "inductive" in that it provides examples of the motives, experiences, reactions, outlook, etc., of five black Americans in Africa and from them makes some generalizations about the relationship of all black Americans to Africa. Write an "inductive" composition in which you make some generalization about people and then support it with three to five specific instances, real or imaginary.

2. There is an implied comparison/contrast in this article between conditions (attitudes, human relations, economic/social circumstances) here and in Africa for American blacks. Write a comparison/contrast essay about any two things (e.g., the place you're in now and the place you came from; the person you are now and the person you'd like to become; two friends, colleges, countries, etc.; conditions here,

conditions elsewhere; etc.). Compare/contrast the two things on at least three points.

3. If you are a member of an ethnic minority, describe your feelings toward your motherland. Compare them to the ones in the article.

4. If you are a member of an ethnic minority, imagine yourself returning to your motherland. What are your feelings, expectations, experiences, reactions, etc.?

5. If you have no strong ties to any American ethnic minority, write a composition describing your thoughts and feelings after reading this article. What is your attitude toward black Americans going to Africa? About a member of any ethnic minority visiting his/her homeland?

6. Pretend you are an American who has just returned from his/her motherland. Describe your experiences. Were you inspired and fulfilled or disappointed and disillusioned? A little of both? How? Why?

their clothes, taking off their clothes, feeding them."

There is no washing machine, but Julia Martinez does have the use of a machine that belongs to a married daughter. There isn't even a decent refrigerator; the freezer works, but the other area doesn't, so when Julia buys a gallon of milk (it takes two gallons a week for the family), she had to freeze it and thaw it out.

The kitchen is a key room because the family never eats out, not even a hamburger, because they cannot afford it. The kitchen walls, made of a plastic resembling wood paneling, are scrubbed clean. In one corner, an old kitchen step-stool serves as a stand for some fake flowers.

Limited Entertainment

A small table in the opposite corner, covered with a spotless cloth, holds the family entertainment center: a small, black-and-white TV set of fairly recent vintage.

Family pictures taken through the years adorn the living-room walls, along with several brightly colored woven rugs with religious themes. Furniture in this room is scant: a reclining chair is shabby and worn and an overstuffed couch is covered with a bright red spread, perhaps, so the holes won't show. One small light bulb hangs from a two-socket fixture in the ceiling. On a red, white and blue pennant on one wall is the Pledge to the Flag.

Ramon and Julia Martinez first brought their family to northern Texas three years ago. The cotton industry is big in Terry County, and that is where he hoped to work.

"I heard some jobs were here, but it didn't work out, so we moved to Florida," Martinez said. His voice was soft, groping for the right words. "I picked tomatoes and cucumbers there, and the kids that were old enough got work, too."

But those weren't the kinds of jobs that put much food on the table, so nine or ten months ago the family came back to Brownfield. Since then Martinez has worked at the cotton gin six days a week on a 10-hour shift that does not provide any time for lunch.

Late in the afternoon, just after 6 p.m., Martinez drives the three miles home in his brown, 1973 Ford pickup, a stylish vehicle that he recently acquired and is making payments on. He is behind in them, too.

By the time the family greetings are done, it is time for the evening meal, usually something hot. Typically, it might be plenty of rice with a little meat, frijoles (beans) and more flour tortillas. "We have some meat maybe two or three times a week," Julia Martinez said.

Ramon and Julia shop together for food every Saturday night. By watching the specials they can hold the bill down to around $70. There is never any candy for the children, but sometimes there are fruit and cookies.

Satisfied With Life

Julia Martinez, 5-foot-5 and 110 pounds, faces heavy burdens, but she says she would change nothing in her life.

"I love them all, and I would still want to have all the children," she said. "The only thing I would want to change is all the troubles we have." She looked away, her eyes brimming with tears.

Three of the Martinez brood were born with the help of a midwife, but Mary Lou, the newest, came into the world at Texas Tech's Health-Science Center Hospital in Lubbock. Hospital spokesmen said nobody is ever turned away, despite the fact that it is not a charity institution. Technically, it is a county teaching hospital connected with Texas Tech, and it does get some funds from Lubbock County.

Because the Martinez children do not go to school, one day is much like the next for them—lounging around the house or watching TV.

Bill Caraway, superintendent of Brownfield schools, admitted he had no idea that some of the school-age Martinez children were not enrolled in school. When Caraway sent an investigator to the Martinez home, he found that last fall the family had tried to enroll one child in intermediate school.

"They were turned away because of our requirements for a birth certificate and immunization records, and they never tried again," Caraway said. "If they were in school, they would be eligible for free lunches and perhaps some clothing, too. But there is nothing we can do unless they are in school."

No. of Words: 1497

Reading Time: _____

Selection 17

Huge Family Takes Hard Times in Stride

VOCABULARY BUILDING

Below are several words used in this article. They are presented in the context of the sentences or phrases in which they occur. If you are unsure of their meanings and cannot define them from the context, look them up in the dictionary. Spaces are provided for additional unfamiliar words from the article to add to your vocabulary.

1. "Adding up the months from *conception* to delivery . . ."

    conception: _____

2. "If life is an *ordeal* for this family . . ."

    ordeal: _____

3. "She was perhaps more *concerned* with what three more in the family would add to her duties . . ."

    concerned: _____

4. ". . . the family entertainment center: a small, black-and-white TV set of fairly recent *vintage.*"

    vintage: _____

5. "On a red, white and blue *pennant* on one wall is the Pledge to the Flag."

    pennant: _____

6. "Three of the Martinez *brood* were born with the help of a *midwife* . . ."

    brood: _____

    midwife: _____

7. "... it is not a charity institution. *Technically,* it is a county teaching hospital ..."

    technically: _____

8. _____ : _____

9. _____ : _____

10. _____ : _____

RETENTION AND COMPREHENSION

A. True/False *(1 point each)*

1. Mr. and Mrs. Martinez do not speak any English.   1. T _____ F _____

2. The Martinez home is very dirty.   2. T _____ F _____

3. Mrs. Martinez would like "an even two dozen" children.   3. T _____ F _____

4. Because there are so many to cook for, the family eats out at least once a week.   4. T _____ F _____

B. Completion *(3 points each)*

5. Eight school-age Martinez children do not _____ .   5. _____

6. Mrs. Martinez said she wouldn't change anything, just all the _____ .   6. _____

7. Mr. Martinez works at a _____ .   7. _____

8. Mr. Martinez and most of the children sleep in the _____ on the _____ .   8. _____

_____

C. Multiple Choice *(2 points each)*

9. The freezer works, but what doesn't work is the (a) toaster, (b) stove, (c) heater, (d) refrigerator.   9. _____

10. The school-age children in the Martinez household (a) love school, (b) can't read or write, (c) do not attend school, (d) hate school.   10. _____

11. Although the Martinez family has a freezer, they do not have (a) a car, (b) a washing machine, (c) a television set, (d) a refrigerator.

11. _____

12. Mr. and Mrs. Martinez (a) shop for food together, (b) agree on everything, (c) are determined to see their children well educated, (d) collect food stamps.

12. _____

13. Mr. and Mrs. Martinez were both born in (a) Mexico, (b) Puerto Rico, (c) Texas, (d) New Mexico.

13. _____

D. Thematic (8 points)

14. Which statement *best* expresses the theme (*main* idea) of the article?
    (a) The Martinezes are basically lazy and backward people, which is the underlying cause of their problems.
    (b) If poor people worked harder, the quality of their lives would improve.
    (c) If life is hard for the Martinezes, it doesn't often show—only in overdue bills and in lack of education.
    (d) Education is a privilege reserved for people who show they can benefit from it.

14. _____

E. Purpose (7 points)

15. The author's *chief* purpose is
    (a) to describe in some detail the life situation of a particular kind of American family.
    (b) to show how desperate the situation of the poor is in some parts of our country.
    (c) to rouse us to take some action on behalf of people who are not getting a fair deal in our society.
    (d) to arouse our sympathy for people, like the Martinezes, who live in great poverty and need.

15. _____

Total Retention and Comprehension Score: _____

QUESTIONS FOR DISCUSSION (MEANING AND TECHNIQUE)

1. The title of this article says the Martinez family takes its "hard times" in stride. What does that mean? Do you agree? Are there indications they don't take their hard times in stride? What are they?

2. Could the Martinez's do anything to alleviate their hard times? What? If you think there are things they could do, why do you think they don't?

3. The writer says, "If life is an ordeal for this family, it doesn't often show." From his description of their life, do you agree it doesn't show? Why or why not? How could their life be worse? Do you know a family whose circumstances are worse? Describe them.

4. Would the circumstances of this family be better or worse if there were fewer children? Why or why not? How do you think Mr. and Mrs. Martinez feel about this question?

5. Would you urge Mr. and Mrs. Martinez to make every effort to enroll their school-age children in school? Why or why not? Why haven't they done so?

6. Should society do anything to help the Martinez family and families like them? If yes, why, what, and how? If no, why not?

7. Would you call the Martinezes poor? Why or why not? How is "poor" defined in America?

8. Do you think Mr. and Mrs. Martinez consider themselves fortunate or unfortunate relative to others?

SUGGESTIONS FOR WRITING

1. Write a composition describing how the Martinezes might "pull themselves up by their bootstraps."

2. Write a composition showing how, no matter what the Martinezes do, they cannot improve their condition.

3. Write a composition explaining why society should (or shouldn't) help families like the Martinezes and what society should (or shouldn't) do?

4. Write a definition of poverty in America and illustrate it with a real or imaginary poor family.

5. Write a "cause-and-effect" essay showing what "causes" brought about the "effect" of a family living in the circumstances the Martinezes find themselves in. Who is to blame for their circumstances?

6. In a way similar to the way the article describes the Martinezes, describe the conditions of your own family or a family you know (the home you/they live in, its furnishing, your/their mother and/or father's occupation, the heating and lighting, the food you/they eat, when and where you/they eat it, the members of the family, its wanderings, etc.).

Overall Reading Performance

Your overall reading performance is a combination of how fast you read and how much you comprehend and retain. The chart below allows you to find out quickly your "overall reading performance."

First enter your "reading time" and your "retention and comprehension" score in the two blanks at the bottom of the page. Then simply lay a straightedge of any kind (the edge of a sheet of paper or a pencil will do) across the chart, placing the left side of the straightedge at the appropriate point on the "Reading Rate" scale, and the right side at the appropriate point on the "Retention and Comprehension" scale. The point at which the paper or pencil intersects the scale in the middle of the page will indicate your overall performance.

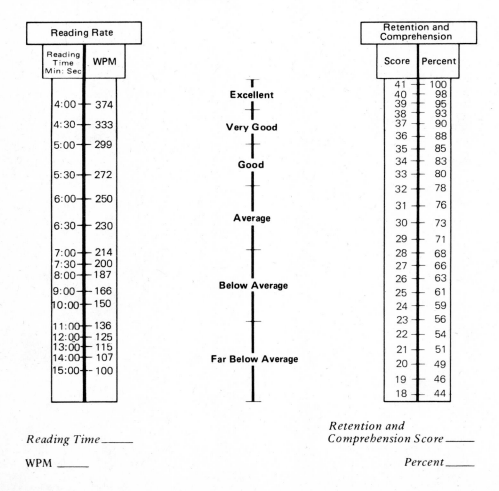

*Reading Time*_____

WPM _____

Retention and
*Comprehension Score*_____

*Percent*_____

Selection 18

Either You Make It or You Don't

AL MARTINEZ

Bob Minor stood for a moment on the windy rim of a 13-story building and looked down.

The street was empty. Traffic had vanished after dark, and stores were closed. In the distance, he could hear a car horn. Once, voices drifted up but he could not place them.

He teetered on the lip of the building, and felt its edge with the toe of his shoe. Then he looked down again. Tomorrow.

Sixteen hours from that moment, Minor would stand again on the precipice of that Los Angeles high rise, but this time he would not so much look down as across.

What he had to do was leap the gap that separated his building from the building across the alley. The distance was 18 feet 6 inches. There would be no net.

At stake was Minor's reputation as the nation's top black stunt man, $4,000 and his life. In that order.

"I was thinking," he says, "that I could do it, that nothing in the world could stop me . . ."

He could see himself, in that second at the rim of the building, hurtling off the edge into space, arms upthrust, head back, and he could see himself landing safely.

But then, if he let the image creep into a corner of his mind, he could also see himself missing, slamming off the side of the other structure and falling, falling . . .

But Minor, 33, a stunt man for seven years, a nice kid from Birmingham, closed his eyes and said the Lord's Prayer.

It was Wednesday.

A stunt man, in his way, lives always at the edge of a precipice. He falls awesome heights, rides cars into twisted metal, sets himself on fire, crashes planes, leaps off trains, is dragged by horses and devoured by sharks.

At the end, he limps off the set or climbs out of the water or rolls off an

Source: Expressions, June 1977. Copyright. 1977, *Los Angeles Times*. Reprinted by permission.

air bag or dusts himself off and counts his blessings. He is alive. So far, so good.

A stunt man is rarely himself on the big screen or on the face of a television set. His credits are small compared to the star that he doubles for (or is his double, depending one one's point of view).

He is that abused, anonymous figure who risks life and limb for the sake of a scene which often, by itself, makes a movie or an episode rise for a moment from mediocrity.

Danger is his specialty, and he glories in the camaraderie he shares with a very small and a very elite fraternity.

Bob Minor is a member. He was the first black man to pierce the barrier of that fraternity five years ago, and since then he has worked in more than 100 movies for the big screen and for television.

At 6-2 and 215 pounds—wide shoulders and narrow hips—Minor is physically equipped for the fights and falls he must endure as part of his trade.

He admits that once you get past 30, the muscles ache a little more and the soreness takes longer to go away, but still it's a business he loves.

"Every stunt is a challenge," he says, standing by on the set of a television show in the basement of a Wilshire Blvd. gym. "You either make it or you don't. It's that simple.

"I'm going more into acting now, but even then I'll do my own stunts. It's something that . . ." He shrugs, unable to find the right words, then adds: "You never get away from it."

It began for Minor in 1969. He had come out of Trade Tech Junior College, where he had run the 100-yard dash in 9.7, high jumped 6-1 and long jumped 23-9.

Body-building, and the gathering of most-perfect-physique trophies, was his main interest then, and it was quite by accident he overheard two men in a gym talking about doing stunts for movies.

"It sounded like something I could do with ease," he says now. "I went up to one of them and said, 'How do you get into that business?'"

They directed Minor to a man who specializes in training stunt men, and a long, rigorous period of training began.

It brought him to the top of that 13-story building on a windy night last year, and the most dangerous stunt he has ever had to perform.

The movie was "Let's Do It Again," and the actor Minor was to double for in the leap between the two buildings was Sidney Poitier.

The right preparation was essential. Three cameras would be running and a net would only be in the way, so Poitier had requested that the leap be made without a net.

There would be an air bag instead 13 stories below, but Minor considered it almost useless.

"If I missed the jump," he says, "I'd have hit the side of the other building and gone into an uncontrollable dive. I'd have been busted up good, and no air bag was gonna prevent that."

There was an even more chilling consequence to missing, but, "You don't talk about things like that, and you try not to think about them.

"I go into every stunt saying I can do it, I know I can do it. There can't be doubt or you're going to get into trouble."

If there was doubt that night atop the downtown building, Minor tried not to show it. He was as prepared for the jump as he would ever be.

He had ordered built a 35-foot ramp up to the lip of the building. He had marked it with tape and had practiced his stride at home. He had tightly bound a pulled leg muscle, and he knew precisely what he was supposed to do.

There had been little sleep the night before ("It was butterflies-in-the-stomach time"), but still he felt ready.

The night past midnight was windy and misty. He rode up the elevator to the roof in silence, not hearing what the elevator operator was saying.

Gathered below were 200 of Minor's friends, some of them fellow stunt men, some neighbors from North Hollywood. Many had told him he was crazy to try the jump, that it couldn't be done, that no amount of money in the world would get *them* to do it.

On the roof, Minor ordered the ramp wiped off thoroughly and tested it again. It was strong. On the opposite building 18 feet 6 inches away, he had placed a white rag. He would jump toward that rag. His target building was 2 feet lower than the jump-off building. That would help.

"Poitier came over and asked if everything was the way I wanted. I said it was. 'Let me know when you're ready,' he said.

"This was maybe 15 minutes before the jump. I told the people up there that if they had anything to say, say it then. After that, I wanted silence. I had to have total concentration."

Minor remembers that silence. Only the sound of the wind could be heard as he walked up the 35-foot ramp to the edge of the building and looked across.

He stood there for a moment. "I said the Lord's Prayer and asked God to look after me one more time. I was still positive, but nervous. I knew everyone was waiting.

"I walked back to the start of the ramp, put my foot on the marker and shook myself loose. Then I turned to the man nearby and said, 'OK.'

"I could hear, 'Camera one rolling, camera two rolling, camera three rolling. Up to speed.' Poitier said 'Action.' I took another 30 seconds to get my concentration back. Then I began the run . . ."

At that point—hurtling full speed up the ramp—there could be no hesitation for Bob Minor. He must commit himself, as a jet roaring down a runway must commit itself to takeoff past point X.

He reached that point and—"I took off. It was perfect. My left foot had hit a tape at the end of the ramp exactly as it should have. I threw my arms up and my head back in a lift, and suddenly I was in midair.

"It was like, man . . . I don't know. Weird. Wild. Free. I was gliding though the air, out of everything, in total concentration."

Minor's jump was more than adequate. He landed at 24 feet, far past the edge of the target building, pitched forward and rolled.

"The first thing I heard was all those people cheering," he says. "They must have clapped and screamed for five minutes. I walked to the edge of the building and I bowed."

On the ground, Poitier hugged him and said, "You're as agile as a cat. I'm glad it was you jumping and not me."

Minor: "I felt great. Relieved, yes, but good. It was another job accomplished.

"Then someone said, 'Bob, I don't know how to tell you this, but camera one malfunctioned. Can you do it one more time?' It's the oldest joke in the world, but for a split second I believed him. 'You gotta be kidding,' I said. He was."

Minor thinks about that. "You know," he finally says, "I probably would have done it again. It's in my blood—the challenge that's gotta be met.

"I wanted to be a cop once, but then the Watts riots broke out and I said to myself, 'No way, baby. Stunting is safer.'"

Minor went from the downtown building directly home. He slept like a baby.

No. of Words: 1590

Reading Time: _____

Selection 18

Either You Make It or You Don't

VOCABULARY BUILDING

Below are several words used in this article. They are presented in the context of the sentences or phrases in which they occur. If you are unsure of their meanings and cannot define them from the context, look them up in the dictionary. Spaces are provided for additional unfamiliar words from the article to add to your vocabulary.

1. "He *teetered* on the lip of the building . . ."

   teetered: _____

2. "Sixteen hours from that moment, Minor would stand again on the *precipice* of that Los Angeles high rise . . ."

   precipice: _____

3. "He [Minor] is that abused, *anonymous* figure who risks life and limb for the sake of a scene . . ."

   anonymous: _____

4. ". . . he glories in the *camaraderie* he shares with a very small and a very *elite fraternity.*"

   camaraderie: _____

   elite: _____

   fraternity: _____

5. "They directed Minor to a man who specializes in training stunt men, and a long, *rigorous* period of training began."

   rigorous: _____

6. "'Bob, I don't know how to tell you this, but camera one *malfunctioned*.'"

malfunctioned: _____

7. _____ : _____

8. _____ : _____

9. _____ : _____

10. _____ : _____

RETENTION AND COMPREHENSION

A. True/False *(1 point each)*

1. Bob Minor had to jump a second time.   1. T _____ F _____

2. Bob Minor was the first black stunt man.   2. T _____ F _____

3. Bob Minor was doubling for Sidney Poitier.   3. T _____ F _____

4. Bob Minor once wanted to be a basketball player.   4. T _____ F _____

B. Completion *(3 points each)*

5. Bob Minor was getting paid $_____ for this stunt.   5. _____

6. The building Bob Minor had to jump from was _____ stories high.   6. _____

7. At the time of the jump Bob Minor was _____ years old.   7. _____

8. Bob Minor thinks stunting is safer than being a _____ in Watts.   8. _____

C. Multiple Choice *(2 points each)*

9. Bob Minor's jump landed him (a) just short of his goal, (b) right on target, (c) far past his target, (d) just a bit beyond his target point.   9. _____

10. During Minor's jump (a) one of the cameras mal-   10. _____

functioned, (b) all cameras worked fine, (c) the film jammed in camera 3, (d) one of the cameramen made a mistake.

11. After Minor's jump (a) there was complete silence, (b) the cameramen congratulated him, (c) Poitier asked him to do it again, (d) the onlookers clapped and screamed for a long time.

11. _____

12. At the bottom, between the two buildings Minor had to jump across, was (a) a net, (b) nothing, (c) a fireman's trampoline, (d) an air bag.

12. _____

13. To become a stunt man, Minor (a) studied stunting at Trade Tech Junior College, (b) decided early to make stunting his career, (c) knew someone in the business who helped him, (d) went through a long, hard period of training.

13. _____

D. Thematic (8 points)

14. Which statement *best* expresses the theme (*main* idea) of the article?
    (a) Even careful preparation and rigorous training cannot assure the successful completion of every stunt.
    (b) A black stunt man is the equal of any stunt man.
    (c) It was a difficult, dangerous stunt—Minor was nervous and tense—but he made it.
    (d) If you do your job well, people will appreciate you.

14. _____

E. Purpose (7 points)

15. The author's *chief* purpose is
    (a) to show that hard work and concentration always pay off.
    (b) to give the reader a glimpse of how one becomes a stunt man, and the risks, work, and rewards that go with the job.
    (c) to encourage people who have the ability to be a stunt man but don't know how to go about becoming one.

15. _____

(d) to show that race is no barrier to success, even in a job as risky and challenging as being a stunt man.

Total Retention and Comprehension Score: _____

QUESTIONS FOR DISCUSSION (MEANING AND TECHNIQUE)

1. Would you do what Bob Minor did for $4000 if you thought you could, but there was a chance you might miss?

2. Do you think it's right to ask anyone to risk his/her life for money?

3. Is 18 feet 6 inches more than most people Bob Minor's age (somewhat past 30) can jump? How far do you think you can jump from a running leap?

4. What reasons does Bob Minor give for doing what he does? Do you empathize with him?

5. What do you think are some characteristics of that "small, very elite fraternity" of stunt men to which Bob Minor belongs?

6. Why do you think there weren't any black stunt men until quite recently?

7. How did Bob Minor become a stunt man? Can anyone become a stunt man or woman? What does it take?

8. How does the writer begin and end this article? Are the beginning and ending effective? Why? How else could he have begun? Ended?

9. The paragraphs in this article are unusually short because it was written for a narrow column in a newspaper. Would you reparagraph it for an essay? If so, how?

10. How long do you think the career of a stunt man lasts? Might there be psychological/emotional burnout as well as physical deterioration with time? Discuss.

SUGGESTIONS FOR WRITING

1. Describe a day on your job in the same way the writer describes a day on Minor's job. Try to make it dramatic (especially the beginning and ending) if possible, even if it winds up being somewhat funny.

2. Describe the stunt from someone else's point of view, say from Poitier's, a cameraman's, a friend's, or a neighbor's.

3. This description/narration of one stunt by one stunt man gives the reader a good idea of what a stunt man is and does. Describe one task (or series of tasks) by one person (yourself or someone else) on one job so that a reader will end up with a pretty good idea of what that job is or entails. You could describe a day or hour in the life of a clerk, a newspaper deliverer, a worker at a fast-food chain (e.g., MacDonald's), or of a worker at any kind of job.

4. Write an "argument" essay in which you attack or defend the idea that anyone should legitimately be allowed to risk his life for money. Give reasons for your positions.

5. Describe a daring/risky thing you once did. Explain why you did it. How did it come about? Describe the act and your feelings before, during, and after, and the attitudes and reactions of those who watched you (if there were any witnesses).

6. Describe a daring/risky thing you saw someone else do. See question 5 above for some ideas on what to write about.

7. Pretend you're a burned-out or old, retired stunt man or woman. Describe your feelings, attitudes, experiences, etc.

8. Pretend you're a stunt man who "chickens-out" just before a really risky stunt. Describe your feelings and actions at the time leading up to the stunt and your feelings and actions during and after you fail to perform the stunt.

9. Write a story showing Bob Minor missing the other building. What would happen (assuming he lived)? How would he feel? How would Poitier and the crowd feel? What would Bob Minor's future be like?

Selection 18

Overall Reading Performance

Your overall reading performance is a combination of how fast you read and how much you comprehend and retain. The chart below allows you to find out quickly your "overall reading performance."

First enter your "reading time" and your "retention and comprehension" score in the two blanks at the bottom of the page. Then simply lay a straightedge of any kind (the edge of a sheet of paper or a pencil will do) across the chart, placing the left side of the straightedge at the appropriate point on the "Reading Rate" scale, and the right side at the appropriate point on the "Retention and Comprehension" scale. The point at which the paper or pencil intersects the scale in the middle of the page will indicate your overall performance.

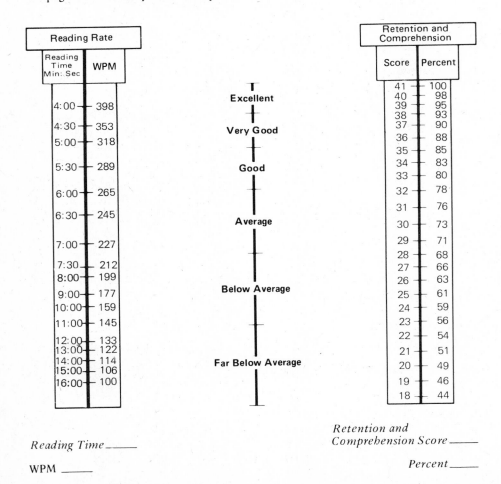

Reading Rate	
Reading Time Min.: Sec	WPM
4:00	398
4:30	353
5:00	318
5:30	289
6:00	265
6:30	245
7:00	227
7:30	212
8:00	199
9:00	177
10:00	159
11:00	145
12:00	133
13:00	122
14:00	114
15:00	106
16:00	100

Excellent

Very Good

Good

Average

Below Average

Far Below Average

Retention and Comprehension	
Score	Percent
41	100
40	98
39	95
38	93
37	90
36	88
35	85
34	83
33	80
32	78
31	76
30	73
29	71
28	68
27	66
26	63
25	61
24	59
23	56
22	54
21	51
20	49
19	46
18	44

Reading Time _____

WPM _____

Retention and Comprehension Score _____

Percent _____

Selection 19

Honesty: Is It Going Out of Style?

STACIA ROBBINS

Since most Americans believe that honesty is an important part of their character, they are not likely to shrug off reports of cheating and lying by elected officials.

An Epidemic of Cheating?

When the Gallup organization recently polled high school students on whether they had ever cheated on exams, 61 percent said they had cheated at least once. It can be argued that such a response may not mean much. After all, most students have, at one time or other, been faced with the temptation to peek at a neighbor's test paper. And students can be very hard on themselves in judging such behavior. However, there are other indications that high school cheating may be on the rise.

More and more states are requiring students to pass competency tests in order to receive their high school diplomas. And many educators fear that an increase in the use of state exams will lead to a corresponding rise in cheating. They cite the case of students in New York State who faced criminal misdemeanor charges for possessing and selling advance copies of state Regents examinations.

Approximately 600,000 students take the Regents exams. And it proved impossible to determine how many of them had seen the stolen tests. As a result, 1,200 principals received instructions from the State Education Commissioner to look for *unusual scoring patterns* that would show that students had the answers beforehand. This put a cloud over the test program. Students making special efforts in preparing for particular exams ran the risk of getting "unusual scores" and thus being suspected of cheating. This showed that a single cheating incident can have a ripple effect—touching the lives of people who had nothing to do with it.

Source: Senior Scholastic, Oct. 31, 1980. Reprinted by permission of Stacia Robbins.

Educators in New York are not the only ones worried. If students can figure out a way to steal closely guarded exam papers in New York State, they can steal them in other states as well. If students are worried enough about their test scores to cheat in New York, they're equally nervous in Idaho or Connecticut.

Cheating is now considered to be a major problem in colleges and universities. How to cope with it has become a favorite topic of conversation at faculty meetings and conferences. Several professors say they've dropped the traditional term paper requirement. Why? Many students buy prewritten term papers. And faculty members say they can't track down all the cheaters anymore.

"I may be wrong," said one professor wistfully, "but I think the situation has gotten worse in the past few years. I used to catch students making up footnotes. Today they simply buy the whole paper."

Some college faculty members across the nation have decided to do more than talk about the rise in student cheating. For instance, professors of the Department of Psychology at the University of Maryland launched a campaign to clamp down on one form of cheating. As 409 students filed out of their exam in *Introduction in Psychology,* they found all but one exit blocked. Proctors (monitors) asked each student to produce an ID card with an attached photo. Students who said they'd left theirs in the dorm or at home had a mug shot taken. The purpose of the campaign was to flush out "ringers," students who take tests for other students.

The majority of students at the University of Maryland applauded the faculty strategy. The campus newspaper editorialized, "Like police arresting speeders, the intent is not to catch everyone but rather to catch enough to spread the word."

Good Old Days

In this season of political campaign rhetoric, it is sometimes implied that in the "good old days" Americans were better, happier, and more honest.

Were they more honest?

Maybe yes, a long time ago when life was very different from what it is today.

Long ago, all school children knew the story of how Abraham Lincoln walked five miles to return a penny he'd overcharged a customer. It's the kind of story we think of as myth. But in the case of Lincoln, the story is true . . . unlike the story of George Washington and the cherry tree. Washington's first biographer, Parson Weems, invented the tale of little George saying to his father, "I cannot tell a lie. I did it with my ax." What is important in both stories, however, is that honesty was seen as an important part of the American character.

And these are just two stories out of many. Students in the last century usually didn't read "fun" stories. They read stories that taught moral values. Such stories pointed out quite clearly that children who lied, cheated, or stole came to bad ends.

Parents may have further reinforced those values. It's difficult to know. We do know that children didn't hear their parents talk of cheating the government on income taxes—there weren't any.

A clue as to why Americans may have been more honest in the past lies in the Abe Lincoln story. Lincoln knew his customer. They both lived in a hamlet. Would a check-out person at a large supermarket return money to a customer? It's less likely. On the other hand, would overnight guests at an inn run by a husband and wife, steal towels? It's less likely.

Recently, a woman who works as a consumer advocate "admitted" that she peels off the higher price stickers to expose the earlier, lower price stickers on many food items. She does that at her local supermarket. But she never does the same thing at her corner delicatessen. "I couldn't do that to Louie," she says. She knows Louie. She doesn't know the owners of the big supermarkets.

Perhaps this tells us that people need to know one another to be at their honest best.

Is Government a Special Case?

Some critics of American society say that dishonesty is rampant in the Federal government. One example they cite took place during March and April, 1980. For a whole month, they say, the United States lied to its allies.

Cyrus Vance, who was then Secretary of State, was given the task of telling Great Britain, Japan, France, West Germany and others that the United States would not take military action against Iran as long as we had the cooperation of our allies. Secretary of State Vance knew that the raid to get out the American captives was already planned while he was talking to our allies. But he also knew that the reason for this deliberate lying was to save lives. The primary purpose of the deception was not to trick our allies but to mislead the Iranian kidnappers so that a rescue attempt could take place.

Many students of ethics believe that lying for the sake of one's country is justified—in certain cases. In this case, having lied for the sake of his country, Secretary Vance secretly wrote a letter of resignation before the raid took place. By submitting his resignation before the raid, he showed that the result had nothing to do with his resignation. It can be said that former Secretary of State Vance deceived other governments only for humanitarian reasons. Then, once he had lied, he resigned.

In that case, it is argued, lying may be justified. Without the deception, the rescue mission could not have taken place.

Of course, dishonesty in government—at local, state and national levels—does not always have such noble reasons. A prime example is the so-called Watergate affair.

During President Nixon's first term (1969–73), a Committee to Reelect the President was formed. The committee is said to have authorized a group of men to break into the Democratic national headquarters in the Watergate hotel. The idea was to take a peek at the files of the Democratic party. When the burglars were caught, many politicians began scrambling to cover up the story. And President Nixon may have been involved.

Most Americans were surprised and outraged by news of the break-in and cover-up. But many Europeans were surprised at our surprise. Some European observers explained that they tend to think of lying, cheating, deception and corruption as part of politics and government.

The vast majority of Americans still believe that honesty is an important part of the American character. For that reason, there are numerous watchdog committees at all levels of society. Although signs of dishonesty in school, business, and government seem much more numerous in recent years than in the past, could it be that we are getting better at revealing such dishonesty?

There is some evidence that dishonesty may ebb and flow. When times are hard, incidents of theft and cheating usually soar. And when times get better such incidents tend to go down.

Cheating in school also tends to ebb and flow. But it doesn't seem linked to the economy.

Many educators feel that as students gain confidence in themselves and their abilities, they are less likely to cheat. Surprisingly, some efforts to curb cheating may actually encourage cheating—a person may feel "they don't trust me anyway," and be tempted to "beat the system." Distrust can be contagious. But, so can trust!

Then there's always that small voice called conscience whispering in everyone's ears. The United States Treasury even gave that name to a special fund—the Conscience Fund—back in 1811. It was started when an anonymous citizen sent in $5, perhaps to ease his conscience over some affair.

Contributions have been steady ever since. A nickel was sent in by a boy who found it on the street. But most contributions are much more substantial than that. At the end of last year the fund stood at $3,824,486.42. Contributions to the fund often come with a conscience-easing letter like this:

"Here's $6,000 I owe for back taxes. I haven't been able to sleep nights. If I still can't sleep, I'll send you the rest."

No. of Words: 1673

Reading Time: _____

Selection 19

Honesty: Is It Going Out of Style?

VOCABULARY BUILDING

Below are several words used in this article. They are presented in the context of the sentences or phrases in which they occur. If you are unsure of their meanings and cannot define them from the context, look them up in the dictionary. Spaces are provided for additional unfamiliar words from the article to add to your vocabulary.

1. "More and more states are requiring students to pass *competency* tests in order to receive their high school diplomas."

    competency: _____

2. "Some critics . . . say that dishonesty is *rampant* in the Federal government."

    rampant: _____

3. "It was started when an *anonymous* citizen sent in $5, . . ."

    anonymous: _____

4. _____ : _____

5. _____ : _____

6. _____ : _____

RETENTION AND COMPREHENSION

A. True/False (1 point each)

1. In a recent poll of high school students, 75% said they had cheated on exams at least once.

    1. T _____ F _____

2. To discourage cheating, psychology professors at the University of Maryland fingerprinted all students as they left the exam room.

    2. T _____ F _____

3. The majority of students at Maryland were in favor of measures taken to discourage cheating.

3. T _____ F _____

4. According to the author, the story of George Washington and the cherry tree was invented by Washington's biographer.

4. T _____ F _____

B. Completion (3 points each)

5. To determine how many students may have seen stolen Regents exams, New York principals were told to check test results for unusual _____

_____.

5. _____

6. The author states that students in the last century did not read "fun" stories but stories that taught

_____.

6. _____

7. When times are hard, dishonesty usually increases; however, cheating in school does not seem linked to the _____.

7. _____

8. Money sent by citizens to the government to pay for dishonest acts is called the _____ _____ Fund by the United States Treasury.

8. _____

C. Multiple Choice (2 points each)

9. The author says that some professors have dropped the traditional term paper requirement because students (a) make up "phoney" footnotes, (b) try to pass off material as their own by not using quotation marks, (c) buy prewritten term papers instead of writing their own, (d) use term papers from the files of fraternity and sorority houses.

9. _____

10. The purpose of making students produce an ID card with photo when taking an exam is (a) to make students more aware of the great amount of cheating going on, (b) to catch bright students not enrolled in a course who sell the information they remember to other students, (c) to compare test results of students who sat near each other, (d) to apprehend students who take tests for other students.

10. _____

11. The woman who peeled off new, higher price stickers to expose old, lower price ones on food items was employed as (a) a consumer advocate, (b) a checkout person in a supermarket, (c) a policewoman, (d) an attorney.

11. _____

12. To show that many people expect the United States government to lie for valid political reasons, the author referred to (a) President Nixon and the Watergate affair, (b) President Truman and the use of the atomic bomb, (c) Secretary of State Cyrus Vance and the raid to free the captives in Iran, (d) the attempts to cover up CIA operations in Cuba.

12. _____

13. The author suggests that the apparent increase in dishonesty in our society may reflect (a) a general breakdown in our moral structure; (b) not an increase, but rather that we are getting better at revealing dishonesty; (c) a reversal by authority figures to enforce strict codes of ethics; (d) an American inability to face up to normal human behavior, unlike Europeans, who expect people to be dishonest.

13. _____

D. Thematic *(8 points)*

14. Which statement *best* expresses the theme (*main idea*) of the article?
    (a) Americans have become more dishonest in order to survive in a system that is corrupt and unfair.
    (b) Students who cheat in school lack confidence in themselves and their abilities.
    (c) Because the federal government and political figures are dishonest, Americans are not upset by the increase in cheating and petty theft in all aspects of our society.
    (d) Evidence seems to show that dishonesty is increasing in America, but Americans still believe that honesty is an important part of the national character.

14. _____

E. Purpose *(7 points)*

15. The author's *chief* purpose is
    (a) to reveal why Americans have become more

15. _____

       dishonest than their forefathers.

    (b) to examine the extent of dishonesty in the United States and its probable causes.

    (c) to make us understand that honesty is an individual choice and not a result of the makeup of American social structure.

    (d) to present methods of discouraging dishonesty in all walks of American life.

Total Retention and Comprehension Score: _____

QUESTIONS FOR DISCUSSION (MEANING AND TECHNIQUE)

1. Is the article a discussion of cheating in America or an attack on cheaters? Are solutions to the problem offered by the writer? Explain your answer.

2. What kinds of evidence are offered to support opinions in the article? Examine the fifth paragraph ("Cheating is now considered . . .") and comment on the information in it.

3. Based on the information in the article, how would you answer the question asked in the title?

4. Explain the events that led to Secretary of State Vance's resignation during the Iranian hostage crisis. Under the circumstances, do you think the American public would have demanded Vance's resignation?

5. What does the story about the consumer advocate who cheats at the supermarket tell us? Is it effective? Why or why not?

6. How does the European view of government officials differ from that of the American?

7. Why does the writer tell us about the Conscience Fund at the end of the article?

SUGGESTIONS FOR WRITING

1. In a paper, discuss the attitudes and practices of cheating on your campus. Talk to students and quote their responses to support your point. Discuss what cheating you have seen or heard about.

2. Under what circumstances do students cheat? Is every student a potential cheater? Write a composition in which you classify academic cheating *or* cheaters.

3. What is the general attitude toward exposers or "finks" in our society? Why? At what point would you take steps to "turn in" a classroom cheat? How would you do it? Write a paper dealing with this problem.

4. Examine your thoughts about cheating. Consider the woman in the article who cheated at the supermarket, but not at the corner grocery. Was she a cheater or a thief? When does cheating become a crime? With the answers to these questions and others, write a paper which deals with this topic. Make sure of your main point before you start writing.

5. If you have ever cheated in school, write an essay about it, including why you felt the need to cheat and what the results would have been if you had not.

6. Have you ever felt "forced" to cheat because an entire class seemed to be cheating? Explain what happened.

7. From your experiences, write about an act of honesty that you or someone performed that was motivated solely by honesty—returning a lost wallet anonymously, for instance. Try to offer an explanation for such behavior.

Selection 19

Overall Reading Performance

Your overall reading performance is a combination of how fast you read and how much you comprehend and retain. The chart below allows you to find out quickly your "overall reading performance."

First enter your "reading time" and your "retention and comprehension" score in the two blanks at the bottom of the page. Then simply lay a straightedge of any kind (the edge of a sheet of paper or a pencil will do) across the chart, placing the left side of the straightedge at the appropriate point on the "Reading Rate" scale, and the right side at the appropriate point on the "Retention and Comprehension" scale. The point at which the paper or pencil intersects the scale in the middle of the page will indicate your overall performance.

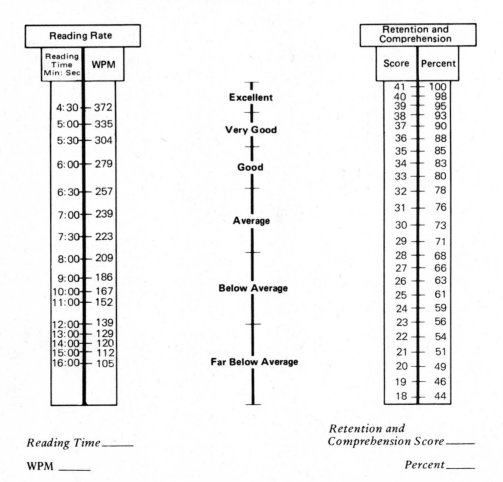

Reading Time _____

WPM _____

Retention and
Comprehension Score _____

Percent _____

Selection 20

Would Americans Man Death Camps?

PAUL GALLOWAY

There are undesirable elements in our nation. You know who they are. They are people who are not good Americans. They are an unstable, potentially disloyal and disruptive group.

Recognizing the enormous problems our country faces, our government leaders have decided that these people should be separated from the rest of us.

These people are to be placed in camps. It may be best to eliminate some of them.

This is a time of crisis. It will be necessary for some of us to supervise these camps. It is our duty. This country has been good to us. We have a responsibility to answer our nation's call in time of need.

"Would Americans man death camps?" Stanley Milgram was asked.

"Under certain circumstances, of course they would," he said. "The capacity for destructive actions is in all of us."

Milgram is professor of psychology at the City University of New York's graduate center. In the early 1950s, while he was on the faculty at Yale University, he developed experiments to measure obedience. He wanted to see how far normal people would go in following orders to carry out destructive acts, to comply dutifully to malevolent authority.

Milgram was surprised and disturbed at the results.

"With numbing regularity, good people were seen to knuckle under to the demand of authority and perform actions that were both callous and severe," he wrote about his findings.

"Men who in everyday life are responsible and decent were seduced by the trappings of authority, by the control of their perceptions and by uncritical acceptance of the experimenter's definition of the situation, into performing harsh acts."

Source: Chicago Sun-Times, April 16, 1978. © Chicago Sun-Times, 1978. Article by Paul Galloway, reprinted with permission.

NBC presented the "Holocaust," a four-part television series on the extermination of 6 million Jews by Nazi Germany.

One reviewer of the series was impressed by the depiction of the Nazis, which, he said, departed from earlier movie and TV stereotypes of "heel-clicking automatons."

"In 'Holocaust,' most Nazis are seemingly normal people who all too easily answer the call of a racist and fascist government," he wrote.

The characterizations, the reviewer continued, also "force us to wonder whether we might collaborate with an immoral government for the sake of opportunism and self-preservation."

We wouldn't! We say it with vehemence. After all, this is the United States of America! We have consciences! We know right from wrong!

So did the persons who volunteered for Stanley Milgram's experiments.

Writer Philip Meyer described Milgram's test in a 1970 *Esquire* magazine article. A paraphrased account follows. Put yourself in the place of those who participated:

You answer an advertisement for an educational experiment at a university. It will only take about one hour and you will be paid.

When you arrive, the man who will conduct the test introduces himself. His name is Jack Williams. You also meet another "volunteer," a middle-aged man with a paunch. He appears nervous.

Williams tells you about the experiment. He says it has been developed to try to understand the effect of negative reinforcement as a learning technique. Instead of rewarding someone for learning something, which is what positive reinforcement does, this experiment will attempt to determine if punishment for failure to learn is effective.

If the learner doesn't answer a question correctly, Williams says, the teacher will administer an electric shock.

One of you will be the teacher and the other will be the learner. You and the other man draw lots. The drawing is rigged so that you become the teacher and the middle-aged man, who is not a real volunteer, becomes the learner.

Williams leads the learner into another room. You can see them through a glass partition. You watch as the learner removes his coat and rolls up one sleeve of his shirt. He is strapped into a chair. You watch Williams administer paste to the learner's arm, then attach an electrode to it.

The electrode is connected to a wire that leads to a shock generator that you, as the teacher, will operate.

You hear the learner tell Williams that he is concerned. He recently discovered that he had a slight heart condition. He asks if the shocks will be dangerous.

Williams says the shocks may hurt but they won't be dangerous.

Williams returns to your room and explains how the experiment will work. It is like a game, he says. You will read a series of word pairs to the learner. Some examples are blue-girl, nice-day, fat-neck.

After you read the list to the learner, you begin reading only the first word in each pair. Then you read a multiple-choice list, one of them the correct pairing.

The learner answers by pushing one of four switches at his chair. If he's right, you move on to the next word. If he's wrong, you push a switch that gives the learner an electric shock.

The control board of the generator has 30 switches, each labeled according to the degree of voltage. The first switch administers 15 volts, and the intensity is increased 15 volts for each switch until it reaches 450 volts. This switch is labeled: Danger—Severe Shock. You are told to increase the voltage for each wrong answer.

Williams gives you a 45-volt shock. It's painful. You do not know, however, that no shock will actually be given to the learner, although he will act as if he is being given a shock.

You begin, and according to plan, the learner consistently gives incorrect answers. If you hesitate to administer the shock, Williams coolly tells you to continue.

As the voltage increases, the learner reacts with growing discomfort. He will writhe in his chair, grimace, then moan, shout and scream in pain. After the voltage has gone over 300 volts, he will not respond at all. He will slump in his chair, apparently unconscious.

Go on, Williams will say. Go on.

Would you go on? Would you go to the end of the board?

Milgram tested almost 1,000 persons. What he found, he said, forced "a painful alteration in my own thinking."

He was dismayed.

"More than 60 percent of the subjects went all the way," Milgram said.

"To our consternation, even the strongest protests from the victim did not prevent all subjects from administering the harshest punishment ordered by the experimenter," Milgram said.

The testing initially used Yale students, then volunteers came from the 20-to-50 age group. A balance of unskilled workers, white-collar workers and professional people was achieved.

Subject 0108 defied the experimenter: "The man is banging. He wants to get out. . . . I'm sorry. If the man wants to get out, I'd just as soon stop. . . . I don't want to administer any more (extremely excited). I will gladly refund the check, but I will not harm this man. . . . I'm sorry, but I will not give him any more if he obviously wants to get out. There is no money in the world that will make me hurt another individual."

But from one of the obedient came this:

165 volts. "That guy is hollering in there. He's liable to have a heart condition. Do you want me to go on?"

180 volts. "He can't stand it! I'm not going to kill that man in there! You hear him hollering? He's hollering. He can't stand it. What if something happens to him? . . . I mean, who is going to take responsibility if anything happens to that gentleman?"

The experimenter says he will accept the responsibility. "All right."

240 volts. "Aw, no! You mean I've got to keep going up with the scale? No, sir. I'm not going to kill that man! I'm not going to give him 450 volts!"

But he did.

In his book, "Obedience to Authority," Milgram writes of one man who was interviewed after he went all the way.

"Great. This is great," he said. "It didn't bother me. I believe I conducted myself well. . . . I did my job."

In a subsequent interview, the man told Milgram of a conversation with his wife. His wife asked whether he had considered that the learner might be dead. "So he's dead," the man said. "I did my job."

Milgram found that defiance increased when the learner was placed in the same room as the teacher. In one situation, the teacher was ordered to force the learner's arm on a metal shock plate to administer the voltage. Nevertheless, 3 of 10 of those in this situation went all the way to 450 volts.

The Milgram experiments were highly controversial. He was sharply criticized for misleading his subjects and placing them in such a position.

"I believe it was a moral experiment," Milgram said recently. "The controversy should not obscure the essential point of the experiment. It shouldn't lose the point of the findings. The subjects could have quit at any time. But we demonstrated the ease with which ordinary human beings can be brought into destructive actions."

He said the experiments have been duplicated by researchers in Munich, Germany, and in Amman, Jordan, with an even higher percentage of obedience than in his experiments.

Milgram emphasizes, however, that a distinction should be made between the laboratory findings and the actual murderous deeds of the Nazis.

Too, we must realize that our history illustrates that Americans have carried out orders from government authority that many individuals would have found repugnant and immoral.

He gives as examples the Indian massacres, slavery, the internment of Japanese-Americans during World War II, My Lai and the free-fire zones of Vietnam.

Milgram said he doesn't want these findings to excuse the horrors of a Holocaust because they show that the capacity to commit evil acts under official orders is a part of human nature. They should instead serve as a warning to us all. He has concluded:

"The results raise the possibility that human nature or, more specifically, the kind of character produced in American democratic society, cannot be counted on to insulate its citizens from brutality and inhumane treatment at the direction of malevolent authority.

"A substantial proportion of people do what they are told to do, irrespective of the content of the act and without limitations of conscience, so long as they perceive that the command comes from a legitimate authority."

"The condition of freedom in any state," Harold J. Laski once wrote, "is always a widespread and consistent skepticism of the canons upon which power insists."

No. of Words: 1735

Reading Time: _____

Selection 20

Would Americans Man Death Camps?

VOCABULARY BUILDING

Below are several words used in this article. They are presented in the context of the sentences or phrases in which they occur. If you are unsure of their meanings and cannot define them from the context, look them up in the dictionary. Spaces are provided for additional unfamiliar words from the article to add to your vocabulary.

1. "They are an unstable, potentially disloyal and *disruptive* group."

   disruptive: _____

2. "...good people were seen to ... perform actions that were both *callous* and severe ..."

   callous: _____

3. "A *paraphrased* account follows."

   paraphrased: _____

4. "He will *writhe* in his chair, *grimace,* then moan, shout and scream in pain."

   writhe: _____

   grimace: _____

5. "To our *consternation,* even the strongest protests from the victim did not prevent all subjects from *administering* the *harshest* punishment."

   consternation: _____

   administering: _____

   harshest: _____

6. "The Milgram experiments were highly *controversial.*"

   controversial: _____

7. "Milgram said he doesn't want these findings to excuse the horrors of a *Holocaust.*"

   Holocaust: _____

8. "... human nature ... cannot be counted on to *insulate* its citizens from *brutality* and *inhumane* treatment at the direction of *malevolent* authority."

   insulate: _____

   brutality: _____

   inhumane: _____

   malevolent: _____

9. "The condition of freedom ... is always a widespread and consistent *skepticism* of the *canons* upon which power insists."

   skepticism: _____

   canons: _____

10. _____ : _____

11. _____ : _____

12. _____ : _____

13. _____ : _____

RETENTION AND COMPREHENSION

A. True/False (1 point each)

1. Most people in Milgram's experiment did as they were told.   1. T _____ F _____

2. Milgram's experiment was duplicated in Israel with similar results.   2. T _____ F _____

3. The "teacher" in the experiment cannot see the "learner."   3. T _____ F _____

4. The "learner" in the experiment couldn't feel the electric shocks.   4. T _____ F _____

B. Completion (3 points each)

5. The experiment was performed on almost _____ persons.   5. _____

6. Milgram is a professor of _____.   6. _____

7. The last switch on the board administers a shock of   7. _____
_____volts.

8. The experiment lasts for about _____hour(s).   8. _____

C. Multiple Choice (2 points each)

9. The subjects used for the experiment were (a) stu-   9. _____
dents, (b) actors, (c) a variety of people, (d) Nazis.

10. When the experiments were repeated elsewhere   10. _____
(a) even more people did as they were told, (b)
even more people refused to do as they were told,
(c) the findings were controversial, (d) three of
ten went all the way to 450 volts.

11. The "learner" in the experiment (a) is chosen at   11. _____
random, (b) is pretending, (c) has just suffered a
heart attack, (d) experiences a great deal of pain.

12. After the voltage has gone over 300 volts (a) the   12. _____
"learner" seems unconscious, (b) the "teacher"
usually wants to stop, (c) most people won't do as
they're told, (d) the "learner" shouts and screams
in pain.

13. In Milgram's experiment (a) 10% refused to do as   13. _____
they were told, (b) 20% refused to do as they were
told, (c) 30% refused to do as they were told, (d)
40% refused to do as they were told.

D. Thematic (8 points)

14. Which statement *best* expresses the theme (*main*   14. _____
idea) of the article?
    (a) The kind of character produced by American
    democratic society insulates its citizens from
    brutality.
    (b) Most people will do cruel things to others if
    someone in authority tells them to.
    (c) The Holocaust could not have happened in
    America.
    (d) There is a distinction between what the Nazis
    did and the laboratory findings.

E. Purpose (7 points)

15. The author's *chief* purpose is   15. _____
    (a) to show that the experiment has very little rele-
        vance to real life.
    (b) to show that the Nazis were people like anyone
        else.
    (c) to report on an experiment that can tell us a
        great deal about how and why people behave
        the way they do.
    (d) to explain that the TV series "Holocaust" is
        based on a deep psychological truth.

Total Retention and Comprehension Score: _____

QUESTIONS FOR DISCUSSION (MEANING AND TECHNIQUE)

1. How does this quotation in the last paragraph apply to the thesis of
   the article:

   > The condition of freedom in any state is always a wide-spread and
   > consistent skepticism of the canons upon which power insists.

2. What are death camps? Where and when did they come into existence? Who was put to death in them? Why?

3. According to what you've learned from this article, do you think
   Americans would operate death camps? All Americans? Would you?

4. How do you think you would have performed as the "teacher" in the
   experiment? Would you have gone "all the way"? Why or why not?

5. Was the experiment fair?

6. What conclusions about people and their attitudes toward right and
   wrong, authority, their own consciences, responsibility, people in
   pain, science, "experiments," etc., can be legitimately drawn from
   Milgram's experiment, if any?

7. What was the Holocaust?

8. How could Milgram's findings be used (as he says he doesn't want
   them to be) to "excuse the horrors of a Holocaust."

9. Do you think the experiment was in some way prompted by the Holocaust. How? Why?

10. What percentage of the "teachers" in the experiment refused to go
    along with the experiment even when prompted and assured by the

experimenter? Is that percentage more or less than you would have expected? Do you find it encouraging or disheartening? Do you think you would have been among those who refused? Why or why not?

11. The first four paragraphs "set a scene." For what purpose? Did this "scene" ever happen anywhere? Where and when? Why?

12. How is this article organized? How is it introduced? What's in the body? How is it concluded?

13. What details are given? Are they sufficient and of the right kind?

SUGGESTIONS FOR WRITING

1. Devise an experiment to explore some aspect of human nature and describe how it would work. You could write it in the form of a "process analysis" (i.e., a "how-to" composition).

2. Pretend you have just been through the experiment as the "teacher" and have "gone all the way." Then write a composition explaining your feelings and actions: Did you hesitate? Why? Why did you continue? How did you react to the writhing and groaning of the "learner"?—to the assurances of the experimenter? This could be written in the form of a narrative.

3. Do the same as in question 2 above but from the point of view of someone who refused to "go along" with the experiment.

4. Write an essay explaining what you think the experiment proves or doesn't prove about human nature.

5. Write a process analysis explaining how this experiment was set up and how it worked.

6. Write an essay defending or attacking the validity of the experiment. Is it legitimate to draw conclusions about how people (or Americans) would act in real life from this experiment?

7. Write an essay explaining why you think Americans would or wouldn't operate death camps. Relate your thinking to the results of the experiment.

Selection 20

Overall Reading Performance

Your overall reading performance is a combination of how fast you read and how much you comprehend and retain. The chart below allows you to find out quickly your "overall reading performance."

First enter your "reading time" and your "retention and comprehension" score in the two blanks at the bottom of the page. Then simply lay a straightedge of any kind (the edge of a sheet of paper or a pencil will do) across the chart, placing the left side of the straightedge at the appropriate point on the "Reading Rate" scale, and the right side at the appropriate point on the "Retention and Comprehension" scale. The point at which the paper or pencil intersects the scale in the middle of the page will indicate your overall performance.

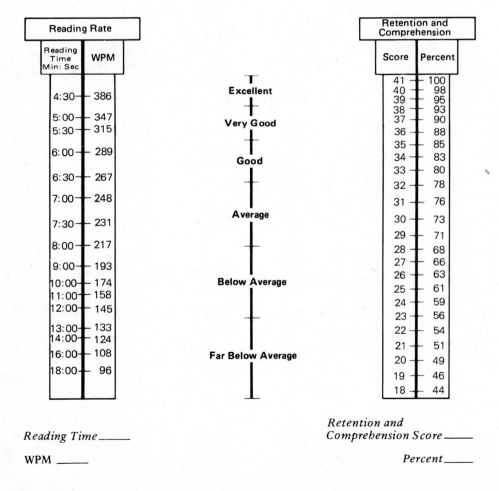

Reading Rate	
Reading Time Min: Sec	WPM
4:30	386
5:00	347
5:30	315
6:00	289
6:30	267
7:00	248
7:30	231
8:00	217
9:00	193
10:00	174
11:00	158
12:00	145
13:00	133
14:00	124
16:00	108
18:00	96

Excellent
Very Good
Good
Average
Below Average
Far Below Average

Retention and Comprehension	
Score	Percent
41	100
40	98
39	95
38	93
37	90
36	88
35	85
34	83
33	80
32	78
31	76
30	73
29	71
28	68
27	66
26	63
25	61
24	59
23	56
22	54
21	51
20	49
19	46
18	44

Reading Time _____

WPM _____

Retention and Comprehension Score _____

Percent _____

Selection 21

Your Name Is Your Destiny

JOE BODOLAI

Research shows that people form opinions about others on the basis of names alone. (Which blind date would you pick: Mortimer or David?) If you've been saddled with an unappealing label, consider switching to a pretty, power-pulling new one . . .

For her first twenty-four years, she'd been known as Debbie—a perky little appellation that didn't suit her dark, willowy, good looks and urbane manner. "My name has always made me think I should be a cheerleader, or go blonde," she complained. "I just don't *feel* like a Debbie!"

One day, while filling out an application form for a publishing job, the young woman impulsively substituted her middle name, Lynne, for the long-deplored Debbie. "That was the smartest thing I ever did," she says now. "As soon as I stopped calling myself Debbie, I felt more comfortable with myself . . . and *other* people started to take me more seriously." Two years after her successful job interview, the former waitress is a successful magazine editor—friends and associates call her Lynne.

Naturally, the name change didn't *cause* Debbie/Lynne's professional coup—but it surely helped, if only by adding a crucial bit of self-confidence to her already abundant talents. Social scientists say that what you're called *can* affect your life. Throughout history, names have not merely identified people but also *described* them. " . . . As his name is, so *is* he . . . " says the Bible (I Samuel 25:25), and Webster's Dictionary includes the following definition of *name*: "a word or words expressing some quality considered characteristic or descriptive of a person or thing, often expressing approval or disapproval." Note well "approval or disapproval": For better or worse, qualities such as friendliness or reserve, athletic ability or a bookish bent, homeliness or allure may be suggested by your name and subliminally conveyed to other people before they even meet you.

Source: Cosmopolitan, Oct. 1980. Reprinted by permission.

What's in an Image?

Names become attached to specific images, as anyone who's been called "a plain Jane" or "just an average Joe" can attest. The latter epithet particularly galls me since *my* name is Joe, which some think makes me more qualified to be a shortstop than, say, an art critic. Yet, despite this disadvantage, I did manage to become an art critic for a time. Even so, one prominent magazine consistently refused to print "Joe" in my by-line, using my first initials, J.S., instead. I suspect that if I were a more refined Arthur or Adrian, the name would have appeared complete.

Of course, names with a *positive* connotation can work *for* you—even encouraging new acquaintances. A recent survey showed that American men thought Susan to be the sexiest female name, while women believed Richard and David were the most attractive for men. One woman I know turned down a blind date with a man named Harry because "he sounded dull." Several evenings after passing up the date, she sidled up to me at a party, pressing for an introduction to a devastating Richard Gere lookalike; they'd been exchanging glances all evening. "Oh," I said. "You mean *Harry*?" She squirmed.

Though most of us would like to think ourselves free from such preconceived notions, we're all guilty of name stereotyping to some extent. Confess: Wouldn't *you* be surprised to meet a construction worker named Nigel? A fashion model called Bertha? A Pope Mel? Often, we *project* name-based stereotypes on people, as one woman friend discovered while minding a day-care center's group of four-year-olds. "There I was, trying to get a little pepperpot named Julian to sit quietly and read a book—and pushing a pensive creature named Rory to play ball. I had their personalities confused just because of their names!"

Apparently, such prejudices can affect classroom achievement as well. In a study conducted by Herbert Harari of San Diego State University, and John McDavid of Georgia State University, teachers gave consistently lower grades on essays supposedly written by boys named Elmer and Hubert than they awarded to the *same* papers when the authors' names were given as Michael and David. However, teacher prejudice isn't the only source of classroom differences; Dr. Thomas V. Busse and Louisa Seraydarian of Temple University found that girls with names such as Linda, Diane, Barbara, Carol, and Cindy performed better on objectively graded IQ and achievement tests than did girls with less appealing names. (A companion study showed that the girls' popularity with their peers was also related to the popularity of their names—although the connection was less clear for boys.)

Changing Fashions

How did your parents arrive at the "sound symbol" that so relentlessly types you? Their method may have been as arbitrary as pointing to a Bible page at random, or as deliberate as a tribute to a favorite ancestor. Not surprisingly, the process of choosing names varies widely from culture to culture. The custom of several tribes of Indians, for example, was to name a baby for a memorable event in one of the parent's lives. In China, an elder dictates names for the next seven generations. As children are born into the family, the parents select a name from the list. Even within a culture, names may go through distinct trends. Prudence, Maude, or Agatha—once as stylish for girls as the current Michelle or Lisa—now seem as antiquated as corsets. Interestingly, girls' names fall in and out of fashion more rapidly than do those of boys, who are often named after fathers or grandfathers—keeping the same names in the family for generations of males.

Even appellations of *recent* vintage can date you. If you're named Debbie or Sherry, for example, you're probably in your midtwenties. In the midfifties, these two names rose to the top of the popularity lists like hit songs—and faded just as fast. (Although in 1950 neither name was in the top *100*, by 1956 Debbie and Sherry were first and second in popularity for newborn girls. By 1960 both names had dropped from the top ten.) A longer-lasting fifties fad was the name Kimberly, no doubt inspired by actress Kim Novak. Newborn Kimberlies abounded until well into the seventies. For boys, Kevin followed a similar pattern. At one time, I didn't know a single Kevin who was more than six, and I still won't vote for any candidate named Kevin because part of me insists he's too young to hold office.

In the sixties, babies were bestowed with imaginative names meant to reflect their parents' spirituality, individuality, or alternate life style. Day-care centers were full of little Sunshines, Frees, Moons, Chastitys, and Geminis. Many such names now carry the same esthetic impact as black-light posters. (One child I know announced upon arriving the first day of school, "My real first name is Tree, but I'd like to be called George, if you don't mind.")

Currently, names beginning with *J* are the rage: Jennifer or Jessica for girls; Jason or Jeremy for boys. (You'd be hard-pressed, though, to find a plain Jane or an average Joe.) Androgynous, "designer" names—Dale, Brit, Brooke, Lane—are also popular for both boys and girls. Despite recent innovations, however, one of the most common female names among all age groups is still Mary; over three-and-a-half million women answer to that well-loved choice, more than twice as many as were christened with the runners-up, Elizabeth and Barbara.

You Can Change Your Name

Though your parents probably meant your moniker to last a lifetime, remember that when they picked it they'd hardly *met* you, and the hopes and dreams they cherished when they chose it may not match *yours*. If your name no longer seems to fit you, don't despair; you aren't *stuck* with the label. Screen stars routinely tailor their names, and with some determination, you can, too.

Legal rules are more flexible in this matter than you might expect. How many newlyweds, for instance, are aware that *no law* requires a woman to assume her husband's name? Not only that, but in most states parents can give their *children* any surname they wish, even if it's not that of either parent. Jane Fonda and Tom Hayden, for example, named their son Tony Garity.

If you do wish to pick a new name, you don't need an attorney to make the switch official. Under common law, all that's necessary is to start *using* the name of your choice. Remember, though, that you must use it *everywhere*—even with your mother—for it to become your legal name. You must also change all your identification papers and records: You'll need a new driver's license, car registration, checking account, insurance, credit cards, voter registration, and telephone listing, to mention only a few. Your Social Security number will remain the same; just fill out form SS-5 at your local Social Security office, and they'll notify the Internal Revenue Service. Be sure to practice your new signature until you write it naturally and consistently.

Getting friends and colleagues to call you Leah instead of Lola may be harder than any paperwork involved, but you'll probably encounter official resistance, too. Be assured that no law prohibits you from using whatever name you've established for any transaction, provided it's not for purposes of fraud, unfair competition, or to otherwise aid any illegal activity. If the gas company tells you that you can't get your bill under a new name, they're wrong. You don't have to show them any sort of court document. You have a right to be called by whatever name you choose.

Once you've changed the records, though, you'll face other problems. Applying for a passport or a new job may call for references or school records that are still in your former name. To forestall bureaucratic complications, however, you may *prefer* to go through legal channels. Although lawyers' fees can amount to several hundred dollars, you'll be able to provide official documentation—a copy of the court order—when the occasion does arise.

Regulations differ from state to state and even between counties; your county clerk can refer you to a civil law book that will explain the procedure in your region. (You should be able to follow the steps on your own, but if legalese intimidates you, by all means, hire an attorney to do the work for you.) If you're a single adult, the process is extremely straightforward. Usually, you must file a petition along with a fee to cover court costs (around $35 in New York State), and in *some* areas, you may be required to print a public notice of your intent to change your name in a local newspaper and appear before a judge—a mere formality that needn't frighten you.

If you have a husband (or ex-spouse) and children, however, these people must be notified of your desire to change your name, and they have a right to object. The court must then approve and sign your petition.

By this time, you've probably realized that changing your name is more complicated than up-grading your wardrobe or changing your hair color, though the effect can be eminently inspiring. Don't be too concerned if you have to keep reminding your man not to whisper "that other woman's name"—persist, and friends and lovers will accept your new identity. Good luck!

No. of Words: 1820

Reading Time: _____

Selection 21

Your Name Is Your Destiny

VOCABULARY BUILDING

Below are several words used in this article. They are presented in the context of the sentences or phrases in which they occur. If you are unsure of their meanings and cannot define them from the context, look them up in the dictionary. Spaces are provided for additional unfamiliar words from the article to add to your vocabulary.

1. "...the young woman *impulsively* substituted her middle name, Lynne, for the *long-deplored* Debbie."

   impulsively: _____

   long-deplored: _____

2. "Naturally, the name change didn't cause Debbie/Lynne's professional *coup*—but it surely helped ..."

   coup: _____

3. "Prudence, Maude, or Agatha—once as stylish for girls as the current Michelle or Lisa—now seem as *antiquated* as corsets."

   antiquated: _____

4. "*Androgynous,* 'designer' names—Dale ..., Brooke, Lane—are also popular for both boys and girls."

   androgynous: _____

5. "To *forestall* bureaucratic complications, however, you may prefer to go through legal channels."

   forestall: _____

6. _____ : _____

7. _____ : _____

8. _____ : _____

RETENTION AND COMPREHENSION

A. True/False (1 point each)

1. One prominent magazine insisted that the author use the name "Joe" because it sounded more masculine than Arthur.

   1. T _____ F _____

2. The woman at the day-care center was guilty of name stereotyping when she selected activities for the two boys named Julian and Rory.

   2. T _____ F _____

3. One of the most common female names among all age groups is Mary.

   3. T _____ F _____

4. The author says that some states require, by law, that the woman assume the husband's name.

   4. T _____ F _____

5. Women with the names "Debbie" and "Sherry" were probably born in the 1950s.

   5. T _____ F _____

B. Completion (3 points each)

6. Lynne said that her original name, Debbie, made her feel that she should have been a blonde or a _____.

   6. _____

7. A recent survey showed that American men thought the sexiest female name was _____ _____.

   7. _____

8. The same survey showed that American women thought the names Richard and _____ _____ were the most attractive for men.

   8. _____

9. The custom of selecting a child's name from a list made up by an elder for seven generations is found in the country of _____.

   9. _____

10. Currently, among the most popular names are those beginning with the letter_____.

    10. _____

C. *Multiple Choice* (2 points each)

11. The university studies referred to show that "appealing" names seem to influence students' (a) popularity, but not academic achievement; (b) popularity and academic achievement; (c) academic achievement, only on subjective material, such as an essay; (d) confidence and self-esteem.

11. _____

12. According to the author, names like Tree, Sunshine, Chastity, and Gemini reflect parental attitudes of the decade of the (a) 1940s, (b) 1950s, (c) 1960s, (d) 1970s.

12. _____

13. The custom of several tribes of Indians was to name a baby for (a) an animal or a plant, (b) an honored relative, (c) a tribal god whose favor was sought by the family, (d) an important event in one of the parent's lives.

13. _____

14. When acquiring a new legal name, a person does *not* have to change (a) voter registration records; (b) a nickname, like "Slim" or "Stubby"; (c) a Social Security number; (d) a previous name when with one's immediate family.

14. _____

15. The author states that a person seeking a name change must (a) hire an attorney, (b) use his old name until he repays any debts, (c) have school and employment records changed, (d) notify an ex-spouse and children.

15. _____

16. In the naming of children most states (a) require that children have their father's surname, (b) require that children have at least either parent's surname, (c) allow the parents to use only close family surnames, (d) let parents use any surname, even if it's not that of either parent.

16. _____

17. Girls' names fade in and out of fashion more rapidly than boys' names because (a) there are fewer boys' names than there are girls' names, (b) boys are often named after fathers or grandfathers, (c) girls are more often named after movie stars and celebrities than boys, (d) parents tend to treat sons more conservatively than they do daughters.

17. _____

18. An example of an androgynous, "designer" name

18. _____

for both males and females is (a) Leah, (b) Brit, (c) Chastity, (d) Mel.

D. *Thematic (11 points)*

19. Which statement *best* expresses the theme (*main idea*) of the article?

   (a) Because names seem to have some influence on how we and others see ourselves, parents should be more careful in the selection of their children's names.

   (b) The popularity of certain names fades so rapidly that most people probably have names that don't fit their personalities.

   (c) People who are uncomfortable with their given names have a right to use legal methods to alter them.

   (d) Changing one's name seems difficult because of social and legal barriers, but it is easy if done in the proper manner.

19. _____

E. *Purpose (9 points)*

20. The author's *chief* purpose is

   (a) to tell us that traditional methods of name selection (the *Bible,* popular entertainers, family names) are no longer satisfactory because people form opinions on the basis of names.

   (b) to outline the necessary legal steps for those people who are unhappy with their names and want a change in their lives.

   (c) to help readers in determining the influence of their given names on themselves and the people around them, as revealed by recent surveys and scientific studies.

   (d) to show that names appear to influence our lives, and if the effects are harmful, steps can be taken to change our "labels" for the better.

20. _____

Total Retention and Comprehension Score: _____

noticed other similarities. Both smoked the same brand of cigarettes. Both liked Italian food and mellow rock music. But the first, brief meeting was relatively superficial. "We could hardly talk," Eddy says, "and my dad kept taking pictures. My parents couldn't believe it."

After an hour Bobby and Mike drove back to school. Later that morning Bobby phoned his home and cried, "Dad, Dad, I just met my twin brother!"

Dr. Shafran replied logically, "Bobby, an adoption agency doesn't separate twins." Neither set of parents had been informed that their sons were multiple-birth babies.

That Sunday Bobby and Eddy met again on Long Island and took turns recounting their life experiences. Both have a high I.Q., yet each had had problems in school at the same time. They'd each had psychiatric therapy in 1977 and 1978 and been told their problems were rooted in their adoption; both called that "baloney." They were similarly attracted to older girls—and had serious relationships with women of 27. Their best sport was wrestling, and they had the same favorite moves and fastest pinning time: 18 seconds. "I discovered that whenever I'd had troubles, Eddy had had troubles," Bobby says. "When I had excelled, he'd excelled. It was overwhelming."

Triple Take

That was only the beginning. The Long Island newspaper *Newsday* heard of the startling reunion about two weeks after it happened and interviewed the twins. The story was picked up by the New York *Post* and the New York *Daily News.*

On the day the article appeared in the *Post,* David Kellman, a 19-year-old college student from Queens, N.Y., saw the picture of Bobby and Eddy. His pulse rate doubled.

"These two people were my mirror image," he says. "But the story didn't give a date of birth, so I tried to keep my emotions low-key and inside till I was sure." That night at home, David hesitantly held out the *Post* and said, "Ma, check this out." Claire Kellman tossed her son a copy of the *Daily News*—which carried no picture but gave a date of birth—and said, "Check *this* out."

"Right then we knew," David says. "We looked up the phone number of the Galland house. Eddy was out, but his mother answered. I said, 'You're not going to believe this, Mrs. Galland, but my name is David Kellman, and I think I'm the third. . . .'"

That evening David and his parents drove over to the Galland home. Eddy watched as the Kellman car parked beside the curb and "still another me climbed out and started up the walk. I opened the door a little, then closed it. I opened it again, saw his face, and closed it again. It was like a

double take, a triple take—and the third time I opened it David was saying, in a voice just like my own, 'I haven't seen you in 19 years—don't slam
the door in my face!' "

Slowly, they moved toward each other. "I can't *believe* this!" they said
simultaneously. Then, again in unison, "I can't believe you *said* that!"—
and fell into each other's arms.

David pulled out his cigarettes—the same brand Bobby and Eddy
smoked. Like his brothers, David had flunked math despite a high I.Q.,
gone through psychiatric care, enjoyed Italian food, wrestling, older
women ("not in that order"), and had dreamed he had a brother who
looked like him.

David felt "euphoria," and Eddy thoroughly enjoyed the night. "We just
kept talking and saying, 'Wow, did you do that too?' "

"Give Us a Chance"

It was probably the first time in history that identical triplets separated in
infancy have been reunited. Each child was brought up in a somewhat
different environment by working parents. The Shafrans are medical and
legal professionals; Richard and Claire Kellman operate a wholesale
housewares business; Elliott Galland is an industrial-arts teacher and his
wife, Annette, is an executive secretary.

Predictably, scientists have now flooded the families with requests to
study the triplets. But the 19-year-olds are too consumed with their joyful,
sometimes zany, self-discovery to hold still for inquiry. "We have never
been genuinely, intrinsically happy like this before," explains David.
"Give us a chance."

The families' first priority was to contact the adoption agency and in-
quire why the boys had been separated. None of the parents was pleased
with the explanation that, 19 years ago, little was known of the potentially
harmful effects of splitting up multiple-birth children. The triplets were
said to be the last such infants separated.

No one can be certain whether they would have led less complex emotional lives if they had stayed together, but the presumption is strong. "We
all had periods of being miserable, a lot of emotional pain, in spite of
having terrific parents," says Bobby. "Psychiatrists told each of us there
was some kind of emotional block."

It is a rare, serious moment in an interview with Bobby, David and Eddy.
Their eccentric sense of humor seems to combine the drollery of the early
Beatles and the horseplay of the Marx Brothers. They often yelp with
laughter, then switch gears to calm, straight-faced conversation that invariably ends in one triplet finishing another's sentence. They confess they
can be "really wild sometimes" when together, but they're trying, gradually, to settle down.

David intends to become a businessman. Bobby, whose mother says he has been cooking since the age of four, plans to operate hotels and restaurants. Eddy will be a doctor. They phone or see one another half a dozen times a day and meet often at one another's homes.

"They're all so happy," says Dr. Shafran with a smile. "But they're rushing to make up for 19 years of being apart. They get kind of fractious. I only hope they won't let all this distract them from their education and goals. You can't make a career out of being a triplet."

In spite of the wonder of finding "our own flesh and blood," the triplets say they have no interest in locating their biological parents. "There may be an underlying curiosity, but it isn't relevant," Eddy says.

Bobby adds, "A woman gave birth to us. We appreciate that. She made sure we got into good homes, and we appreciate that. But we all have intelligent parents who cared for us, went through trials and heartaches with us. They are our real parents."

All three of the triplets agree with that.

No. of Words: 1834

Reading Time: _____

Selection 22

Triplets . . . And They Didn't Know It!

VOCABULARY BUILDING

Below are several words used in this article. They are presented in the context of the sentences or phrases in which they occur. If you are unsure of their meanings and cannot define them from the context, look them up in the dictionary. Spaces are provided for additional unfamiliar words from the article to add to your vocabulary.

1. ". . . it appealed to his *quirky* sense of humor and strong sense of individuality."

   quirky: _____

2. "'He was always *precocious*, but also restless and *hyperkinetic*.'"

   precocious: _____

   hyperkinetic: _____

3. "Everything in *unison*, as though professional *mimes* were doing this."

   unison: _____

   mimes: _____

4. "'We have never been genuinely, *intrinsically* happy like this before . . .'"

   intrinsically: _____

5. "Their eccentric sense of humor seems to combine the *drollery* of the early Beatles and the horseplay of the Marx brothers."

   drollery: _____

6. "'But they're rushing to make up for 19 years of being apart. They get kind of *fractious*.'"

fractious: _____

7. _____: _____

8. _____: _____

9. _____: _____

RETENTION AND COMPREHENSION

A. True/False (1 point each)

1. As a teenager, Bobby Shafran blamed his difficulties in school on his adoptive parents.

    1. T _____ F _____

2. Bobby Shafran and Eddy Galland, his brother, were attending the same community college when they discovered their relationship.

    2. T _____ F _____

3. David Kellman, the other triplet to discover his relationship to Bobby and Eddy, was identified by a newspaper reporter.

    3. T _____ F _____

4. The adoptive parents of Bobby, Eddy, and Dave had no idea that the boys were related.

    4. T _____ F _____

5. At the time of their discovery, the triplets were living in the state of New York.

    5. T _____ F _____

B. Completion (3 points each)

6. The triplets all shared an interest in the sport of _____.

    6. _____

7. Also, they all enjoyed a taste for _____ food.

    7. _____

8. One area in which the triplets seem to differ is in their choice of _____.

    8. _____

9. The presumption is strong that their separation somehow influenced the triplets' early _____ problems.

    9. _____

10. The triplets *are/are not* interested in finding their biological parents.

10. _____

C. Multiple Choice (2 points each)

11. Bobby's first real indication that something about him was unique occurred when he (a) dreamed of a boy who looked like he did, (b) saw a psychiatrist for school problems, (c) was a freshman in high school, (d) was called by a different name at college.

11. _____

12. Bobby met one brother with the aid of (a) the adoption agency which separated them, (b) a mutual friend who showed Bobby some photographs, (c) a sociologist, (d) an industrial arts teacher in college.

12. _____

13. Eddy Galland's first indication that something unusual was about to happen started with (a) "weird" phone calls from friends, (b) a letter from Bobby Shafran, (c) a newspaper interview, (d) a strange dream about people who resembled him.

13. _____

14. The statement ". . . an adoption agency doesn't separate twins . . ." was whose reaction to the first meeting between Bobby and Eddy? (a) Eddy's, (b) Bobby's, (c) Eddy's mother, (d) Bobby's father.

14. _____

15. Another similarity of the triplets was (a) attendance at the same college, (b) an attraction to older women, (c) rather average IQs, (d) an inability to appreciate their situation.

15. _____

16. Even after seeing a photo of Bobby and Eddy, David took no action to contact them until he (a) was called by an old college buddy, (b) learned of their birth date, (c) was notified officially by a representative of the hospital where they were born, (d) read an article about them in *Newsweek*.

16. _____

17. According to the article, the triplets are (a) undergoing extensive scientific examination, (b) not going to let themselves be studied by scientists, (c) writing a book on their lives, (d) not quite ready to submit to study until they have discovered each other more.

17. _____

18. The adoption agency's reason for separating the triplets was that (a) nineteen years ago little was known of the harmful effects of splitting up multiple-birth children, (b) the biological mother had requested the separation, (c) no one family wanted the financial burden of adopting triplets, (d) it had been a decision by an agency administrator who saw no harm in separation at an early age.

18. _____

D. Thematic (11 points)

19. Which statement best expresses the them (*main* idea) of the article?
    (a) The information to be gathered from the triplets' experiences will influence how social scientists view the importance of environment in shaping human life.
    (b) Environment does not influence our lives as much as inherited genetic characteristics do.
    (c) The triplets' discovery of each other was truly fortunate because it gave them happiness, a sense of well-being, and an explanation for their emotional difficulties as youths.
    (d) The triplets will never be the same now that they know of each other's existence.

19. _____

E. Purpose (9 points)

20. The author's *chief* purpose is
    (a) to assure that multiple-birth children are not separated as the triplets were.
    (b) to help us appreciate the feelings of the participants in an event that has probably never happened before and will probably never happen again.
    (c) to convince us that scientists still do not know the effects of environment and heredity on our lives.
    (d) to suggest that there are forces which influence human life and which we do not understand.

20. _____

Total Retention and Comprehension Score: _____

QUESTIONS FOR DISCUSSION (MEANING AND TECHNIQUE)

1. Is the writer more concerned with *what* happened or *how* it happened? Why? Consider the title and the first sentence before you answer.

2. Why is it important for the story to develop without confusion? What techniques does the writer use to keep the narrative easy to follow? Does it become hard to keep the triplets straight? If so, at what point?

3. Find paragraphs that compare the brothers. In what ways are the brothers alike? Different?

4. How did each of the triplets react when they were told (before the discovery of their relationship) that their problems in school were caused by their adoptions? Offer an explanation for their reactions.

5. Why does the writer quote the triplets often?

SUGGESTIONS FOR WRITING

1. If you have friends who are of multiple birth, how are they alike or different? What problems are caused by their similarities, or, perhaps, their attempts to be different? Compare them in an essay.

2. Does the information learned from the triplets' discovery provide support for environment or heredity as the dominant factor in determining one's life? In an essay support your answer with references from the article.

3. If you know an adopted person who located his/her natural parents, write a narrative telling how it happened, including how it affected the lives of the people involved.

4. What are the procedures for adopting a child in your state? What kind of adoption agencies exist in your area? Do adoption agencies have too many or not enough children for people to adopt? Write an informative composition dealing with one or more of these questions.

5. Write a paper arguing for or against the idea that adopted children have a right to know who their natural parents are.

Selection 22

Overall Reading Performance

Your overall reading performance is a combination of how fast you read and how much you comprehend and retain. The chart below allows you to find out quickly your "overall reading performance."

First enter your "reading time" and your "retention and comprehension" score in the two blanks at the bottom of the page. Then simply lay a straightedge of any kind (the edge of a sheet of paper or a pencil will do) across the chart, placing the left side of the straightedge at the appropriate point on the "Reading Rate" scale, and the right side at the appropriate point on the "Retention and Comprehension" scale. The point at which the paper or pencil intersects the scale in the middle of the page will indicate your overall performance.

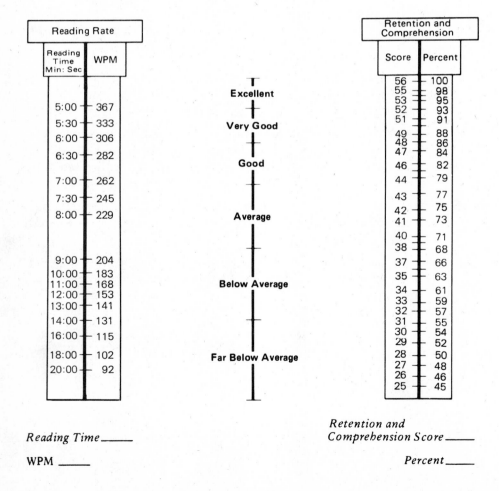

*Reading Time*_____

WPM _____

Retention and
*Comprehension Score*_____

*Percent*_____

Selection 23

What's in Paycheck Varies With Skill, Schooling, Sex

DALE SINGER

How much money do you make?

If you are Jimmy Carter,* your job pays $200,000 a year, plus such "perks" as a rent-free lease at 1600 Pennsylvania Ave. But the hours are long and there's no overtime pay.

The average slam-dunker in the National Basketball Assn. earns $143,000—a sky-high leap from $20,000 in 1967. Touchdown passes in the National Football League go from a $113,932 quarterback to a $64,631 receiver.

Actor Steve McQueen, reportedly the highest-paid worker in the United States, commands $5 million a picture plus a percentage of the profits—a level which allows him to work only three or four months a year.

But before you head for Hollywood, heed these average annual income figures compiled by the Screen Actors Guild: $7,380 for actors, $4,908 for actresses.

Comparing salaries among various occupations is difficult. Figures pulled together from various sources—government reports, professional organizations and other groups—may represent different time periods or different methods of computation.

But when they are put together, they provide an interesting answer to an interesting question: Are wages equitable?

United Press International reporters interviewed workers in various fields as well as economists who have studied the issue of wages, trying to find out what jobs earn how much money and why.

The answers reveal a wide range of factors that influence salaries and just as wide a range of satisfaction or dissatisfaction felt by workers whose paychecks are eroded daily by the highest inflation in 33 years.

*Jimmy Carter was president in 1980, when this article appeared. Wages have changed somewhat since then, but, not, in general, relative to each other.

Source: Los Angeles Times, Feb. 17, 1980. Reprinted by permission of United Press International.

Consider the joke about the doctor shocked by the bill he gets from the plumber. "This is outrageous," he sputters. "I'm a doctor, and I don't earn this much."

"When I was a doctor," the plumber replies, "neither did I."

Doctors earn a reported average of $55,000 a year. Some specialists earn more, as much as $71,000 reported for orthopedic surgeons, but others earn less, including psychiatrists, whose income is said to average $45,000.

Now listen to Chuck Ollinger, a plumber in Erie, Pa., whose average 60-hour workweek brings in $45,000 a year, which he shares with his wife and son who help him in the business.

"We make a decent living these days," Ollinger says, "but we don't get rich. The money doesn't add up compared to the time you put in and what you have to go through to make it. It's just not worth it anymore. In just the last three or four years it's been a hassle."

Figures from the Census Bureau show that in early 1979 the average yearly income of the American family headed by a full-time worker was $18,000—about 20% higher than the figure for the mid-1970s.

Families headed by white workers in white-collar jobs averaged $25,500, with blue-collar families averaging $18,600. Blacks earned less in both categories.

The highest-paid hourly employees were construction workers, with wages of $8 an hour. At the other end were waiters and waitresses, who earned $2.90 an hour before tips.

Education is a factor in determining salaries, with college graduates consistently earning more than workers whose education stopped at high school. But increasing salaries for technical jobs has caused the gap between salaries based on level of education to shrink in recent years.

Some other figures:

A schoolteacher in Mississippi earns an average of $9,000, which is $4,500 less than the average teacher's salary nationwide and even farther behind the $16,000 earned by teachers in New York.

Firefighters and police officers in large cities make $17,000, the same as the average postal worker. The average scientist earns $24,000, ranging from $30,000 for physicists to $20,000 for geographers.

The president of a large corporation earns $250,000 in salary, not including benefits, but he (or she) works an average of 60 hours a week. In major television markets, the person who anchors the local news show earns an average of $200,000 a year.

File clerks average a little more than $7,000 a year, while the top level of computer operators have salaries averaging $17,250. Secretaries range from $10,300 to $15,700, while attorneys average from $18,700 right out of law school to nearly $57,000 at the top of their field.

One important factor in salaries, of course, is success. In 1931, when the presidency paid only $75,000, much of the country was shocked when baseball star Babe Ruth was offered $80,000 to play for the New York Yankees.

Asked if he deserved to earn more than President Herbert Hoover, Ruth is said to have replied: "Why not? I had a better year than he did."

Why does your job pay as much—or as little—as it does? Adam Smith, whose pioneer work "Wealth of Nations" helped form economic thinking more than 200 years ago, listed some criteria that are still accurate today.

First, Smith wrote, wages are determined by how agreeable or disagreeable a job may be. This principle is further influenced by the law of supply and demand: If a job is so desirable that everyone wants it—and anyone can do it—the wages it brings are likely to be low, if all other factors are equal.

But all other factors rarely are equal. Smith's second principle is that wages depend on how easily and cheaply a skill can be learned. Everyone might want to be paid as well as a doctor, but not everyone is able or willing to go through years of exacting medical training.

A third factor cited by Smith also points up why professions such as medicine and the law command such high fees.

"We trust our health to the physician," Smith said, "our fortune and sometimes our life and reputation to the lawyer and attorney. Such confidence could not safely be reposed in people of a very mean or low condition.

"Their reward must be such, therefore, as may give them that rank in society which so important a trust requires."

Two other important factors that Smith says shape a worker's paycheck are how steady the work is and how easy it is to succeed in any given field.

"Put your son apprentice to a shoemaker," Smith said, "there is little doubt of his learning to make a pair of shoes; but send him to study the law, it is at least 20 to 1 if ever he makes such proficiency as will enable him to live by the business."

Today's economists tend to echo Smith's thoughts in general, but they point out the modern equation is changed by many circumstances, including education and organized labor.

Dick Henderson, management professor at Georgia State University in Atlanta, says where there are strong unions or a predominant number of white males, jobs bring higher wages than non-union jobs heavily populated by either minorities or women.

"At first glance, in jobs that are occupied by females and minorities, there is great likelihood that the pay is less than the worth of the job," Henderson said. "At face value, there is some type of basic discrimination."

He said the disparity in pay between jobs dominated by white males and those with a large number of women and minorities generally ranges between 50% and 70%.

Gary S. Becker, a professor of economics at the University of Chicago, says wages in America are equitable. "Overall, wages work out pretty well in the equity sense, meaning those people who work hard, are more skilled and more productive usually get paid more."

But he concedes that salaries paid to black workers often are limited by racial prejudice. He also cited a trend toward employees at larger companies earning more money than those at smaller companies.

Education helps someone earn more money, but Becker added that the rate at which earnings rise tends to get lower at higher levels of education. A high-school graduate may earn 30% more than someone with a grade school education, but a college degree does not ensure another 30% jump.

One final factor might be noted: special talents. In Adam Smith's time, performers were engaged in what he called "a sort of public prostitution." He may have been taking an accurate look into today's climate of movie and sports stars whose lives are subject to a new wave of gossip.

Smith put his theory this way:

"The exorbitant rewards of players, opera-singers, opera-dancers, etc., are founded upon these two principles: the rarity and beauty of the talents, and the discredit of employing them in this manner.

"It seems absurd at first sight that we should despise their persons and yet reward their talents with the most profuse liberality. While we do the one, however, we must of necessity do the other."

Now you know how much other people earn, and something about why. Are you satisfied with your paycheck? If not, join the crowd.

Salary may not be the most important thing to look for in a job. Surveys by *Playboy* magazine and placement specialist Frank S. Endicott of Northwestern University rate salary as less important than the type of work, the opportunities for advancement, job security and friendly co-workers.

Still, those features don't pay the bills, and in a time when bills are becoming bigger all the time, satisfaction with salary is not easy to find.

"It's not enough," says New York police officer Michael Parente of his $20,000 annual pay. "I was better off as a rookie when I was earning $9,500."

Noting that six officers have been killed since 1970 in his precinct in the city's Lower East Side, Parente complained about his salary as compared with that of other city workers.

"I don't want to cut anyone else down," he said, "but you have responsibilities. You're on duty 24 hours a day. You can't say, 'I'm off duty. I don't feel like it.'"

Trudy Posey, a Red Cross nurse in Atlanta, also said the nature of her job should bring her more money. "It's quite rewarding to take care of sick people," she says, "but it's frustrating because we're not being paid a lot.

"I've talked to others like a cleanup lady at General Motors who makes more than our starting salaries. Why that's true, I don't know."

Jim Kindregen, principal administrative analyst in the office of San Francisco Mayor Dianne Feinstein, feels he is a victim of the tax-cutting fervor of Proposition 13.

Kindregen studies budget requests for city departments, then helps decide where the money should go—including $24,600 that goes into his paycheck every year.

"If you're going to look at it from the standpoint of comparing my salary to, let's say, a plumber's, you're going to have to say that virtually every white-collar job is underpaid," he says.

"If a Muni (bus) driver gets $70 a day or over $18,000 a year, then I say that as one of two people in the entire city who does what I do, I should be getting $40,000. But if you make such a statement, you risk being very unrealistic because of political realities."

In Columbus, Ohio, waitress Joanne Blue works for $1.89 an hour, plus tips. An average 40-hour week brings in between $125 and $150. A former elementary school teacher with a 2-year-old daughter, she tried babysitting in her home, but wanted an outside job to help with the bills.

"I'm satisfied with my pay," she says. "I'm not griping. We've got great management. They're not picky. They don't make you wash walls if there is a lull in business.

"I found it necessary to work to pay bills. I skimp a lot at the grocery store. Don't get me wrong—I won't feed my family peanut butter to pay the bills. I don't buy those untasty foods. I shop specials and use coupons. It's hard to shop."

Ernest Gardner, a librarian in San Francisco, has a master's degree. He says his job in the reference department helps make society work. He earns less than $12,000 a year.

"We don't make enough money in proportion to what we do and how we serve society." he says. "The reason is that it's a woman-dominated profession. Librarians are not looked upon as a doctor or a lawyer is.

"We are very underpaid," he says.

No. of Words: 1986

Reading Time: _____

Selection 23

What's In Paycheck Varies with Skill, Schooling, Sex

VOCABULARY BUILDING

Below are several words used in this article. They are presented in the context of the sentences or phrases in which they occur. If you are unsure of their meanings and cannot define them from the context, look them up in the dictionary. Spaces are provided for additional unfamiliar words from the article to add to your vocabulary.

1. "... heed these average annual income figures *compiled* by the Screen Actors Guild ..."

   compiled: _____

2. "Are wages *equitable*?"

   equitable: _____

3. "The answers reveal a wide ... range of satisfaction or dissatisfaction felt by workers whose paychecks are *eroded* daily ..."

   eroded: _____

4. "... it is at least 20 to 1 if he ever makes such *proficiency* as will enable him to live by the business."

   proficiency: _____

5. "He said the *disparity* in pay ... generally ranges between 50% and 70%."

   disparity: _____

6. "But he *concedes* that salaries paid to black workers often are limited by racial prejudice."

   concedes: _____

7. "The *exorbitant* rewards of players, opera-singers, opera-dancers, etc. ...."

   exorbitant: _____

217

8. "'They don't make you wash walls if there is a *lull* in business.'"

   lull: _____

9. _____ : _____

10. _____ : _____

11. _____ : _____

12. _____ : _____

13. _____ : _____

14. _____ : _____

15. _____ : _____

RETENTION AND COMPREHENSION

A. True/False (1 point each)

1. According to the article, the highest paid hourly workers are construction workers.   1. T _____ F _____

2. Teachers earn the same in various parts of the country.   2. T _____ F _____

3. People consider salary the most important thing to look for in a job.   3. T _____ F _____

4. College graduates average 30% more in salary than high school graduates.   4. T _____ F _____

5. Most people are satisfied with their pay.   5. T _____ F _____

B. Completion (3 points each)

6. The lowest paid hourly employees are _____ .   6. _____

7. One thing that brings higher wages is a strong _____ .   7. _____

8. Two groups that are paid less than others are _____ and _____ .   8. _____

9. The article quotes from the work of an economist who lived more than 200 years ago named _____ .   9. _____

10. When this article was written, the highest paid   10. _____
    worker in the United States was apparently
    _____.

C. Multiple Choice (2 points each)

11. Professor Gary Becker says that (a) wages are gen-   11. _____
    erally inequitable; (b) overall, wages are equitable;
    (c) wages aren't and shouldn't be equitable; (d)
    players, opera-singers, opera-dancers, etc., are
    overpaid.

12. According to Ernest Gardner, librarians are under-   12. _____
    paid because (a) it's a woman-dominated profes-
    sion, (b) they are not as educated as doctors and
    lawyers, (c) their work isn't very important to soci-
    ety, (d) they don't work as hard as people with
    other kinds of jobs.

13. Average annual incomes for actors and actresses   13. _____
    are (a) higher than rookie policemen's, (b) higher
    than firemen's, (c) higher than bus drivers', (d)
    none of the above.

14. A factor in determining salaries is (a) education,   14. _____
    (b) sex, (c) race, (d) all of the above.

15. In general, white-collar workers earn more than   15 _____
    (a) doctors, (b) blue-collar workers (c) lawyers,
    (d) T.V. newscasters.

16. Compared to the mid-70s, in early 1979 the average   16. _____
    yearly income was (a) about 30% higher, (b) about
    20% higher, (c) about 10% higher, (d) about the
    same.

17. According to the article, in 1980 the inflation was   17. _____
    (a) the highest since the mid-70s, (b) beginning to
    decline, (c) leveling off, (d) the highest in thirty-
    three years.

18. A schoolteacher in Mississippi (a) wants to teach in   18. _____
    New York, (b) earns more than a bus driver in San
    Francisco, (c) earns less than the average teacher's
    salary nationwide, (d) earns more than the average
    postal worker.

D. Thematic (11 points)

19. Which statement *best* expresses the theme (*main*
idea) of the article?
    (a) Most people feel they are underpaid, even
    though salary is not the most important thing
    about their jobs.
    (b) Wages have generally been going up, but their
    purchasing power has been greatly eroded by
    inflation.
    (c) Jobs with strong unions and a predominant
    number of white males bring higher wages
    than non-union jobs with large numbers of mi-
    norities or women.
    (d) Although wages are generally equitable, they
    vary according to education, sex, race, and part
    of the country.

19. _____

E. Purpose (9 points)

20. The author's *chief* purpose is
    (a) to encourage people to gain an education in
    order to obtain higher wages.
    (b) to show how prejudice and bias influence the
    amount of wages paid and create inequities.
    (c) to report his findings on the range of salaries in
    the nation, and the reasons for variations or
    seeming inequities.
    (d) to persuade the public that wages are generally
    equitable but that they need to be made more
    so.

20. _____

Total Retention and Comprehension Score: _____

QUESTIONS FOR DISCUSSION (MEANING AND TECHNIQUE)

1. Discuss this proposition: If you're a woman and/or a member of a
minority, all the education in the world won't help you get a better
paycheck.

2. Is it fair for women and minorities to be, in general, paid less than
others? Why is it that way? Is it changing? If so, how or why?

3. Why should someone with more education be paid more? Is it possi-

ble for someone with less education to be better at the same job than someone with more education? And if so, should that person be paid less?

4. Do you think the size of the paycheck is the most important thing about a job? If not, what other factors are? Would you accept less pay in exchange for these other factors?

5. How should pay scales be determined? How are they determined now?

6. Was Adam Smith right in the five points he gave that determine the size of a paycheck? What did he say they were? What points did he leave out that are important now but that weren't factors then, or that he didn't consider?

7. What do you think is a fair range of salaries? In other words how wide a spread should there be between salaries? Should anyone make more than, say, five times as much as someone else? Ten times? Twenty? Fifty? One hundred? Is anyone's work worth fifty times as much as anyone else's? Should the spread be controlled somehow or not? Why or why not? If yes, how? Have other democratic countries (not in the Soviet or communist bloc) done anything to control the spread between incomes? If so, which ones? How?

8. Even if going to high school or college didn't improve the size of your paycheck at all, would it be worth doing? Why or why not?

9. Are you surprised by any of the figures given? Which ones? Why?

10. Do you think salaries are fairly equitable or not? Why or why not?

11. Is the sentence with which the article begins (*How much money do you make?*) a good way to start? Why?

12. At what point do you think the introduction to this article ends and the body begins? How do you know?

13. Does the article end well? Could it use a better conclusion?

14. Are there enough facts and details given to help answer the question "Are wages equitable?" What kinds of support (facts and details) does the writer give, and where did he get them? Would the article have had much value without them?

SUGGESTIONS FOR WRITING

1. Write an essay defending the value of an education, even if it didn't increase the size of your paycheck.

2. Write an article defending the position that getting an education beyond a certain point (tell what point) is a waste of time.

3. Write an essay explaining how minorities and/or women as a group can go about increasing their paychecks.

4. Write an essay explaining why no one should earn more than X-times more than anyone else and how this could be controlled.

5. If you hold a job, describe some of the things (good or bad) about that job (other than the size of the paycheck) that you find important and tell why. If they were changed (for better or for worse) would you trade those changes for a bigger or smaller paycheck? Explain.

6. Should librarians (like Ernest Gardner in the article) be paid more? Why? Discuss in writing.

7. Should Kindregen (the city budget analyst in the article) be paid (as he would like) more than twice as much as a city bus driver (instead of about 30% more)? Why? Explain your position in writing, giving reasons either for or against.

8. If you work, do you think you're paid equitably? Explain why you should be paid more, less, or the same. Support your argument with reasons.

9. Write a good concluding paragraph for this article.

Overall Reading Performance

Your overall reading performance is a combination of how fast you read and how much you comprehend and retain. The chart below allows you to find out quickly your "overall reading performance."

First enter your "reading time" and your "retention and comprehension" score in the two blanks at the bottom of the page. Then simply lay a straightedge of any kind (the edge of a sheet of paper or a pencil will do) across the chart, placing the left side of the straightedge at the appropriate point on the "Reading Rate" scale, and the right side at the appropriate point on the "Retention and Comprehension" scale. The point at which the paper or pencil intersects the scale in the middle of the page will indicate your overall performance.

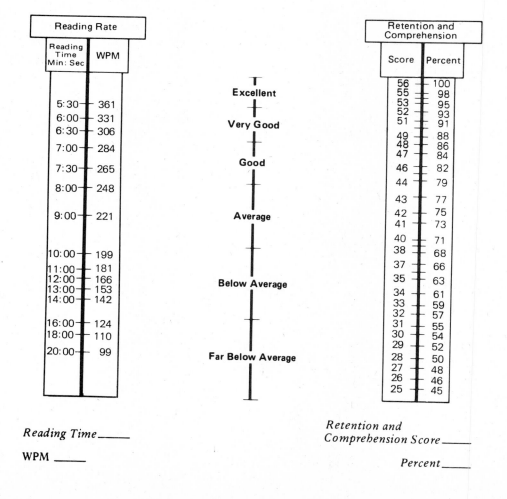

Reading Time _____

WPM _____

Retention and Comprehension Score _____

Percent _____

Selection 24

Archives: The Camels Are Coming

ROSE L. ELLERBE

The camels are coming, hurrah, hurrah! exclaimed the citizens of Los Angeles, until the beast turned burden

In 1858 Los Angeles was yet a Mexican pueblo, centered about the Plaza, or scattered along *Calle Principal* (Main Street), which was merely a road, muddy or dusty—as was the rainfall. Dwellings and buildings were of adobe, mostly whitewashed and one story in height. Residents included a few American families; several Americans who had married native Californians; some families of Spanish blood and the rest of the population Mexican, *mestizo* or Indian. The common speech of all was Spanish.

On a January morning of this year a procession passed along Main Street that sent a wave of excitement to every household of *el ciudad*. Headed by a handsome young officer on horseback and a few soldiers came a line of great shaggy, dusty creatures, carrying knotty loads heaped upon their humpy backs and accompanied by a couple of dusky-skinned men who talked an unknown tongue to their charges. It is likely that by the time this caravan had crossed the river and reached the plaza, the greater part of the people of the town were looking on as the strange beasts filed along to a corral.

This was the first appearance of Uncle Sam's camels in Los Angeles. They were in charge of Lieutenant Ned Beale, who was later a general and an ambassador, and who remains one of the most interesting characters of California history. He was also owner of Tejon Rancho—a nice little principality of 200,000 acres.

The *Los Angeles Star,* of January 27, 1858, thus describes this event:

"Col. Beale and about fourteen camels stalked into town last Friday week and gave our streets quite an Oriental aspect. It looks oddly enough to see, outside of a menagerie, a herd of huge, ungainly, awkward but docile camels move about in our midst with people riding them like horses and bringing up weird and faroff associations to the eastern traveler, whether by book or otherwise, of the lands of the mosque and crescent, with visions of Mecca and Jerusalem. These camels under the charge of Col. Beale are all grown and serviceable and most of them well broken to the saddle and very gentle. All belong to the one-hump species except one, which is a cross between the one- and two-hump species. This fellow is much larger and more powerful. He is a grizzly looking hybrid—a camel-mule of huge proportions. This mule, as they call this hybrid, will pack 2200 pounds.

"The animals are on their way to the Colorado River for the purpose of carrying military supplies and provisions for Col. Beale and his military escort which it is conjectured will penetrate from thence as far as possible into the Mormon country. Afterward Col. Beale will return by the new wagon route that he has lately surveyed" (to Fort Tejon).

After this date, for a number of years, camels were quite often seen in Los Angeles streets. In 1860 the papers reported that Captain W. S. Hancock, then in charge of the Southern Department military affairs and a resident of Los Angeles, was seeking to establish an express route between Los Angeles and Fort Mojave and had sent out a camel in charge of Greek George.

In 1861, a military camp—the first established during the civil war in Southern California—was located on the *Ballona Rancho* near the present site of Culver City. This was named Camp Latham. Before the end of the year more than a thousand men were encamped here. Newmark, in his "Sixty Years in California," says:

"Fort Tejon was pretty well broken up by June (1861), when a good deal of the army property was moved to Los Angeles. Along with Uncle Sam's bag and baggage came thirty or more camels, including 'young 'uns.' These were for some time quartered near the genial quartermaster's Main Street office. (W. S. Hancock was the quartermaster referred to.) In October they were removed to a yard fixed up for them opposite the Second Street school."

There is a difference of opinion as to just where this corral was located, but it was out "in the country" south of First Street—perhaps as far south as Second—and between Main and Broadway.

Charles J. Prudhomme says he remembers seeing the camels browsing on the hills back of North Broadway and the old cemetery and a "big herd" pastured out toward what was once Colegrove and is now Hollywood.

Joseph Mesmer recollects the keen interest which he, with other small boys of the town, took in these visitors, which were corralled near his home on the site where the Natick House now stands. He also states that some of the camels were stationed at Camp Latham.

Troops from Camp Latham were mostly moved on to Arizona and the camels were used to transport supplies. It will be remembered that the territories of Arizona and New Mexico were saved to the Union and the troublesome Indians of that period held in check almost entirely by the California Volunteer forces, nearly all the regulars in the Indian service being sent east. In January, 1863, note is made of a camel express serving between San Pedro and Tucson. Just how large a part the "camel corps" played in the service does not appear, although army officials agreed in extolling their ability to travel in desert regions with heavy loads and at a remarkable speed.

The history of the "Forgotten Camel Corps" is an interesting chronicle. According to Bonsall, biographer of General E. F. Beale, the idea of using camels came to Beale while exploring Death Valley with Kit Carson. The War Department was at that time struggling with the difficulties of army transportation in the arid regions of the Southwest. "When Beale presented himself at the department with his suggestion of a camel corps, it was regarded as Quixotic, but at all events having as much substance as a relayed line of balloons which at this time was warmly advocated for the same purpose."

The matter was discussed in Congress and in 1854 Jefferson Davis introduced a bill for an appropriation to purchase camels—which failed to pass. In 1855 the *Los Angeles Star* said editorially:

"We predict that within a few years these extraordinary and useful animals (camels) will be browsing upon our hills and valleys and numerous caravans will be arriving and departing daily. Let us have the incomparable dromedaries, with Adams Express Company's men, arriving here tri-weekly with letters and packages in five or six days from Salt Lake and fifteen or sixteen days from the Missouri. Then the present grinding steamship monopoly might be made to realize that the hard-working miner, the farmer and the mechanic were no longer completely within their grasping power.

"We might have an overland dromedary express that would bring us the New York news in fifteen to eighteen days. We hope some of our energetic capitalists or stockbreeders will take this speculation in hand, for we have not much faith that Congress will do anything in the matter."

This has a familiar sound, even though written in 1855. In spite of the *Star's* pessimism, however, Congress did, under the Davis administration as War Secretary, make an appropriation of $30,000 to buy camels. An army transport, the *Supply,* under command of Col. David D. Porter, was promptly dispatched to Egypt and Arabia. Beale's biographer says that Porter first stopped at Tunis and bought two camels as an experiment; then he went to Constantinople, where he met British officers who told him of the valuable service rendered by their camel corps of 500 animals used in the Crimean campaign. After this he purchased and sailed with 33 camels, which he landed at Indianola, Texas; then made a second trip, returning with 44 "very sea-sick camels."

In February, 1857, the animals were brought across the country to Albuquerque, where they were divided, part being sent to San Antonio, where they were to be used as transport animals by the troops in Southern Texas. The balance, under the charge of Lieutenant Beale, accompanied by 44 citizens and 20 soldiers, were despatched to Fort Tejon, California.

Theoretically, the camel should have proved a God-send to the army and the country. But, as a matter of fact the experiment turned out a most dismal failure. Soldiers, and more important still, horses and mules exhibited a deep-seated antipathy to these ships of the desert. Other animals bucked and vamoosed at the sight of the hump-backed strangers. Men detailed to assist the two camel-drivers, Hi Jolly and Greek George—both of whom were well known in Los Angeles—deserted rather than wait on the camels. Mexicans and professional "mule skinners" had no use for an animal that didn't kick back nor understand their brand of "cussing." The camel possesses a most ferocious looking set of teeth which "it exhibits with a roar like that of a royal Bengal tiger—yet they are entirely harmless." The soldiers and drivers were afraid of them, they claimed. They mistreated the brutes so that many of them died.

Perhaps the fault was not entirely with the drivers, however. The camel could make good time under a load—when he was turned loose to forage on a terrain where one mouthful might be scattered over an acre of ground, he could make even better time. Tired herders often had to spend most of the night rounding up the strayed animals. J. M. Guinn says: "Of all the impish, perverse and profanity-provoking beasts of burden that ever trod the soil of America, the meek, mild-eyed, soft-footed camel was the most exasperating. That prototype of perversity, the army mule, was almost angelic in disposition compared to the hump-backed burden-bearer of the Orient."

Perhaps the camel was homesick! At any rate, when the war ended, the powers-that-be decided that camels could not be utilized to advantage, condemned those remaining and put them up for sale at Benicia. Beale's biographer says that the General purchased some of them and kept them on his Tejon Rancho and tells a story of Beale driving with his son, Truxton, a tandem team of camels before a sulky to Los Angeles—a trip that would have delighted the heart of any small boy.

Perhaps under other conditions the camel might have proved worthy of his keep as a beast of burden in the arid regions of this country. There was certainly an unreasonable prejudice against them among the soldiers and drivers of our army. It is hinted, too, that the "Missouri mule trust" of that day may have had something to do with their failure to give satisfaction.

In many countries the camel is admittedly an almost indispensable animal; his ability to store his own water and food; his strength and speed; his adaptation to intense heat or extreme cold, are all valued. His meat is said to be tender and juicy; his hair is utilized in textiles. And his intelligence and docility make him beloved of his owners and drivers. Within recent years the camel has been successfully introduced into South Africa and Australia, proving especially a most valuable factor in transportation in the great sparsely settled regions of the African continent. Mexico is said to have considered seriously the possibility of using camels in Lower California and other arid districts. Even our government has discussed giving the beasts another trial. Possibly we may yet find these burden bearers competing with the motor truck and the electric road in the desert regions of our own country. Certainly they could not stampede the automobiles— although they might upset some of their drivers, particularly those who had taken contraband aboard.

But no matter how scientifically and efficiently and successfully a camel herd might be developed under modern methods and conditions, never again will it be possible to create such an interesting and romantic camel corps as Jefferson Davis and Ned Beale dreamed of and brought into being.

No. of Words: ___2000___

Reading Time: _____

Selection 24

Archives: The Camels Are Coming

VOCABULARY BUILDING

Below are several words used in this article. They are presented in the context of the sentences or phrases in which they occur. If you are unsure of their meanings and cannot define them from the context, look them up in the dictionary. Spaces are provided for additional unfamiliar words from the article to add to your vocabulary.

1. "... a herd of huge, *ungainly,* awkward but *docile* camels ..."

    ungainly: _____

    docile: _____

2. "a cross between the one- and two-hump species. ... He is a grizzly looking *hybrid*—a camel-mule ..."

    hybrid: _____

3. "... it is *conjectured* [that Col. Beale and his military escort] will penetrate ... as far as possible into Mormon country."

    conjectured: _____

4. "... although army officials agreed in *extolling* their ability to travel in desert regions with heavy loads ..."

    extolling: _____

5. "The War Department was at that time struggling with the difficulties of army transportation in the *arid* regions of the Southwest."

    arid: _____

6. "When Beale presented ... his suggestion of a camel corps, it was regarded as *Quixotic* ..."

    Quixotic: _____

7. "... the experiment turned out a most *dismal* failure."

    dismal: _____

8. "Soldiers . . . horses and mules *exhibited* a *deep-seated antipathy* to these ships of the desert."

   exhibited: _____

   deep-seated: _____

   antipathy: _____

9. "Of all the *impish, perverse* and *profanity-provoking* beasts of burden that ever *trod* the soil of America, the . . . camel was the most *exasperating.*"

   impish: _____

   perverse: _____

   profanity: _____

   provoking: _____

   trod (tread): _____

   exasperating: _____

10. _____ : _____

11. _____ : _____

12. _____ : _____

13. _____ : _____

14. _____ : _____

15. _____ : _____

RETENTION AND COMPREHENSION

A. True/False *(1 point each)*

1. The meat of the camel is said to be tender and juicy.   1. T _____   F _____

2. Although strong, camels are rather slow.   2. T _____   F _____

3. Kit Carson got the idea for a camel corps while exploring Death Valley.   3. T _____   F _____

4. Jefferson Davis was opposed to the idea of a U.S. camel corps.   4. T _____   F _____

5. Camels roar like tigers.   5. T _____   F _____

B. Completion (3 points each)

6. The first shipment of camels was brought to the state of _____ .

6. _____

7. The first appearance of camels in Los Angeles took place in the year _____ .

7. _____

8. An army transport was dispatched to _____ _____ and _____ to buy camels.

8. _____

9. The common language in Los Angeles in the 1850s was _____ .

9. _____

10. The only "hybrid" camel seen in Los Angeles in 1858 was a cross between the _____ and _____ species.

10. _____

C. Multiple Choice (2 points each)

11. When Col. Beale first suggested a camel corps, the army was also considering (a) a mule train, (b) a relayed line of balloons, (c) a pony express, (d) a railroad.

11. _____

12. One of the earliest advocates of a U.S. camel corps was (a) Abraham Lincoln, (b) Ulysses S. Grant, (c) Jefferson Davis, (d) Kit Carson.

12. _____

13. The U.S. Camel Corps failed because (a) camels are too slow, (b) camels are not intelligent enough, (c) camels are hard to handle, (d) none of the above.

13. _____

14. The hybrid camel first seen in Los Angeles in 1858 was able to carry (a) around 500 pounds, (b) between 500 and 1000 pounds, (c) 1200 pounds, (d) 2200 pounds.

14. _____

15. After their first entrance into Los Angeles, camels (a) were never seen there again, (b) were seen there quite often for a while, (c) were shipped back to Albuquerque, (d) were sold to British officers for the Crimean campaign.

15. _____

16. The first congressional bill to buy camels, introduced in 1854, (a) was sent to committee, (b) passed with a large majority, (c) barely passed, (d) failed to pass.

16. _____

233

17. One real problem camel herders had with the camels was (a) they kicked, (b) they bit, (c) they strayed too far when grazing, (d) they were frightened of other animals.

17. _____

18. After the war the camels were (a) destroyed, (b) used for textiles and meat, (c) shipped back to Algeria, (d) sold.

18. _____

D. Thematic (11 points)

19. Which statement *best* expresses the theme (*main* idea) of the article?
    (a) Camels and politics didn't mix well in the United States of the 1850s and 1860s.
    (b) A U.S. camel corps could never have worked well here because conditions were too different.
    (c) A U.S. camel corps was a good idea that failed mainly because of prejudice against a new, strange animal.
    (d) Using camels in the arid Southwest was an idea more romantic than practical.

19. _____

E. Purpose (9 points)

20. The author's *chief* purpose is
    (a) to show how prejudice and obstinancy can frustrate a good idea.
    (b) to give an entertaining and informative account of a curious bit of American history.
    (c) to convince Americans that even today camels could provide a useful service in our arid states.
    (d) to correct some mistaken ideas people have had about the U.S. Camel Corps during the Civil War.

20. _____

Total Retention and Comprehension Score: _____

QUESTIONS FOR DISCUSSION (MEANING AND TECHNIQUE)

1. Does this article have an interesting introduction? What is it? What makes it interesting? Can you imagine some much less interesting way to begin?

2. Does the article have a satisfying conclusion? If so, what about the last paragraph makes us feel "satisfied"?

3. Make a list of the sources the author quotes or refers to. How many did you find? Do these quotes make the article more interesting and believable?

4. Why is it curious/interesting/romantic to think of a camel corps in America? What does the word "romantic" mean in this context?

5. Who was Jefferson Davis? Kit Carson?

6. Why do you think the camel corps failed in America? Was it the nature of the camel or the reaction of the people dealing with the camels? Both? Neither?

7. The article speaks of "Mormon country." Where is that? Who or what are Mormons?

SUGGESTIONS FOR WRITING

1. Write an "argument" essay in which you argue for (as Jefferson Davis did in Congress in 1854) or against the use of an American camel corps—either for the 1850s and 1860s or now.

2. Write a "camel-eye's" view of this episode in American history.

3. Write an account of this episode in American history from the point of view of Col. Beale, Jefferson Davis, Kit Carson—or an ordinary camel driver or keeper—or a small boy who "hangs around" the camels and the soldiers and keepers.

4. Write an imaginary newspaper account of an imaginary U.S. "elephant corps."

5. Write an account of the U.S. Camel Corps that ends with the imaginary "success" of the corps instead of its failure.

6. Pretend you're an officer in charge of the U.S. Camel Corps in the 1860s. Write a memo to Washington explaining your difficulties with the camels, your successes with them, or your recommendations regarding their future use, etc.

7. Write a composition explaining what could have been done to make the U.S. Camel Corps a success.

Overall Reading Performance

Your overall reading performance is a combination of how fast you read and how much you comprehend and retain. The chart below allows you to find out quickly your "overall reading performance."

First enter your "reading time" and your "retention and comprehension" score in the two blanks at the bottom of the page. Then simply lay a straightedge of any kind (the edge of a sheet of paper or a pencil will do) across the chart, placing the left side of the straightedge at the appropriate point on the "Reading Rate" scale, and the right side at the appropriate point on the "Retention and Comprehension" scale. The point at which the paper or pencil intersects the scale in the middle of the page will indicate your overall performance.

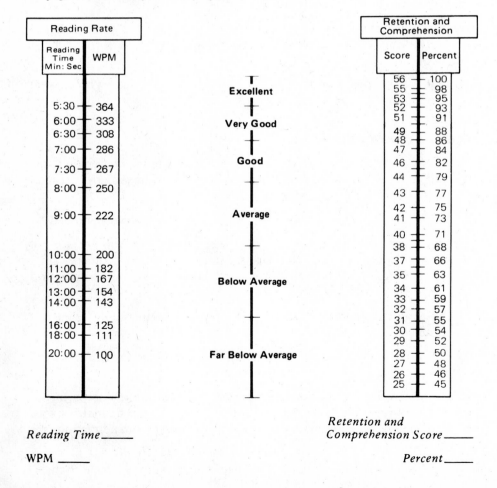

Reading Time_____

WPM _____

Retention and
Comprehension Score_____

Percent_____

Selection 25

Tarahumara:
Runners of the West

BERNARD L. FONTANA

Run, run, run! Joggers lope along on city streets or country roads, putting in their daily two miles, five miles, or eight miles. Strenuous. A new exercise. The modern way to health.

Before there were airplanes or cars or pickup trucks, even before there were horses, people ran over the deserts and mountains of Arizona and the American Southwest. It was the old way to health. It was, in fact, the only way to get around in a hurry. Children, as soon as they learned to walk, began training for a lifetime of getting from one place to another on foot. And the strong ones, the swift ones, became track stars.

The Papago Indians of southern Arizona used to run kickball races over courses from 10 to 15 miles long and return. The contestants, usually several on a side, used their feet to toss a wooden ball or pitch-covered stone ball ahead of them as they hurried forward. The Pima Indians, living along the Gila River in central Arizona, ran the same kind of races.

There were relays, too, without the ball. The races could be over a marked course to the finish line or they might end when the sun went down. Sometimes the athletes continued until the last person was left standing. Survival of the fittest. On occasion a team member died of exhaustion. There is a shrine on the Papago Reservation that is said to mark the spot where a runner dropped dead in his tracks.

Papago and Pima women ran too. Instead of kicking a ball, they used a stick to toss ahead of them: two small sections of cactus rib tied together with a cord.

The runners were barefoot. Men often painted themselves with white clay. Every Papago summer village had a racetrack near it where people could practice, and the betting on races was intense.

In 1902 an observer of Pima Indians wrote, "The custom of using these

Source: Arizona Highways, May 1979. Excerpted from *Tarahumara—Where Night Is the Day of the Moon,* Northland Press. Reprinted by permission.

[kick] balls is rapidly disappearing, as it is to be regretted, are the other athletic games of the Pimas."

By 1920, according to calendar records kept by Pimas and Papagos the running stopped. So, too, had it stopped among most other Arizona Indians except where it continued as a game in schools. Horses had come. Trains had come. There were automobiles and paved roads. Diet had changed. Men, women, and children had become overweight.

But in another part of the "Greater Southwest," running and racing continue unabated. The area is fewer than 300 airline miles from Tucson, Arizona. It is in the 20,000 square miles of the mountains and canyons of the Sierra Tarahumara of southwestern Chihuahua, Mexico. The people who run are the Tarahumara, linguistic and cultural relatives of the Pimas and Papagos. Their name is a corruption of the term they use for themselves, *Rarámuri*. It means "footrunner."

Of all the Indians who live in what anthropologists call the Southwest Culture Area, Tarahumaras have changed the least over the last 300 years. They are truly a mirror on the past. To see them is to pay a visit to most Arizona tribes about 100 years ago. They are corn farmers, about 50,000 of them, who live in widely scattered settlements and whose houses are separated from one another by the limits of shouting distance. They are also pastoralists who raise sheep and goats for their manure, wool, and hair. Oxen are yoked to wooden plows. They are foragers who supplement their diet of corn, beans, squash, chilis, and a little meat by gathering wild potherbs and by fishing the numerous streams and rivers of their mountain fastness.

They are involved in the cash economy of Mexico only in a minor way, trading or selling their crafts and labor in order to buy clothes, axes and other steel tools, soap, needles, matches, soft drinks, canned lard, and luxuries such as harmonicas and portable radios. In years when crops are bad, money is a greater necessity. Few Tarahumaras are in schools and fewer still are literate. Most speak Spanish as their second language, but Tarahumara remains the everyday language of the home.

Tarahumaras are among the greatest endurance runners in the world. Women, girls, men, and boys continue to race just as Arizona Indians did in times gone by. Having heard this, on one of our trips into the Sierra Tarahumara, my friends and I wanted to see for ourselves. We arranged a race between two pairs of girls. One pair older than the other, lived near a Mexican settlement where their lives were fairly sedentary. The second lived in a remote canyon, connected to the outside world only by narrow and steep trail.

The outcome of the race was a forgone conclusion, but we went ahead anyway, offering 100 pesos to each of the winners and 50 pesos to each of the losers. It seemed like a good investment of some $13 or $14.

We chose a short course along the river's edge where the girls could run over existing trails. The trails moved up and down, in some places over rocks. Each girl carried a slightly curved stick about three-feet long, and each two girl team had a small hoop made of beargrass. One of my friends stood about a half-mile from the starting point as the turnaround marker. The race was to be over when the runners completed three circuits, or about three miles. They were too polite to tell us that such a short race is silly.

On your marks, get set, go! The girls dashed along using their sticks to throw their hoops ahead of them. They were supposed to take turns lifting the hoop with their sticks and tossing it ahead of them again, but in this race the first team member to reach the hoop picked it up, even if she was the person who had thrown it. Sometimes they ran for several yards, carrying the hoops on the stick before they threw it again.

The "city" girls soon dropped far behind. However, they never stopped and no one showed any signs of lagging on purpose. Once in a while they smiled as they ran past us, but generally their minds were on the business of running. Three girls were barefooted; one wore sandals. All breathed heavily. And why shouldn't they—at approximately 7000 feet above sea level and running with all their might?

The contest seemed to be over almost before it began. We didn't clock it, but certainly the time was excellent. The local "country" girls won handily, almost a half-mile ahead of the other team. Within less than a minute after the race had ended, all four runners sat on the grass at the finishing point and smiled shyly as they received their reward money. They were no longer breathing heavily and, in fact, gave no indication that they had just run three miles. A real effort, after all, would have lasted for many miles and for many hours, sometimes all night.

The endurance of Tarahumara runners is legendary, and justifiably so. Late in the last century or early in this one, Alexander R. Shepherd, a mining magnate, had an upright piano shipped from *Carichic,* a town high in the mountains of northern *Chihuahua,* to his home in *Batopilas* at the bottom of Mexico's Grand Canyon, the *Barranca del Cobre.* He hired Tarahumaras to do the job. Shepherd's son, Grant, described in later years how such a feat could be accomplished:

> They get under the poles in a squatting position; at the word "*Va-manos!*" they straighten up. The piano is off the ground, and the carriers move off with the inward satisfaction of knowing that all they have to do now is carry this great box for 185 miles in 15 or 20 days. There will be at least 24 carriers—that makes three sets—and they spell each other every 20 or 30 minutes. . . . Each man is paid at the rate of $1 a day. At the end of the journey he takes his "easy money" and trots back home a 180 miles or more in about three days, and he has a happy time for some months on his ill-gotten gains!

The men's kickball race—and Tarahumaras use a wooden ball just as Pimas and Papagos used to do—is run over a "track" likely to include streams, gullies, rocky slopes, fences, meadows, and brush-strewn hill-sides. It is normally anywhere from two to twelve miles long. The number of laps depends on whether the race is to last only a few hours or a day and a night or more.

In the 1890s the naturalist Carl Lumholtz clocked a race in which the runners, kicking a ball ahead of them, covered 21 miles in two hours. The lead man ran 290 feet in 19 seconds on the first lap and the next in 24 seconds. Lumholtz also recalled a Tarahumara who took five days to carry a letter from *Guazapares* to Chihuahua City and return, a trail distance of nearly 600 miles.

In 1926, two Tarahumara men ran from *Pachuca* in the State of Hidalgo, Mexico, to Mexico City, 65 miles away, in nine hours and thirty-seven minutes. A year later two other racers covered the 89.4 miles between San Antonio and Austin, Texas, in 14 hours and 53 minutes.

It was also in 1927 that a Tarahumara named José Torres broke a world's record that had stood since 1882 when he ran the 51 miles between Kansas City and Lawrence, Kansas, in 6:46:41, shaving a little more than an hour off the old time. Purcell Kane, a 17-year-old Apache student from the Fort Apache Indian Reservation in Arizona, missed a turn, had to double back, and came in about 20 minutes later to place second ahead of two other Tarahumaras. The Navajo in the contest had to drop out. "The flat-footed, steady jogging of the Tarahumaras," noted a newspaper reporter, "was a decided contrast to the long, smooth striding of the Arizona Indians."

For good measure, these fifth annual Kansas relays featured two Tarahumara girls who ran the Topeka to Lawrence part of the course, 29 miles. The winner finished in 5:37:45.

The endurance of Tarahumaras as runners has made them the objects of modern medical and physiological studies. A heart specialist, writing in 1971, said, "Probably not since the days of the ancient Spartans has a people achieved such a high state of physical conditioning."

We once visited the home of an elderly Tarahumara and discovered he had an enormous earthenware cooking jar in his house. Although it was cracked and a piece was gone from its rim, we wanted to buy this 30- to 40-gallon container for the Arizona State Museum. The problem, though, was how to get this huge pot, which weighed 65 pounds, from his house at the bottom of a canyon to a mountain top where we had a truck parked. The distance was fully six miles by the shortest possible route over the face of a cliff; seven or eight miles by a longer trail that avoided the cliff. And it was all uphill.

We asked the man, grey-haired and bent over from years of hard work, if he knew anyone who might be willing to take the pot up to the truck for $100 pesos (a little more than $4). Much to our surprise, he said he would be glad to. But he would need a blanket or tarpaulin to carry it. We agreed that the next day he should come by our camp to get a blanket. We paid him in advance and left.

When he failed to show up by the next noon, we went back to his house to see what had happened. When we walked inside, he was there but the pot was gone! "Where's the pot?" we wanted to know.

"Oh," he answered, "I took that up there last night."

He had made a 12- to 16-mile round trip in the pitch dark over a narrow footpath on a rainy night carrying this heavy and cumbersome jar. Just how we will never know. Moreover, he was as casual about it as if he had merely walked across the street to buy a loaf of bread.

"How could that old man have done it?" I asked.

"Maybe," came the answer, "no one has ever told him he is old."

And another 100 years from now it is likely there will still be young men like this old man. Tarahumaras, independent and resourceful people, Southwestern footrunners par excellence.

No. of Words: 2092

Reading Time: _____

Selection 25

Tarahumara: Runners of the West

VOCABULARY BUILDING

Below are several words used in this article. They are presented in the context of the sentences or phrases in which they occur. If you are unsure of their meanings and cannot define them from the context, look them up in the dictionary. Spaces are provided for additional unfamiliar words from the article to add to your vocabulary.

1. "But in another part of the 'Greater Southwest,' running and racing continue *unabated*."

    unabated: _____

2. "They are also *pastoralists* who raise sheep and goats for their manure, wool, and hair."

    pastoralists: _____

3. "They are *foragers* who supplement their diet . . . by gathering wild potherbs and by fishing . . ."

    foragers: _____

4. "Few Tarahumaras are in schools and fewer still are *literate*."

    literate: _____

5. ". . . lived near a Mexican settlement where their lives were fairly *sedentary*."

    sedentary: _____

6. "The local 'country' girls won *handily*. . ."

    handily: _____

7. "The endurance of Tarahumara runners is legendary, and *justifiably* so."

    justifiably: _____

8. "Shepherd's son, Grant, described in later years how such a *feat* could be accomplished. . ."

   feat: _____

9. "Probably not since the days of the ancient *Spartans* . . ."

   Spartans: _____

10. "He had made a 12- to 16-mile round trip in the pitch dark . . . carrying this heavy and *cumbersome* jar."

   cumbersome: _____

11. _____ : _____

12. _____ : _____

13. _____ : _____

14. _____ : _____

15. _____ : _____

RETENTION AND COMPREHENSION

A. True/False (1 point each)

1. The Tarahumara Indians live in the mountain areas of Arizona.   1. T _____ F _____

2. The Tarahumara are related in language and culture to the Papago and Pima Indians of Arizona.   2. T _____ F _____

3. Spanish is the first language of the Tarahumara.   3. T _____ F _____

4. The Tarahumara live today as most Arizona tribes lived 100 years ago.   4. T _____ F _____

5. The author suggests that in another 100 years the Tarahumara will become "citified" and lose their ability to run long distances.   5. T _____ F _____

B. Completion (3 points each)

6. The Papago Indians used to run races over courses that were from 10 to _____ miles long.   6. _____

7. As they ran long races, the Papago would "toss" a ball with their_____.

7. _____

8. One example of Tarahumara endurance was the carrying of_____over a distance of 185 miles.

8. _____

9. Another example mentioned was of the Tarahumara man who covered a distance of 600 miles in _____days.

9. _____

10. "Tarahumara" is based on the word "raramuri," which means_____.

10. _____

C. Multiple Choice (2 points each)

11. Relay races among the early Papagos and Pimas sometimes continued until (a) even the children were exhausted, (b) the women forced the men to quit, (c) the last person was left standing, (d) the sun came up on the next day.

11. _____

12. A shrine on the Papago Reservation marks the spot where (a) the longest race ended, (b) a runner dropped dead in his tracks, (c) the last racetrack remains, (d) a heavily contested relay race ended in a brutal fight.

12. _____

13. Which was *not* a reason for the disappearance of running among the Arizona Indians? (a) changes in diet, (b) greater use of automobiles, (c) elimination of running in the schools, (d) travel by train.

13. _____

14. Even today, the Tarahumara still use (a) oxen and wooden plows, (b) bows and arrows to hunt, (c) smoke signals, (d) ancient ceremonies before each race.

14. _____

15. In the race arranged by the author, two "country" girls ran against two "city" girls who lived (a) in Tucson, Arizona, (b) near Mexico City, (c) in a remote canyon in the mountains, (d) near a settlement where they led less active lives.

15. _____

16. In this match race both pairs of girls also (a) threw a leather ball to the other member of her relay team, (b) tossed grass hoops ahead of them with

16. _____

sticks, (c) kicked a soccer ball as they ran, (d) passed a baton at the turnaround markers.

17. A newspaper reporter at the Kansas Relays in 1927 described the running style of the Tarahumara contestants as (a) a "long, smooth striding," (b) a "flat-footed, steady jogging," (c) "a cat-like loping," (d) a "deceivingly quick shuffling movement."

17. _____

18. The old Tarahumara man who carried the 65-pound cooking pot up the cliff at night had (a) to walk up a narrow path in the rain, (b) to face the possibility of delivering it to the wrong place, (c) not accepted any money for the task, (d) used his own blanket to carry the pot.

18. _____

D. Thematic (11 points)

19. Which statement *best* expresses the theme (*main idea*) of the article?
    (a) The comforts of modern life have destroyed the high state of physical conditioning of the Southwest's "running" Indians.
    (b) The Tarahumara culture, although surrounded by civilization, is too remote and independent to be negatively influenced and will probably continue to produce excellent distance runners.
    (c) Once the Tarahumara Indians get into the economic mainstream of the surrounding settlements, they too, like the Papagos and Pimas, will stop being so healthy and strong.
    (d) The Tarahumara Indians are very simple and unsophisticated, and they have taken something as natural as running and made it into a near science.

19. _____

E. Purpose (9 points)

20. The author's *chief* purpose is
    (a) to trace the effects of progress on native American cultures.
    (b) to show the differences between one group of Indians who refuse to be civilized and other groups who have lost their heritages.

(c) to arouse the reader's sympathy for the even-
tual disappearance of an interesting group of
people.

(d) to tell how one group of native Americans has
been able to withstand the negative influences
of progress and retain a unique level of endurance.

Total Retention and Comprehension Score: _____

QUESTIONS FOR DISCUSSION (MEANING AND TECHNIQUE)

1. How has the writer grouped the Indians of the "Greater Southwest"?
What was his reason for doing so?

2. As presented to the reader, are the Tarahumaras interesting for other
reasons besides their running ability? If so, what are those reasons?

3. Could this article have started with the second paragraph? What is the
reason for the first one?

4. What were the effects of civilization on the other running Indian
tribes? What does the writer see in the future for the Tarahumaras?

5. What does the account of the relay race between the "country" girls
and the "city" girls show? The story about the old man who carried
the pot in the rain—what does it show?

SUGGESTIONS FOR WRITING

1. Write a paper convincing the reader of the benefits of regular exercise.

2. Try to recall the most physically demanding experience you ever had.
It need not have been in an athletic contest or on a planned outing
(long hike or mountain climb). Try to describe particularly how you
felt in mind as well as body.

3. Have you witnessed changes resulting from the advance of civilization or "progress" (the building of a dam in a wilderness area; a new
industry in a small town)? In an essay discuss what the positive and
negative effects were on the area, the people, and the way of life.
Include its effects on you also.

4. If you know someone who has become an exercise enthusiast after
leading an inactive life, compare/contrast what the person was like
before and after the change.

Selection 25

Overall Reading Performance

Your overall reading performance is a combination of how fast you read and how much you comprehend and retain. The chart below allows you to find out quickly your "overall reading performance."

First enter your "reading time" and your "retention and comprehension" score in the two blanks at the bottom of the page. Then simply lay a straightedge of any kind (the edge of a sheet of paper or a pencil will do) across the chart, placing the left side of the straightedge at the appropriate point on the "Reading Rate" scale, and the right side at the appropriate point on the "Retention and Comprehension" scale. The point at which the paper or pencil intersects the scale in the middle of the page will indicate your overall performance.

Reading Rate	
Reading Time Min: Sec	WPM
5:30	380
6:00	349
6:30	322
7:00	299
7:30	279
8:00	262
9:00	232
10:00	209
11:00	190
12:00	174
13:00	161
14:00	149
16:00	131
18:00	116
20:00	105
22:00	95

Excellent

Very Good

Good

Average

Below Average

Far Below Average

Retention and Comprehension	
Score	Percent
56	100
55	98
53	95
52	93
51	91
49	88
48	86
47	84
46	82
44	79
43	77
42	75
41	73
40	71
38	68
37	66
35	63
34	61
33	59
32	57
31	55
30	54
29	52
28	50
27	48
26	46
25	45

*Reading Time*_____

WPM _____

*Retention and Comprehension Score*_____

*Percent*_____

Selection 26

The Mystery of Rommel's Missing Treasure

KEN KRIPPENE

Did the desert finally outfox Rommel, recapturing the spoils of war and burying them beneath its shifting, uncharted dunes?

Buried somewhere among the windswept sand dunes of Southern Tunisia are 90 small metal trunks, filled to the brim with gold coins. In addition, there is one steel box about two feet in diameter in which can be found a veritable fortune in priceless jewels—sparkling diamonds, blood-red rubies, scintillating emeralds and star sapphires, as well as dozens of other precious stones. All together, the cache is valued at approximately $100 million.

Why should such a valuable treasure as this lie buried in the burning sands of the Sahara? For one thing, not many people know about the buried loot, and, if they do, they think it's at the bottom of the Mediterranean Sea. And those who know about it have so far conceded victory to the unyielding desert and searched for other treasures elsewhere.

But where did this bounty come from? To whom does it belong, and why was it buried in such a forbidding place? To find the answer to this enigma it is necessary to turn back the pages of history to the early morning hours of March 8, 1943. Just as the dreaded ides of March had once come for the indomitable Julius Caesar, so, too, were they about to descend upon the illustrious Field Marshal Erwin Rommel, unquestionably one of the most astute generals ever to come out of Hitler's Third Reich.

On that morning, Rommel and a small but trusted group of officers and one young enlisted soldier were gathered in the spacious living room of a beautiful villa overlooking the blue waters of the Mediterranean in Hammamet, just a short distance south of Tunis. The ornate villa with its high white walls covered with purple bougainvillea had been used by Rommel for the previous month as his base of operations. It was and is one of the

Source: The Saturday Evening Post, Jan./Feb. 1980. Reprinted with permission from The Saturday Evening Post Company © 1980.

showplaces of the Tunisian countryside. Rommel, always meticulously dressed, sat dejectedly in a large leather chair, his throat heavily bandaged, his face and body spotted with ugly sores from his strenuous campaign in the unfriendly desert. The end had come. He knew it and so did the others surrounding him. Only three days before he had fought and lost his last battle near Medenine, a small desert outpost on the rim of the Sahara. Desperate, and with only 140 tanks remaining in his arsenal of field weapons, he had attacked British General Montgomery's desert forces in a final effort to turn the tide of battle which had been running against him. But it was to no avail. As night approached, 52 of his tanks had been destroyed and the panzer units had retreated in the direction of Tunis.

Sadly, Rommel contemplated the past. Just a few short months before, his *Afrika Korps* had brilliantly won battle after battle. An open road to Egypt, Palestine and the Middle East lay before him. Even as the allied forces were pouring in troops, tanks and cannon, Rommel had begged Hitler for replacements. But none were available, so he was left to fight alone with what remained of his once invincible *Afrika Korps* against almost insurmountable odds.

In the beginning, of course, everything had gone well. U-boats based in southern Italy had carried to Tunis a fortune in gold coins which Rommel was to use to pave the way to his glorious victory on his march to the Nile. Important Arab sheikhs and pashas were to be bribed in order to win them over to the Nazi cause, and Arab mercenaries were to be given weapons and trained to join in the fight against the ever-expanding allied forces. But even this proved difficult, as some of the powerful Arab rulers preferred to remain politically neutral. In many instances when they refused to fight under the banner of the Third Reich, they were summarily executed or imprisoned, their palaces burned and looted. It was in this manner that over the years Field Marshal Rommel was able to gather his collection of some of the world's most precious jewels, adding them to his ever-growing hoard of gold.

Now, with defeat imminent, Rommel was determined not to let his treasures fall into the hands of his adversaries. Many times he had thought of shipping them by sea from Tunis to southern Italy, but as the war in North Africa was drawing to a rapid conclusion, he found that this was now impossible. With complete control of the air and sea, the British were creating havoc among all shipping in the Mediterranean, and one out of every two U-boats attempting to make the short run across the sea was being destroyed. Little wonder, then, why Rommel sought some other means of saving the bulk of his treasure.

Of the seven men who were gathered in the living room of that seaside villa in Hammamet, Heinrich Suter, a photographer, is still alive, and was able to give an eye-witness account of what transpired. Let it be said immediately that "Heinrich Suter" is a pseudonym. At the age of 18, he became a member of the notorious SS and, because he was an expert movie cameraman as well as still photographer, was sent to North Africa to document Rommel's glorious victory and, it was hoped, his conquest of the Middle East.

"You know, Ken," he said, "many people believe that this story about Rommel's treasure is a lot of bunk, but I know it's true. I was present at the villa in Hammamet on the night when a convoy of army trucks—maybe 15 or 20 of them, carrying Rommels' fortune in gold coins and jewels, as well as many other priceless treasures—pulled away into the night and disappeared in the darkness bound for a secret destination in the desert. One of Rommel's most trusted field officers, Colonel Hans Neidermann, was in charge of the convoy under orders to bury the treasure as quickly as possible in some safe spot on the Sahara to keep it from falling into the hands of the British and New Zealand forces who, at that time, had nearly surrounded us and were on the verge of final victory."

"But, Heinrich," I interjected, "from the stories I've read I was always under the impression that Rommel's treasure was put aboard some speed boats and under cover of darkness made the run across the Mediterranean to Italy. Then as dawn broke, the small fleet was discovered by British bombers and the crews were ordered to dump the treasure into the sea in the shallow waters just off Corsica. I have heard many times that's where skin divers have been searching for it ever since."

"That's partially true," Heinrich admitted, "but you know they didn't call Rommel the 'desert fox' for nothing. He was well aware of the fact that British Intelligence knew all about his gold supply and that they were making every effort to capture it."

Heinrich explained that in order to confuse the enemy, Rommel put into effect a diversionary tactic: sending a fleet of fast power boats bearing several crates of *objets d'art* which his troops had purloined from museums and palaces to a secret destination on the coast of Italy. The allies had been waiting for just such a move and were ready to intercept, if possible, or sink, if necessary, these small boats once their observation planes had spotted them.

Rommel's diversionary tactic worked perfectly, and while the British bombers were making a desperate attempt to capture the swift treasure-laden ships, the convoy of trucks bearing the bulk of Rommel's fortune were speeding along secondary dirt roads in a southwesterly direction toward Douz, a small desert outpost where, according to plan, the gold was to be transported by camel caravan to a safe location and buried under one of the hundreds of large sand dunes dotting the area. At least, that was the plan.

"That's all I know about it," Suter said, "except that a few weeks later, we picked up a radio news broadcast from England stating that British forces had intercepted and killed, during a daylong battle on the rim of the desert near Douz, a well-equipped contingent of German soldiers who evidently had been assigned to some remote outpost and were attempting to rejoin their units. According to the broadcast, there were no survivors, the German soldiers having fought to the death."

What actually happened, according to Suter, was quite clear. They had succeeded in safely burying the treasure on the Tunisian Sahara and on their return to Douz were ambushed by a contingent of British troops. In the ensuing battle they died to the last man. So, ironically enough, no one—not even General Rommel—knew where his gold and jewels had been buried.

To check out Heinrich's fantastic story, and to pick up further information, if possible, on this unusual camel caravan that had left the oasis of Douz on or about the 10th of March, 1943, for a rendezvous with death in the desert, I took a month's holiday in Tunisia. More than anything else, I wanted to separate fact from fiction in an effort to establish the validity of this fabulous saga.

South of Tunis is the beautiful white city of Hammamet and the magnificent seaside villa which, at different times, had been the headquarters of both Generals Rommel and Montgomery. The low, rambling, white stucco house, now owned by the Tunisian government, has been transformed into an International Culture Center and has changed little since it was constructed in 1930 by Georges Sebastian, a Rumanian refugee who later fled to America during Rommel's invasion of Tunisia.

To the southwest and not far from Hammamet is the small oasis of Douz, a sun-baked village located on the fringe of the scorching Sahara Desert. A handful of Arabs have lived at this palm-studded oasis for many years. While most of them remembered very little about the incident of the truck convoy, one old man of about 70 by the name of Youssef said that back in those days he had been working at the camel market and personally sold five of his camels to a group of foreigners. Although they had purchased several animals—perhaps 60 or 70, he thought—he did not know where they had gone after leaving the market. He remembers the incident because the strangers were dressed in military uniforms and wore short light-brown pants that barely covered their knees, and it was the first time he had ever seen men with straw-colored hair, although their bodies were bronze from exposure to the desert sun. But they were very kind and courteous, he remembers, and paid well for the animals.

Aging Mohammed Saidi remembers that several large trucks had entered their village at about that same time and were parked on the outskirts of the oasis where they remained for several weeks before they were taken away by some British soldiers who had arrived unexpectedly at Douz.

Douz is not as desolate and foreboding as it may sound. Once the sun sinks, a cooling breeze whips across the barren stretches of land, and as night falls Berber girls perform their sensual dances on the edge of the oasis in the hope of receiving a few coins from those who come to watch them. Some of these tawny young women are strikingly beautiful, with their long, coal-black hair cascading around their shoulders, while their trim figures are almost completely enveloped in long red tribal dresses adorned with myriad hand-fashioned silver jewelry.

The gigantic sand dunes surrounding Douz stretch out in every direction as far as the eye can see. The Sahara is a pitiless inferno—a land where only desert nomads can survive, and yet, it is not without an intrinsic though solitary and lonely beauty. Nomads call it the "Garden of Allah," and rightfully so. During the daylight hours, temperatures often rise to well over 100 degrees F., and now and then we were forced to seek the sanctuary of small oases—clumps of palm trees and muddy waterholes— that offered a shady respite from the searing rays of the sun. And yet, at this very moment, thousands of nomads—Taurogs, Berbers and Bedouins— roam these sandy wastes forever on the move, traveling from one oasis to another where their flocks of sheep and goats can graze on the coarse grass.

Rommel's camel caravan probably left Douz on or about the 10th day of March, 1943, and traveled no more than two days into the desert. There was no need to go further in order to safely hide the treasure. But where is it? That remains the unanswered question.

No. of Words: __2120__

Reading Time: _____

Selection 26

The Mystery of Rommel's Missing Treasure

VOCABULARY BUILDING

Below are several words used in this article. They are presented in the context of the sentences or phrases in which they occur. It you are unsure of their meanings and cannot define them from the context, look them up in the dictionary. Spaces are provided for additional unfamiliar words from the article to add to your vocabulary.

1. "To find the answer to this *enigma* it is necessary to turn back the pages of history . . ."

    *enigma:*_____

2. "Just as the dreaded *ides of March* had once come for the *indomitable* Julius Caesar, so, too, were they about to descend upon . . . Rommel . . ."

    *ides of March:*_____

    *indomitable:*_____

3. "Rommel, always *meticulously* dressed, sat dejectedly . . ."

    *meticulously:*_____

4. ". . . and Arab *mercenaries* were to be given weapons and trained to join in the fight against the . . . allied forces."

    *mercenaries:*_____

5. "In many instances when they refused to fight under the banner of the Third Reich, they were *summarily* executed . . ."

    *summarily:*_____

6. ". . . sending a fleet of fast power boats bearing several crates of *objets d'art . . . purloined* from museums and palaces . . ."

    *objets d'art:*_____

    *purloined:*_____

7. "... long red tribal dresses adorned with *myriad* hand-fashioned silver jewelry."

   *myriad:*_____

8. "... clumps of palm trees and muddy waterholes—that offered a shady *respite* from the *searing* rays of the sun."

   *respite:*_____

   *searing:*_____

9. _____:_____

10. _____:_____

11. _____:_____

12. _____:_____

RETENTION AND COMPREHENSION

A. True/False (1 point each)

1. Rommel's missing treasure is valued at $10 million.

   1. T _____ F _____

2. The author believes the treasure is buried in the Sahara desert in Southern Tunisia.

   2. T _____ F _____

3. All of the German soldiers who buried the treasure died soon afterwards in a battle with the British.

   3. T _____ F _____

4. Only General Rommel knew where the treasure was buried, and with his death, the secret was lost forever.

   4. T _____ F _____

5. Arabs who live near the area of the supposed buried treasure appear to spend a great amount of time and energy searching for it.

   5. T _____ F _____

B. Completion (3 points each)

6. The treasure was made up of gold coins and _____.

   6. _____

7. The gold coins in the treasure were meant to be used to bribe Arab _____ to side with the Nazis.

   7. _____

8. In Rommel's final battle in Africa, he was defeated by British desert forces led by General _____.

8. _____

9. Before its burial in the desert, the treasure was transferred near an oasis from military trucks to _____.

9. _____

10. The author bases much of his article on an eyewitness who was a member of the infamous Nazi group called the _____.

10. _____

C. Multiple Choice (2 points each)

11. The gold coins in the treasure had been shipped from (a) southern Italy by U-boat, (b) Swiss banks, (c) France by destroyers, (d) Berlin by air transport.

11. _____

12. Arab rulers who refused to join the German forces were (a) exiled to neutral countries, (b) executed or imprisoned, (c) sent to European concentration camps, (d) forced to fight at gunpoint.

12. _____

13. The Germans made no serious attempt to send the treasure out of Africa because (a) their air force was destroyed, (b) the British controlled the Mediterranean, (c) they wanted to ship it to South America instead, (d) they were too busy fleeing the British Army.

13. _____

14. The eyewitness quoted in the article was sent to Africa to (a) train Arab soldiers, (b) document Rommel's battles, (c) spy on British headquarters in Tunis, (d) arrange for the treasure's burial in the desert.

14. _____

15. According to the eyewitness's account, British Intelligence (a) knew all about the treasure and was making an effort to capture it, (b) knew about it but underestimated its worth, (c) knew nothing about it, (d) intercepted the treasure convoy and captured the wealth.

15. _____

16. The German eyewitness to the events in the article (a) is still hunting for the treasure, (b) is referred to with a false name, (c) had been tried for war crimes, (d) escaped to Central America with some of the treasure.

16. _____

17. Additional support for the author's thesis is provided by (a) actual films taken of the treasure's burial, (b) a Rumanian refugee who saw the convoy leaving Douz, (c) Bedouins who witnessed the battle between the British and the German burial party, (d) an old Arab who said he sold camels to people who looked like German soldiers.

17. _____

18. Many people believe that Rommel's treasure (a) never existed, (b) was really meant to be used as bribes to the Arabs by fleeing Nazi war criminals, (c) was dumped into the sea just off the coast of Corsica, (d) was discovered by Arab nomads and divided among their leaders.

18. _____

D. Thematic (11 points)

19. Which statement *best* expresses the theme (*main idea*) of the article?
    (a) Rommel's plan to keep the treasure for himself was spoiled when a British Army unit accidentally came upon the German burial party.
    (b) Contrary to popular belief, a huge amount of treasure was buried by the defeated Germans in the Sahara where it still awaits discovery.
    (c) Rommel's decision to bury the treasure was a mistake, especially after speedboats with some of the treasure did get through safely to France.
    (d) A definite possibility exists that the treasure was not buried but flown out through West Africa to an unknown island in the Caribbean.

19. _____

E. Purpose (9 points)

20. The author's *chief* purpose is
    (a) to explain the reasons why the Germans were unable to enlist the Arabs to fight against the allied forces in Africa.
    (b) to show how General Rommel's concern for the treasure probably caused him to lose the final battle at Medenine.
    (c) to examine the possibility that a vast amount of wealth was buried in the North African desert in an unknown location.

20. _____

(d) to make us realize that many professional treasure hunters are making a huge mistake by not searching the desert around Douz for Rommel's missing treasure.

Total Retention and Comprehension Score: _____

QUESTIONS FOR DISCUSSION (MEANING AND TECHNIQUE)

1. With what events does the story of the disappearance of Rommel's treasure begin and end? How is the narrative presented? By order of time? Importance of the event? As remembered by witnesses? Is the narrative easy to follow? Why or why not?

2. Does the writer use many adjectives and descriptive phrases? Do they add interest to the article? How? Select a passage that is especially descriptive and discuss how it achieves its effect.

3. What is the reliability of each person who offered information in support of the existence of the treasure?

4. Is the way Rommel and the German soldiers are depicted by the writer favorable? unfavorable? objective?

5. Based on the information we have in the article, what was the extent of the writer's research? Was it sufficient in the light of his main idea? Explain. What else should he have done?

6. Is it possible that everything happened just as the writer presented it even though there is no hard evidence (photographs, inventory lists, maps, eyewitnesses) to support his claim? Defend your opinion with reasonable explanations.

SUGGESTIONS FOR WRITING

1. Select a local, favorite, nature spot and describe it in such a manner that others might be interested enough to go there. Use vivid adjectives, rather than words such as "terrific," "great," and "super." Include directions and other useful information for a first-time visitor. Or, write the same type of paper for an *event*.

2. If you have been involved in a search or hunt for something or somebody that was supposed to have been in a particular place but was not found, tell what went on and give an explanation why the search was unsuccessful.

3. Get information on a creature whose existence is debatable (the

Abominable Snowman; the Loch Ness Monster; Bigfoot), and write an argument for or against the creature's existence.

4. Stories of buried treasure, hidden riches, lost gold mines, and sunken ships are very popular. If you are familiar with such a local legend, try to uncover its origin and ask others about it. Write a composition about it.

Selection 26

Overall Reading Performance

Your overall reading performance is a combination of how fast you read and how much you comprehend and retain. The chart below allows you to find out quickly your "overall reading performance."

First enter your "reading time" and your "retention and comprehension" score in the two blanks at the bottom of the page. Then simply lay a straightedge of any kind (the edge of a sheet of paper or a pencil will do) across the chart, placing the left side of the straightedge at the appropriate point on the "Reading Rate" scale, and the right side at the appropriate point on the "Retention and Comprehension" scale. The point at which the paper or pencil intersects the scale in the middle of the page will indicate your overall performance.

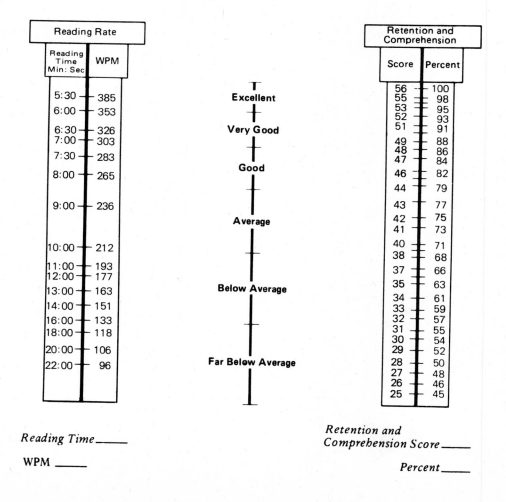

Reading Time _____

WPM _____

Retention and
Comprehension Score _____

Percent _____

Selection 27

Hello! My Name Is 1069

JOHN CAMPBELL

The use of numbers to identify people has been widely condemned as dehumanizing and insulting. But becoming a number might not be so bad if proper attention is paid to choosing an appropriate one.

Michael Peter Dengler, an art dealer and substitute teacher who lives in Minneapolis, Minnesota, started a controversy that could have important implications for the future when he decided a few years ago to change his name to the number 1069. He encountered considerable resistance from employers and utility companies, to name just a few, and the phone company even refused to list him in the phone book. The Minnesota Supreme Court finally ruled that Dengler could use the name One Zero Six Nine on a common law basis only, but that he could not use the numerals, for the statutes prohibit the use of numbers as names. The case has now been appealed to the U.S. Supreme Court.

Overall, the reaction to Dengler's attempt to become a number has been quite negative. Editorial writers throughout the United States have questioned the propriety of such a change. A typical reaction was that of *Saturday Review* magazine, which lamented that "a decision in his favor would accelerate the process of dehumanization that has already gone much too far" and declared that "There is something unholy and inhuman about digits when they are used as identifiers, whether on a Buchenwald registry or a Minnesota court order." This view, however, is quite limited in scope and overlooks the fascinating possibilities involved in such a change. If the proper guidelines were established, such a conversion to numbers could become the most rewarding, enlightening, and earthshaking experience to affect mankind since 1066.

First, it must be realized that name-changing is a fairly common occurrence in the United States, and frequently a person not only gets a new name but becomes a very confident somebody else. Examples of name-changing abound: Cassius Clay changed to Muhammad Ali for religious reasons; Ellen Cooperman became Ellen Cooperperson in order to become a liberated woman; Sanche de Gramont changed to Ted Morgan

Source: The Futurist, Oct. 1980. Reprinted by permission of *The Futurist.*

when he became an American citizen because he "wanted to make his name rather than inherit it"; movie stars change their name so that they can better charm the public; Hitler could not have ruled in tyranny if his name had been Shicklgruber; and Joe Pfsbilitik could not have been an overachiever had he not changed his name to Bill Pfsbilitik because he hated the name Joe. Just as Sanche de Gramont changed his name, many other citizens changed their names at naturalization ceremonies and many others had their names changed by immigration officials when they arrived as refugees from Europe. All this shows that one's name from birth is not sacrosanct but used until changed. If a number is "an offense to human dignity" as many maintain, what about a name such as Penicillin Smith—so named because his parents saw the name "Penicillin" on a hospital chart. Moreover, there is now a baby girl outlandishly named Equal Rights Amendment. Also, there are other names that might be considered an affront to human dignity; consider I.M. Hipp, A. Moron, Henry Will Burst, E.Z. Rider, Lettuce Godebed, and Humperdink Fangboner.

Putting Humanity into Numbers

Name-changing is certainly not anathema to us, and name-changing-to-a-number-name, if done with forethought and ground rules, could easily become acceptable and very beneficial. We would probably all agree that our humanity is worth protecting and that we are all encumbered by an ever expanding computerization of society. All too often, we are treated as just another digit by the forces that control our lives. But if we were able to put humanity into numbers, if we were able to humanize figures, if we were able to personalize the mathematical process, we could influence every computer's respect for our humanity and the opinion of anyone who looks at a person and sees only a cipher.

The first step in providing for the transition to number-changing is to require a number that has redeeming social values. The number would need to be related to a historical event or to an epoch-making moment, and thus, a person upon being introduced would bring knowledge and enlightenment to everyone present since the number by etiquette would need to be discussed at length before moving on to other topics. (I suggest that the words *name* and *number* be combined to form a new word—*namber.*)

The choice of nambers is, of course, unlimited and ranges from the esoteric to the mundane. You could choose 2141473 if you had always been fond of Copernicus or simply if you were a heliocentric individual. The date marks the birth of the founder of astronomy, who published a treatise on the revolution of the earth and the other planets around the sun. This namber would be a lovely conversation piece and you could go on for hours digressing about the sun, the moon, or the stars whether you were talking to a group of astrophysicists or a nubile young thing at a cocktail party.

The historical basis for one's number, of course, could not be a commonplace one such as 101563 (the day I could legally drink) or 917331904 (the first day plus the school's zip code that I started teaching at Brookstone), for one does not learn anything of significance from those nambers. The basis for choosing a number should also not be a religious one, and the courts should not allow a religious fanatic to select a futuristic number such as 2285800 (signifying the month, day, year, and exact time when he believes the world will end) since that date cannot be verified in advance. Besides, that day will arrive and the world will carry on as usual and then that person would return to court to select another number stating the reasons why the inspired date failed. The courts are crowded enough. Moreover, can you imagine the concern or panic if someone like Jeanne Dixon were allowed to pick a doomsday namber! The future is out and we must look to the past for redeeming social nambers.

You would not need to have any special reason for making a selection; however, if you were William or if you were a history invasion buff, you could adopt 1066 as your number. The redeeming benefits would be immediate. For example, the person choosing the number must do adequate research. A court hearing would be held before a judge, defense and prosecuting attorneys, and a court-appointed historiographer. In order to obtain approval for your namber, you would need to be knowledgeable and competent in answering questions concerning the history of your chosen period. Everyone present would need to be thoroughly prepared on the meaning of 1066, and as a result a complete review and in-depth study would be achieved by all. If the person failed to defend adequately his number, he could reapply several months later after research and study.

Nambers Could Bring Revolutionary Changes

The effect upon society of namber-changing would be quite striking. The printed word would be more overwhelmed with attention than it is at the moment. This happening would be more revolutionary than the invention of the printing press. Libraries, book stores, publishing houses, and especially history book clubs would experience an unprecedented boom as everyone searches for an appropriate namber. Other changes would be just as revolutionary. For instance, night school courses would be crammed as everyone strives to become more competent historians at parties, teas, showers, and bridge clubs. Likewise, television talk shows would become even more popular as hosts introduce guests chosen more for the excitement engendered by their nambers than because of their dexterity at boring chitchat. Viewers will seek edification and will appreciate the plethora of historical data that will enrich their lives. TV hosts will need to be more competent historically speaking. They will need to be able to ad-lib a summit conference rather than a song-and-dance routine. Probing questions will be the key to their success as seriousness replaces frivolity. These hosts will need to select carefully their namber because of such close public scrutiny, although Johnny Carson might appropriately select 5,000,004 as his namber, indicating that he is the first TV personality ever to make that much money working just four hours a week.

The nature of education will undergo a major restructuring due mainly to the talk show influence. No longer would bleary-eyed but avid students need to rise at 5:00 to take history courses on *Sunrise Semester,* for the talk shows will have developed a relationship with colleges and universities to offer college credit contigent upon the right selection of guests. If a show, for example, picked at least one guest every day for six months with a historical reference to the Spanish Inquisition, one college credit would be given for EUR 446. Since talk shows usually have several guests during a show, five or six semester credits could be given during a six-month period. The increased revenue from credits would be a tremendous boon to the colleges and to the talk shows.

Eventually, everyone will have a namber and every encounter with another individual will increase one's knowledge of history and the world and open up new avenues for reflection. Besides credit earned for watching talk shows, each individual could arrange for high school or college credit based simply on meeting with and discussing another person's namber. Of course, proper documentation and appropriate guidelines would need to be established, but high schools could give credit for, say, 300 personal interviews, colleges could give credit for 600, and there could be a doctoral degree credit for 1,200 interviews. We would eventually become a country of historians and not jocks, and Arnold Toynbee munchies would replace the Reggie Jackson candy bar.

No More History Teachers

But the namber-changing revolution would not be without its problems. Foremost among them would be the elimination of history courses in schools and universities since everyone would be so well informed without needing formal schooling. Social studies departments would cease to exist, and teachers would be dismissed. But this will be a blessing in disguise and these teachers need not bemoan their fate as they would automatically qualify for more lucrative positions as court consultants, aides to prosecuting and defense attorneys, talk-show directors, hosts, or guest hosts, and coordinators for developing programs for credit with the schools—and there are many more positions too numerous to catalogue. Moreover, namber counselors would be as important as marriage counselors and would be concerned with preventing historical mishaps, such as advising against a 5191536 (the day on which Anne Boleyn was executed) from marrying a 6281491 (Henry VIII), especially so if she is head over heels in love. In addition, number counselors would also become as important as astrologers and would help with wise counsel in the selection of nambers for babies.

Jobs would be created even at the highest levels because the president would certainly need some sage counselors in namber matters in order to provide the proper inspiration for this steam-rolling American movement. The United States under his leadership would be the first country that would go totally metric and nambric. In choosing his own number, it is a foregone conclusion that President Reagan's nickname would be 40th or just plain 40 for short, since he is the 40th president of the United States. The president would also need a competent administrator in charge of his Namber Knowledge Program (a spinoff of the Physical Fitness Program), which would award history medals for meeting a certain number of people and discussing their nambers in a designated period of time.

This article just touches on a few of the more exciting aspects of a movement that would profoundly restructure political, social, and economic patterns in the United States and perhaps in the world. The excitement produced by such a move could be the necessary panacea to the loss of identity affecting the 1970s. This confused and uncertain era in which we live—with low productivity, mounting inflation, fuel shortages, and a myriad of international problems besetting us—is a time without a focus and a time needing an inspiration, a movement. A "Namber Revolution" could get us through the worst of times in the 1980s as the next 10 years pass almost unnoticed. This namberphoria (*namber + (eu)-phoria*) is the new foundation this country needs and one that should be encouraged, especially by influential magazines and newspapers that so blatantly erred in their editorial support for the preservation of the banal syndrome of keeping names like Tom, Dick, and Harry and that refused even to consider the more stimulating and educational path of a number revolution.

But then, one day, after everyone has adjusted well to the number revolution that has swept the country, and after everyone has received a surfeit of high school and college credit and become mind boggled with historical facts, and the number society is well esconced, you can believe that some smart aleck will come along and want to change his number back to a real honest-to-goodness name like John, and the struggle to change society will begin anew. It's difficult if not impossible to foresee what reaction this counter-revolt might produce.

No. of Words: ___2134___

Reading Time: _____

Selection 27

Hello! My Name Is 1069

VOCABULARY BUILDING

Below are several words used in this article. They are presented in the context of the sentences or phrases in which they occur. If you are unsure of their meanings and cannot define them from the context, look them up in the dictionary. Spaces are provided for additional unfamiliar words from the article to add to your vocabulary.

1. "...we could influence...the opinion of anyone who looks at a person and sees only a *cipher*."

    cipher: _____

2. "The choice of nambers...ranges from the *esoteric* to the *mundane*."

    esoteric: _____

    mundane: _____

3. "...if you had always been fond of Copernicus or simply if you were a *heliocentric* individual."

    heliocentric: _____

4. "...you could go on for hours *digressing* about the sun, the moon, or the stars ..."

    digressing: _____

5. "...guests [would be] chosen more for the excitement *engendered* by their nambers than because of their *dexterity* at boring chitchat."

    engendered: _____

    dexterity: _____

6. "Viewers will seek *edification* and will appreciate the *plethora* of historical data . . ."

   *edification:*_____

   *plethora:*_____

7. ". . . seriousness replaces *frivolity*."

   *frivolity:*_____

8. ". . . such a move could be the necessary *panacea* to the loss of identity affecting the 1970s."

   *panacea:*_____

9. "This confused . . . *era* in which we live—with a . . . *myriad* of international problems besetting us . . ."

   *era:*_____

   *myriad:*_____

10. ". . . [the] influential magazines and newspapers that so *blatantly erred* in their . . . support for the preservation of the *banal syndrome* of keeping names like Tom, Dick, and Harry."

   *blatantly:*_____

   *erred:*_____

   *banal:*_____

   *syndrome:*_____

11. _____ :_____

12. _____ :_____

13. _____ :_____

14. _____ :_____

RETENTION AND COMPREHENSION

A. True/False (1 point each)

1. The author is serious about his proposal.   *1*. T _____ F _____

2. The Minnesota Supreme Court ruled that Michael Peter Dengler could not use numerals for his name.   *2*. T _____ F _____

3. The *Saturday Review* magazine was in favor of Dengler's desire to use a number.   3. T _____ F _____

4. Name changing is a fairly common occurrence in the United States.   4. T _____ F _____

5. Hitler refused to change his name.   5. T _____ F _____

B. Completion (3 points each)

6. The word "namber" is a combination of the words _____ and _____.   6. _____

7. A number should be related to_____.   7. _____

8. Copernicus wrote a treatise about_____.   8. _____

9. Colleges and universities could offer_____for watching talk shows.   9. _____

10. In schools and universities_____courses would be eliminated.   10. _____

C. Multiple Choice (2 points each)

11. Before a person could adopt a namber, he would have to (a) get the approval of a knowledgeable scholar, (b) register it with the appropriate department, (c) appear at a court hearing, (d) have a good and sufficient reason.   11. _____

12. A good reason for picking a certain number might be that it (a) reminded you of a significant date in your life, (b) related to an important address, (c) related to your social security number, (d) related to a historical event.   12. _____

13. Nambers would (a) increase knowledge, (b) dehumanize society, (c) result in mass confusion, (d) help in the census.   13. _____

14. Number counselors would (a) help construct usable nambers, (b) advise against using certain nambers in some cases, (c) appear as consultants at court hearings, (d) function as marriage counselors in marital disputes caused by mismatched nambers.   14. _____

15. After the new number society is well established, it   15. _____
is possible that (a) there will be many people with
the same number, (b) computers will be better
able to process population information, (c) some
people will want to change back to simple word
names, (d) people will want to change from one
namber to another.

16. The *Satuday Review* magazine felt that nambers   16. _____
(a) would hinder the spread of education, (b)
would help modernize society, (c) were not anathema to us, (d) were dehumanizing.

17. In picking acceptable nambers, religious convic-   17. _____
tions (a) are helpful, (b) should be avoided, (c)
add color, (d) provide a desirable moral tone.

18. Nambers could (a) cause some political problems,   18. _____
(b) bring about great unemployment, (c) cause libraries to "boom," (d) arouse greater interest in
mathematics.

D. Thematic (11 points)

19. Which statement *best* expresses the theme (*main*   19. _____
idea) of the article?
    (a) Word-names (such as A. Moron) can be just as
        dehumanizing as number-names.
    (b) If certain unlikely assumptions are granted,
        nambers could benefit society in many ways.
    (c) Nambers could work just as well as word-
        names.
    (d) People would get tired of nambers and go back
        to word-names.

E. Purpose (9 points)

20. The author's *chief* purpose is   20. _____

    (a) to make a serious proposal in humorous way.
    (b) to explain possible future changes brought
        about by computers in an amusing way.
    (c) to show in a half-serious way that words can be
        just as "dehumanizing" as numbers.
    (d) to make certain assumptions and work them
        out in an amusing way.

Total Retention and Comprehension Score: _____

QUESTIONS FOR DISCUSSION (MEANING AND TECHNIQUE)

1. How early in the article is its thesis (main idea) stated? What is it? What kind of "background" precedes it? Was it wise to build up to the thesis in that way? Do some of the other articles do it too? Which ones? How?

2. Is this article meant to be taken seriously? Where do we first become aware of its real tone? How?

3. "Hitler could not have ruled in tyranny if his name had been Shicklgruber" says the writer of this article. Do you agree? Why or why not? Refer to Selection 21, "Your Name Is Your Destiny."

4. What is a *namber*?

5. Why do you think the *Saturday Review* magazine (and other editorialists) did not like Michael Peter Dengler's attempt to change his name to a number?

6. What does the author mean by "putting humanity into numbers" and being able to "humanize figures." How does he suggest we do that? Why is that called "humanizing" them? Why aren't numbers considered "human" to begin with? What does "humanize" mean?

7. What does the number 1066 at the end of the second paragraph refer to?

8. Who are Arnold Toynbee and Reggie Jackson and why does the author say "Arnold Toynbee munchies would replace the Reggie Jackson candy bar"?

9. There is *irony* and *satire* in this article. What do these terms mean? How does the article display them? Name some of the things satirized.

10. Does the article have a fitting conclusion? Why or why not?

11. Does the article seem to get "farther out" (more absurd, outrageous) as it progresses? In what ways? How?

SUGGESTIONS FOR WRITING

1. Write a "cause-and-effect" essay, serious or satiric or comic, showing the effect on society of a similar kind of change (everyone dressing completely alike, no one going to school, everything being handmade, men holding "women's jobs," women holding "men's jobs," camels instead of cars, etc.).

2. Argue for or against a particular change by showing a number of specific consequences of that change (as the author of this article

does). Your argument can be serious or satiric and/or comic.

3. Write a refutation of the thesis of this article by showing how dehumanizing even this author's humanized "nambers" would become.

4. Pretend you are Michael Peter Dengler's lawyer. Write an appeal to the court showing why Dengler has a constitutional right to change his name to a number and what the broader implications are of allowing the courts to veto one's choice of a name, be it a proper noun or a number.

5. Pretend you are writing the dialogue for a play or movie and write the script for a conversation between a "nubile young thing at a cocktail party" and yourself (or anyone and yourself) about her and/or your "namber."

Selection 27

Overall Reading Performance

Your overall reading performance is a combination of how fast you read and how much you comprehend and retain. The chart below allows you to find out quickly your "overall reading performance."

First enter your "reading time" and your "retention and comprehension" score in the two blanks at the bottom of the page. Then simply lay a straightedge of any kind (the edge of a sheet of paper or a pencil will do) across the chart, placing the left side of the straightedge at the appropriate point on the "Reading Rate" scale, and the right side at the appropriate point on the "Retention and Comprehension" scale. The point at which the paper or pencil intersects the scale in the middle of the page will indicate your overall performance.

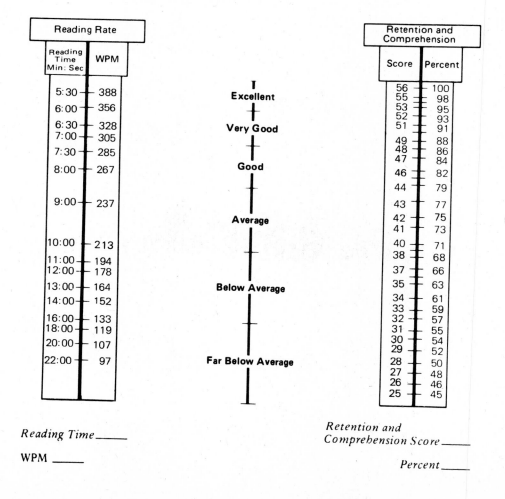

*Reading Time*_____

WPM _____

*Retention and Comprehension Score*_____

*Percent*_____

Selection 28

Is the Perfect Worker a Mindless Idiot?

RICHARD WOLKOMIR

At Citicorp's headquarters in Manhattan, the mailman dresses in sheet metal. And he knows only one word, which he always says twice, "Beep, beep."

Actually, the mailman is a mail *thing*—a robot made of wires, transistors, and computer chips. This automated filing cabinet rolls through offices following a chemical trail on the floor, stopping at preassigned stations to pick up and deliver mail, flashing its blue lights.

Speedier than its human predecessors on the mail route, it gets no fringe benefits, no wages, no vacations, no coffee and doughnuts. All it asks is a nightly plug-in and a jolt of juice. And that is why robots are coming on strong.

Over 2,000 of the mechanical hulks are on the job already in the United States, 1,000 in Europe, and about 2,000 in Japan. More join the workforce every week. And countries on both sides of the Iron Curtain are investing big bucks in robots—the magic word is productivity. For instance, auto industry experts estimate that robots—even at prices up to $100,000 apiece—punch in for $4.80 an hour, compared to as much as $14 per hour in wages and fringe benefits for human workers.

Still, these motorized hulks are spectacularly stupid. As Joseph Engelberger, president of Unimation, Inc., the largest robot manufacturer, puts it, "Even today's most sophisticated industrial robot would have to accept being called a mere oaf as a high accolade."

Unimation makes today's worldwide best-seller, the Unimate, which looks like a tank turret with a gun barrel ending in a steel claw. An oaf it is, stone dumb. But the Unimate, like other industrial robots, is a whiz of a worker.

At an International Harvester plant in Canada, for instance, Unimates endlessly swing heavy harrow discs into a hearth for tempering, then snatch them up as they emerge, white-hot. At a Xerox photocopier factory in Rochester, N.Y., the robots insert parts into processing machines, like

Source: Mechanix Illustrated, Jan. 1981. Reprinted with permission of *Mechanix Illustrated.*
Copyright 1980 by CBS Publications.

mother robins feeding worms to their chicks. On a Chrysler assembly line, Unimate welders peck away at new K-Car chassis like a flock of hostile parrots.

Is the work dirty? Dangerous? Numbingly repetitive? Is the workplace searingly hot? Toxic with fumes? Deafeningly noisy? Robots are too stupid to care. They just keep on swiveling their arms, clacking their claws, at your service.

"A new slave class," Unimation's Joseph Engelberger calls them. These first-generation industrial robots are just the thing for such dreary tasks as spray-painting car bodies or ceaselessly moving parts from here to there. Compared to ordinary machines, they look like mechanical Einsteins, smartly welding each chassis in just the right spots as it inches along the assembly line. Actually, they're mindless idiots. If the next car is slightly out of place the robot gleefully welds the air.

Some are a bit brighter than others. Binks Manufacturing Company makes a robot paint sprayer that is talented enough to paint cartoons for kicks, if someone shows it the moves. Cincinnati Milacron's T³ (a jointed arm waving atop a pedestal, it looks like a cobra undulating in a snake charmer's basket) has an even brighter computer brain.

T³ can figure the most efficient arm movement to use, whether it's spray painting, stacking-and-packing, or welding. It can weld as many as 15 different auto body styles, all coming down the assembly line at random. It tells machines it bosses when to stop and start. And it even diagnoses its own disorders, giving technicians the word via a video display.

The secret? Most of today's robots, as one industry expert has put it , are legless, blind, and deaf, trying to use chopsticks with a hand numbed by novocaine. The T³'s hand is just a bit less numb—sensors feed data into its brain, allowing it to track moving objects and modify its movements accordingly.

For first-generation robots, that's it for tricks. No match for Fido. But a second generation of robots now is coming on the job market. And these machines are an evolutionary leap—they have eyes.

Auto-Place, Inc., a small robot manufacturer, brought out the first industrial seeing-eye robot in 1976. Called Opto-Sense, it combines a robot that looks like a woodworking lathe with a video camera and a microcomputer. The device wowed spectators at an international robot conference by shooting craps and sorting a deck of cards into hearts, diamonds, clubs, and spades.

When it isn't fooling around with card tricks, Opto-Sense can do all the usual robot chores, like feeding parts into presses or moving gin bottles along an assembly line. But it also can perform inspections. Via its TV eye, it can pick up a part no matter how askew it is on the conveyor belt, check for flaws, and then either pass the part on for further processing or toss it in a reject bin.

Chesebrough-Pond's has used the sighted robots to inspect medical thermometers. Bulova Watch's Systems & Instruments Division has used them to set fuse timers on military explosives.

But Opto-Sense is not a star performer because it lacks real hand-eye coordination. Like other first-generation robots, it can only pick up parts that are presented to it just so, although it's a bit more talented than most. What manufacturers need is a robot that can peer into a bin of miscellaneous parts, spot the particular item needed—even if it's upside down, sideways, or half buried—pick it up, turn it until it's oriented correctly, then proceed to the next step. For example, next the robot may insert the part in a grinding machine or screw it into another part.

Such robots are in the works. University of Rhode Island engineers have an experimental model, the Mark IV, that actually can select parts from a jumble in a bin. Researchers at California's SRI International have developed a robot that uses an overhead TV camera to guide its arm. To demonstrate its powers, this experimental model can bolt down a small engine's cover, using a wrench it selects from a jumble of tools on a table.

Meanwhile, General Motors engineers, working in conjunction with Unimation, have designed an advanced seeing robot. The GM engineers started with Unimation's PUMA, which is basically an animated arm. The robot is fairly cheap, about $30,000. And it is designed to join forces with human workers on light assembly jobs, handling pieces weighing under five pounds (GM estimates that 95% of all parts circulating through its factories are in that flyweight category). Like most of the new first-generation robots, PUMA can choose any of several work sequences—give it part A and the robot goes through one series of steps, give it part B and it goes through a different series of steps.

But GM—working with Cincinnati Milacron—has taken PUMA one step further and equipped it with eyes. To do that, the engineers hooked PUMA up to a digital camera, which looks at an object (a wrench, for instance) and converts the various shades of light it sees into numbers. If 0 represents black and 63 represents white, then a number like 25 represents a certain shade of gray. The camera converts what it sees into a pattern of such numbers and feeds them into a computer.

In the computer's mind the numbers become a picture clear enough to guide PUMA's hand toward the wrench. At $10,000, the vision hardware costs only a tenth what it did a decade ago, when GM first began the research. And, given today's explosion in electronic technology, GM expects the price to drop still further. With economics behind it, the second generation of robots is about to debut.

Meanwhile, Unimation has given PUMA ears. Most robots learn tasks via the monkey-see technique. That is, a trainer guides the robot's hand through the new motions it must learn, such as reaching out to a certain spot, grasping a connecting rod gliding by on an assembly line, then reaching up and hooking the rod onto another conveyor passing overhead. But the new PUMA system, thanks to its computer brain, has learned some rudimentary English, enabling programmers to type directions directly into the computer.

At Carnegie-Mellon University, researchers are teaching computers— robots' brains—to take orders from humans in spoken English. So far, their machine recognizes some 1,000 words. It even ignores coughs and sneezes.

An Ohio State University professor, Robert McGhee, is developing a robot that walks. The Bionic Bug looks like a six-legged beetle. Sensors in its feet measure each foot's pressure against the ground and against obstacles, enabling the machine to pick its way along a test trail littered with stumps. At Purdue University, researchers have developed a robot sophisticated enough to write Chinese characters.

Like it or not, the mechanical men are coming. In fact, they're here. At Chrysler's assembly plant in Newark, Del., robots already handle 98 per cent of all spot welds on the new K-Car bodies. Productivity has jumped from 60 to 70 cars per hour.

What will happen to people? For certain jobs, robots work cheaper, faster, more efficiently. And they can turn out better quality work because they don't get tired or bored. Will people become obsolete?

According to industry experts, humans will be around for a long time, handling the more complicated tasks that are too much for a robot's feeble brain. At the same time, robots will be taking over the dangerous, boring, or uncomfortable jobs for which it's tough to recruit people, like spray painting the insides of vans. But mass unemployment as the mechanical men take over seems unlikely.

"We're not going to suddenly, in one year, install hundreds of these things," says GM's Donald E. Hart. "They're going to start moving out one at a time until they've proved themselves, and then they'll gradually move into new areas."

"No one absolutely must have a robot when there's willing human labor about," says Unimation's Joseph Engelberger.

However, a Rand study has predicted that, by the year 2000, only 2 per cent of the country's workers will be employed in manufacturing. And an SRI International automation expert recently told a United Auto Workers conference that, to stem rising unemployment as robots take over jobs in the next 25 years, we will need earlier retirement, shorter work weeks, retraining programs, and more service jobs. Ultimately, he said, robots could handle up to 90 per cent of all assembly jobs. But he added, "We can't hope to remain competitive in world markets without them."

Meanwhile, robots themselves have come to an evolutionary fork. Call it the HAL vs. C3P0 question.

HAL, the robot in *2001 A Space Odyssey*, was nowhere to be seen. He was, in effect, the entire space ship, controlling everything. C3P0, in *Star Wars,* was a stand-alone robot—he marched around like a man. And real robots could go in either of those two directions.

Currently, the Westinghouse Electric Corporation, working with a National Science Foundation grant, is taking a step toward HAL. Westinghouse researchers are developing a system that would triple the productivity of certain types of manufacturing, such as the production of small electric motors. Robot systems would do almost everything. And Westinghouse expects a pilot plant to be in operation in 1982.

Japan is going further. A government-funded team in that country is now building a totally automated factory, where only two or three humans will work, punching computer keys. The factory itself will be a huge robot, turning raw materials and components into finished products. General Motors has developed a HAL-like paint-spraying system—a centralized computer which works its will through an array of robot arms. The U.S. Air Force also is developing an automated factory.

Which will win, HAL or C3P0?

"It's a grand, everybody-wins fight between the forces that would make artificial humans and the forces that would make manufacturing completely inhuman," says Joseph Engelberger. "Robots of one form or the other, stand-alone or distributed, are in one destiny—bully for both!"

His prediction? Both types of robot are needed. And he says that as the new robots that can see, hear, feel, understand a bit of English, and walk around come into their own, the machines will move beyond industry.

He foresees, perhaps in this decade, robot gas stations, robot garbage collection, robot fast-food stands. In fact, a Massachusetts inventor already has developed a robot that makes sandwiches.

Ultimately, says Engelberger, our homes will be HAL-like robots, with a centralized computer doing the thinking and also controlling a C3P0-type robot, which will handle household chores ranging from vacuuming to mowing the lawn. It might even play ping-pong. But it won't be a real chum. "We have a powerful, but docile, slow-witted, but untiring, worker that is just barely sensate," says Engelberger.

Meanwhile, the central computer would keep an inventory of household supplies, down to the salt and pepper, and order them automatically when they got low. Engelberger assumes that store computers and your house will be able to chat.

"If the Ms. of the household should cook some exotic dish, she could feed the recipe to the robot and it would gather the ingredients, ordering anything which happened not to be on hand," he says.

The robot house also would routinely handle its own repairs and maintenance, with those sessions scheduled for off hours so as not to disturb human activities. And, besides operating a fire alarm and sprinkler system, the robot would catch burglars in a gentle bearhug and call the cops.

What would people do in such a robot house?

As Joseph Engelberger puts it, "Anything they damn please!"

No. of Words: 2284

Reading Time: _____

Selection 28

Is the Perfect Worker a Mindless Idiot?

VOCABULARY BUILDING

Below are several words used in this article. They are presented in the context of the sentences or phrases in which they occur. If you are unsure of their meanings and cannot define them from the context, look them up in the dictionary. Spaces are provided for additional unfamiliar words from the article to add to your vocabulary.

1. "'Even today's most sophisticated industrial robot would have to accept being called a mere oaf as a high *accolade*.'"

   accolade:_____

2. ". . . Unimates endlessly swing heavy *harrow* discs into a *hearth* for tempering, then snatch them up as they emerge, white-hot."

   harrow:_____

   hearth:_____

3. "(. . . it looks like a cobra *undulating* in a snake charmer's basket) . . ."

   undulating:_____

4. ". . . it can pick up a part no matter how *askew* it is on the conveyor belt, . . ."

   askew:_____

5. _____ :_____

6. _____ :_____

7. _____ :_____

8. _____ :_____

RETENTION AND COMPREHENSION

A. True/False (1 point each)

1. At an international robot conference, one robot surprised spectators by playing poker.

   1. T _____ F _____

2. A recent study has predicted that, by the year 2000, only 10% of the country's workers will be employed in manufacturing.

   2. T _____ F _____

3. There are already over 2000 mechanical robots on the job in the United States.

   3. T _____ F _____

4. The cheapest robot still costs about $100,000.

   4. T _____ F _____

5. Presently, robots are used mostly in the automotive industry.

   5. T _____ F _____

B. Completion (3 points each)

6. Auto industry experts estimate that robots cost about $4.80 an hour compared to as much as _____ per hour in wages and benefits for humans.

   6. _____

7. Carnegie-Mellon University researchers have developed a robot that responds to about _____ English words.

   7. _____

8. Purdue University researchers have developed a robot sophisticated enough to write characters in the _____ language.

   8. _____

9. One Massachusetts inventor has developed a robot that makes _____.

   9. _____

10. The author suggests that a house robot could be a fire alarm and might even catch _____ _____.

    10. _____

C. Multiple Choice (2 points each)

11. Citicorp's robot mailman is directed by (a) a radio control system, (b) a chemical trail on the floor, (c) a computerized video camera, (d) a word processor attached to its transistors.

    11. _____

12. The most popular robot looks like (a) C3P0 from *Star Wars,* (b) HAL from *2001: A Space Odyssey,* (c) a tank turret with a gun barrel-like steel claw, (d) a six-legged beetle.

12. _____

13. The Binks Manufacturing Company robot paint sprayer is talented enough to (a) remember and mix the right colors, (b) anticipate problems in the assembly line, (c) paint cartoons if shown how, (d) decrease or increase the thickness of paint it sprays.

13. _____

14. Unlike the "first" generation of robots, the "second" generation of robots will have (a) "eyes," (b) "brains," (c) "arms," (d) "thumbs."

14. _____

15. Manufacturers need perfected robots that can (a) diagnose their own disorders; (b) stop welding when, for instance, cars are slightly out of place; (c) select and pick up parts that are not exactly just so; (d) work with humans and other robots.

15. _____

16. An example of a job which most humans do not like but is perfect for robots is (a) mowing the lawn, (b) sorting nuts and bolts, (c) delivering the mail, (d) spray painting the insides of vans.

16. _____

17. The "HAL versus C3P0 question" refers to (a) the older and more modern robot forms, (b) creating robots that can work side by side with humans, (c) whether robots will be employed only by manufacturers or only by consumers, (d) what form future robots will take.

17. _____

18. Which is *not* mentioned as a solution to unemployment caused by the use of robots? (a) early retirement, (b) shorter work weeks, (c) creation of more people-centered jobs, (d) retraining programs.

18. _____

D. Thematic (11 points)

19. Which statement *best* expresses the theme (*main* idea) of the article?

   (a) No mater how humanlike robots become, they will never replace actual people in factories.

   (b) As robots become cheaper and more sophisticated, they will relieve human labor from doing unpleasant tasks.

19. _____

(c) Foreign countries have made greater advances in the design, manufacture, and use of robots than the United States has.

(d) Robots may make man's life easier at work and at home, but no robot can exist without human control.

E. Purpose *(9 points)*

20. The author's *chief* purpose is   20. _____

(a) to present an argument for the increased use of robots in the United States.

(b) to tell how robots will change the work habits of American assembly line and office employees.

(c) to explain the difference between self-contained, manlike robots that need human commands and vast, single-unit computers that are not dependent on human direction.

(d) to inform the reader of current examples of robot use and possible developments in the employment of robots.

Total Retention and Comprehension Score: _____

QUESTIONS FOR DISCUSSION (MEANING AND TECHNIQUE)

1. What did you think robots did and looked like before you read this article? On what did you base your ideas?

2. What robot characteristics determine its sophistication? What does T³ look like and what can it do? How sophisticated is it compared to other robots?

3. What are the differences between a HAL-type robot and a C3P0-type robot? Why are they at an "evolutionary fork"?

4. Whose views are presented on the question of unemployment created by the replacement of human workers by robots? Are these views representative of other segments of people engaged in production?

5. In describing one type of robot, the writer said they worked "like mother robins feeding worms to their chicks." Does that help you to visualize how robots function? Find other similes or comparisons that help you understand more about robots.

6. What do the authorities quoted in the article predict for the future of robots in the world and in the United States?

7. Are robots becoming more or less expensive? Is there a parallel in the history of cost between transistor radios and robots? Explain.

SUGGESTIONS FOR WRITING

1. Is a computer a robot? How about an automatic garage door opener? A remote control parking lot sweeper? Write a paper telling what a robot is so that most people could distinguish between simple machines and robots.

2. If you have experience working where an actual robot was used, describe what it looked like and what it did. Was its job formerly done by a human? What were the problems? Benefits?

3. Write a composition explaining how an automatic bank teller or change-making machine works. Describe its advantages and disadvantages.

4. Will robots put people out of work or not? Explain.

5. Imagine doing your tasks at work or at home without machines. Write a paper showing how things would be different for you.

6. Is your place of employment up-to-date or behind the times in the use of computers and electronic equipment? Can you compare it to other places that do the same kind of work? Give your opinion and the reasons for it in an essay.

7. In a paper, describe a funny, frightening, or frustrating experience you had with a mechanical or electronic device (a computerized chess game, for example).

8. The word "robot" is sometimes used to describe a person. Do you know someone you consider a "robot"? In a paragraph, explain why.

9. What occupations do you think will never be completely replaced by machines or computers? Think of several and explain why in a paper.

10. Suppose that the decisions baseball umpires make could be automated. Write a composition explaining how it might be done.

Selection 28

Overall Reading Performance

Your overall reading performance is a combination of how fast you read and how much you comprehend and retain. The chart below allows you to find out quickly your "overall reading performance."

First enter your "reading time" and your "retention and comprehension" score in the two blanks at the bottom of the page. Then simply lay a straightedge of any kind (the edge of a sheet of paper or a pencil will do) across the chart, placing the left side of the straightedge at the appropriate point on the "Reading Rate" scale, and the right side at the appropriate point on the "Retention and Comprehension" scale. The point at which the paper or pencil intersects the scale in the middle of the page will indicate your overall performance.

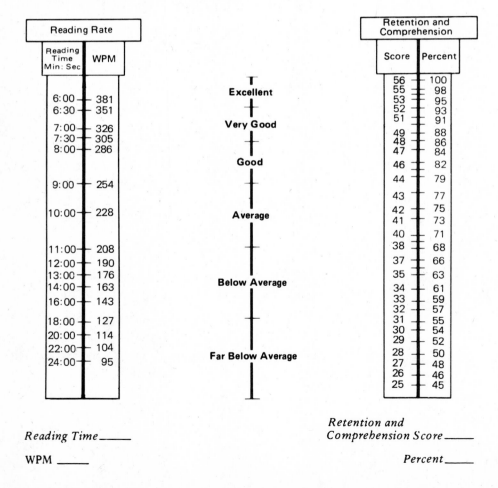

Reading Rate	
Reading Time Min: Sec	WPM
6:00	381
6:30	351
7:00	326
7:30	305
8:00	286
9:00	254
10:00	228
11:00	208
12:00	190
13:00	176
14:00	163
16:00	143
18:00	127
20:00	114
22:00	104
24:00	95

Excellent

Very Good

Good

Average

Below Average

Far Below Average

Retention and Comprehension	
Score	Percent
56	100
55	98
53	95
52	93
51	91
49	88
48	86
47	84
46	82
44	79
43	77
42	75
41	73
40	71
38	68
37	66
35	63
34	61
33	59
32	57
31	55
30	54
29	52
28	50
27	48
26	46
25	45

*Reading Time*_____

WPM _____

Retention and
*Comprehension Score*_____

*Percent*_____

Selection 29

Minuteman Crews Await Armageddon

MICHAEL SEILER

MINOT, N.D.—Under 60 feet of concrete, soil and rock, Mike Perkins and Scott Berry sit in a metal container called Oscar.

They are at the approximate hub of 10 silos, each of which holds a Minuteman 3 missile. Each silo is at least three miles from the next, and from three to seven miles from Oscar. Perkins and Berry are responsible for all 10.

Every minute of every day, there are 28 other men like Perkins and Berry sitting in vaults buried under the North Dakota plains—15 crews in all, responsible for a total of 150 missiles. Each missile is armed with three independently targeted nuclear warheads.

If it ever had to be given, the presidential order would come to the 15 containers; the men inside would push the switches—at least they all say they would—and Perkins, Berry and the rest would have no reason to bother climbing out.

Of course, the theory behind the presence of the men, the containers and the missiles scattered under 8,000 square miles of wheat and cattle country just south of the Canadian border is that their readiness guarantees that the order never need be given.

They are the third leg of the nation's nuclear deterrent—Polaris and Poseidon missile-carrying submarines are one, the Air Force's B-52s are the other—and it is this triad concept that has come under increasing scrutiny lately.

Last month, the Pentagon began a major review of the United States' strategic posture. The study, ordered by President Carter, is supposed to determine how much deterrent is enough.

At the heart of the review is the concern that by the mid-1980s the 1,000 Minuteman missiles in their concrete silos at Minot and elsewhere under the Great Plains will be up against larger, more accurate Soviet missiles than those the U.S.S.R. has now.

Source: from *Los Angeles Times,* Jan. 1, 1978. Copyright, 1978, *Los Angeles Times.* Reprinted by permission.

The Pentagon already has a replacement in mind for the Minuteman. In October, Defense Secretary Harold Brown gave the go-ahead to the Air Force to begin preliminary work on the MX missile, larger and more powerful than the Minuteman.

The MX system, if it ever is built, would be composed of mobile missiles moved around in concrete-lined underground trenches several miles long. The system eventually could cost as much as $40 billion.

With MX still only a drawingboard concept, the Minuteman remains important—and impressive. The best place to see it and understand it, the Strategic Air Command (SAC) people say, is here. And the best time to see and understand the men who make it work is now.

Winter came to North Dakota early this year, leaving a 2-foot-deep layer of snow over the gently rolling hills and plateaus around Minot Air Force Base. The snow will remain until spring.

There are no thaws in a North Dakota winter, say the Air Force personnel who work here. There is only the snow and cold. Temperatures as low as minus 40 are common, and often the winds blow down from Canada so strongly that the wind-chill reading approaches minus 80.

It is hardly the ideal place for an Air Force base. But the location—only 80 miles from the geographic center of North America—gives Minot more advance warning of a potential enemy attack than any other SAC installation in the country.

Capt. Doug Martin, in charge of a Minuteman maintenance crew at Minot, was standing inside the 10-foot-high fence surrounding a missile silo one day recently, talking about the weather in a soft Tennessee accent.

Routine maintenance of the missiles in their silos becomes a complicated task in winter and often has to wait until the weather improves, he said.

"We had four days last week it was so cold that we didn't send a (maintenance) team off base," Martin said. "Once it (the wind-chill reading)—gets down to minus 65, we button up the hole and send the (maintenance) guys back to base," he said while his men worked over the open silo. "People are more important than missiles."

On a bad day, when the wind-chill approaches but doesn't quite reach minus 65, Martin said his men can work for only 20 minutes at a time. Then they have to climb back into their trucks to warm up.

The weather is a constant enemy in winter, Martin said. Little pieces of equipment—bolts and nuts—freeze, and the snow is always there to be cleared away before the maintenance men can open the 100-ton concrete hatch to get to the missile itself. Snow and ice removal normally takes about five hours—first with bulldozers, then picks and axes.

If the Minuteman actually had to be fired, the hatch over its silo would be blown open by an explosive charge and the weight of the snow and ice would have no effect.

The launch site itself is an acre of land with almost nothing visible above ground, except a light post and three radar devices to spot intruders.

The radar is supersensitive, Martin said, and routinely sounds an alarm when tumbleweeds, ducks, rabbits or even field mice find their way inside the perimeter.

Teams of Air Force security guards armed with M-16 rifles are dispatched to the unmanned sites when the alarm goes off, usually to find nothing more challenging than a flock of geese.

When maintenance men open the hatch, they almost always discover nests of mice that have taken refuge in the top of the silo.

Each Minuteman missile is protected from the shock of a nuclear explosion by a spring-suspended base that can move as much as 4 feet up or down. A cushion of foam rubber, which lines the inside of the concrete hole is there for the same purpose.

The missile itself—6 feet wide, 60 feet long and weighing 78,000 pounds—has a range of more than 6,000 miles and attains a speed of 15,000 m.p.h. Its three one-megaton warheads will fall within yards of their targets.

But first, people such as Mike Perkins and Scott Berry have to throw the switch.

Perkins, 31, the launch control facility commander, is a first lieutenant from Greeley, Colo. Berry, 24, is a first lieutenant from Salem, Ore.

They have both thought about their job, the power behind their launch switches, the possibility that one day the message from the President through SAC headquarters might be the real thing.

But worry about it? Anticipate the unthinkable? Not quite.

"Do you worry about driving the Los Angeles freeways?" asked Perkins, rhetorically. "It scares the devil out of me. I'm sure on a day-to-day basis people in L.A. don't think about driving on the freeways. They think about doing their jobs. Their jobs require them to get from point A to point B. Our jobs require us to be here."

Berry said, "When you look at those 10 green lights (indicating that Oscar's 10 Minuteman missiles are functioning normally and can be launched, if the order comes), it's really difficult to believe there are missiles and nuclear weapons out there.

"We work with that knowledge, day in and day out, so much that we don't really look at it that way. We just deal with what we can see in here, and what I see is 10 green lights and it's my job to keep them green as much as possible."

But what if the order really came?

"The shock would undoubtedly surprise everyone," said Perkins. "But I don't think there would be any hesitation, any stopping for a second to think about it, any moral deliberation."

"I agree," said Berry. "Five minutes after it's all over, I'd wonder if it really happened. I think you have to have that initial certainty to work here. The minute you let doubt start, it's going to snowball. You have to believe that when the President says go to war, we're going to war. Otherwise everything out here is useless."

Perkins and Berry are scheduled to work 24 hours straight—alternating with 24 hours off—but North Dakota winters being what they are, launch crews frequently are marooned in their capsules for 48 or even 72 hours.

Often, the county roads, some unpaved, that serve the area ice over and relief crews remain at the base—more than 20 miles away.

Entrance to Oscar is through a small frame building housing several security guards, a cook and other support personnel, down a concrete shaft in a slow-moving freight elevator and then through two 8-ton blast doors.

Oscar itself is a small container suspended on shock absorbers inside a concrete-and-steel vault that has walls 4 feet thick. The capsule's interior is painted lime green, as are the computer components and control panels that fill the room.

The monotony of the green is broken only by the soft red covering of two padded chairs, one for the crew commander, one for his assistant.

There is a chemical toilet at one end of the room, a cot further down along the opposite wall. Neither is curtained off from Oscar's bright neon lights.

Until a policy change last summer, crew members worked 12-hour shifts and were not allowed to nap on duty.

Now, with the 24-hour schedule, they routinely take turns sleeping.

A small oven for heating the frozen dinners sent down from the support building above, an AM-FM radio and a 9-inch, black-and-white television set comprise Oscar's spartan creature comforts.

But Oscar isn't there for comfort. Basically, its crew serves two functions.

The first is to monitor messages coming over five different communications links—high frequency, very high frequency and ultra-high frequency radio systems, a teletype and land telephone lines (Minot's command capsules and silos are connected by 1,500 miles of protected underground cables).

The second function is obvious enough: to be ready to launch the 10 missiles. Obvious, but not simple.

The procedure, in case of a presidential launch order, goes roughly like this:

The two crew members decode the message, which includes an "enabling" code, then turn to a small red metal box located above the assistant's console. The box is secured by two combination locks (each crew member knows only his lock's combination).

Inside the box are two keys and authentication documents that enable the crew to prove that the go-to-war order is real.

The two men sit in front of their consoles and feed the "enabling" code into their computer (in effect, arming the missiles).

An alarm bell rings. The men insert their keys—the keyholes are 12 feet from each other so that one man cannot insert both.

The commander starts his countdown:

"Five . . . four . . . three . . . two . . . one . . . Key turn."

The two men turn their keys simultaneously and hold them in the launch position for a five-second count by the commander:

"One . . . two . . . three . . . four . . . five . . . Release."

The light on the console panel that says "Missile Away" lights up. It is all over—unrecallable and quite final.

"It is ingrained in us, month after month after month, that we can do it—boom, boom, boom," said Berry, quickly snapping his fingers three times.

But there is one final safeguard. It would take more than just the two-man crew of Oscar to launch the 10 Minuteman missiles. At least one other crew in one of the four other launch control capsules in Oscar's squadron would have to go through the same process with its own 10 missiles for Oscar's Minutemen to be fired.

All the Minuteman crews are subject to the Air Force's "human reliability program." Crew members are routinely taken off the alert cycle in case of death in the family, serious illness or marital problems.

SAC officers say initial screening for Minuteman training at Vandenberg Air Force Base in California tends to weed out those who might have fundamental doubts about their ability to do the job or who have any tendencies toward instability.

Under the human reliability program, officers who acquire those doubts or tendencies later in their careers are reported by their superior officers or peers.

Senior officers here insist, in the words of one squadron commander at Minot, "There's not a sense of ratting on your buddies." Nor, they say, is there any moral stigma attached to being removed from alert duty.

It is simply an accepted fact of life that men dealing with nuclear weapons must be subject to close scrutiny and that their mental health and stability are not strictly a personal matter.

The average age of a Minuteman crewman is 25. For their age, they seem to deal well with the essentially static nature of their jobs.

Crew members of a missile-launching submarine can at least take some pride in completing another 60-day cruise, even though that cruise might not amount to anything more than circling in the middle of the North Atlantic.

And the men who fly B-52s can find satisfaction in a practice mission—including some stomach-jolting low-level simulated bomb runs—successfully completed.

But a Minuteman crew's only satisfaction is knowing that the missiles are ready to go, if needed.

"The more sophisticated the equipment is, the more you are bored," admitted one Minuteman squadron commander.

Said another missile officer, "Occasionally you get to the point where you hope something will break, so you will have something to do."

There's at least one partial cure for this frustration. Several times a year, a Minuteman is removed from its silo, its warheads are placed in storage here and the missile itself shipped to Vandenberg.

A launch crew and supporting personnel travel with the missile and launch it over the Pacific from Vandenberg.

Almost invariably, the Minuteman performs as expected and the men get the satisfaction of knowing the missile works. "It's really enjoyable to see the thing you've been working on for years fly," said one maintenance sergeant with a smile.

And that, they all agree, is better than the possibility Mike Perkins was discussing with a visitor to Oscar.

"Five or 10 minutes after a real launch," he said, "we'd start wondering what precipitated this action and start worrying about our families."

He wasn't smiling.

No. of Words: 2299

Reading Time: _____

Selection 29

Minuteman Crews Await Armageddon

VOCABULARY BUILDING

Below are several words used in this article. They are presented in the context of the sentences or phrases in which they occur. If you are unsure of their meanings and cannot define them from the context, look them up in the dictionary. Spaces are provided for additional unfamiliar words from the article to add to your vocabulary.

1. "Minuteman Crews Await *Armageddon*."

   *Armageddon:*_____

2. "They are the third leg of the nation's *nuclear deterrent* . . . and it is this *triad concept* that has come under increasing *scrutiny* lately."

   *nuclear:*_____

   *deterrent:*_____

   *triad:*_____

   *concept:*_____

   *scrutiny:*_____

3. ". . . tumbleweeds, ducks, rabbits, or even field mice find their way inside the *perimeter*."

   *perimeter:*_____

4. "'Do you worry about driving the Los Angeles freeway?' asked Perkins, *rhetorically*."

   *rhetorically:*_____

5. "'But I don't think there would be any hesitation, any stopping for a second to think about it, any moral *deliberation*.'"

   *deliberation:*_____

6. "'I think you have to have that *initial* certainty to work here.'"

   *initial:*_____

7. "... launch crews frequently are *marooned* in their capsules for 48 or even 72 hours."

   *marooned:*_____

8. "... [various conveniences] *comprise* Oscar's *spartan creature comforts.*"

   *comprise:*_____

   *spartan:*_____

   *creature comforts:*_____

9. "Nor ... is there any moral *stigma* attached to being removed from alert duty."

   *stigma:*_____

10. "'Five or 10 minutes after a real launch ... we'd start wondering what *precipitated* this action ...'"

    *precipitated:*_____

11. _____:_____

12. _____:_____

13. _____:_____

14. _____:_____

15. _____:_____

RETENTION AND COMPREHENSION

A. True/False (1 point each)

1. "Oscar" is the name of a Minuteman missile.   1. T _____ F _____

2. Each missile is armed with three independently targeted nuclear warheads.   2. T _____ F _____

3. The missile warheads can travel over 6000 miles and land within yards of their targets.   3. T _____ F _____

4. Only the capsule crew commander can launch the missile with his key.   4. T _____ F _____

5. The Minot Air Force Base is about 1000 miles from the geographic center of North America.

5. T _____ F _____

B. Completion *(3 points each)*

6. The launch keyholes are _____ feet from each other.

6. _____

7. The average age of a Minuteman crewman is _____.

7. _____

8. The number of missiles controlled by each launch capsule is _____.

8. _____

9. The number of "legs" in the nation's nuclear deterrent force is _____.

9. _____

10. The missile system which may eventually replace the Minuteman is called _____.

10. _____

C. Multiple Choice *(2 points each)*

11. When the radar sounds an alarm (a) the capsule commander prepares to launch the missiles, (b) the commander opens the small red metal box, (c) teams of security guards are sent to investigate, (d) a presidential aide is notified immediately.

11. _____

12. When maintenance men open the hatch at the top of a silo (a) they almost always find nests of mice, (b) they usually find a flock of geese, (c) the crews know something is up, (d) the missile is about to be launched.

12. _____

13. The launch capsule is equipped with (a) a color television, (b) two cots, (c) a complete kitchen, (d) none of the above.

13. _____

14. To launch a capsule requires the participation of (a) three crew members, (b) two control capsules, (c) the Air Force base commander, (d) the human reliability program director.

14. _____

15. The Minuteman missiles (a) are never launched without a presidential order, (b) have never been flown so far, (c) always perform as expected, (d) are launched every so often over the Pacific from Vandenberg.

15. _____

16. The green lights on the launch control panel indicate that (a) the missiles are functioning normally and are ready to be launched, (b) the crew members should decode the "enabling" message, (c) the crew should take the first step in the lauching procedure, (d) the missiles have been launched and all is well.

16. _____

17. The human reliability program is supposed to (a) assure that missiles are launched only when ordered, (b) weed out unreliable applicants, (c) monitor the mental health and stability of crew members, (d) provide counseling help to disturbed crew members.

17. _____

18. There are fifteen crews at Minot Air Force Base, monitoring a total of (a) 15 missiles, (b) 45 missiles, (c) 150 missiles, (d) 1500 missiles.

18. _____

D. Thematic (11 points)

19. Which statement *best* expresses the theme (*main idea*) of the article?
    (a) The Minuteman crew members are young but highly trained to be reliable, ready, and willing to launch the missiles whenever the order comes through.
    (b) Although the Minuteman missiles buried in the earth in North Dakota are highly accurate, fast, and deadly, they may have to be replaced soon by a new missile system.
    (c) There are many highly accurate, fast, and deadly missiles buried in the earth in North Dakota, always ready to be launched by crew members—with safeguards to prevent an accidental or unauthorized launch.
    (d) The severe winters in North Dakota and the isolation the crew members experience there makes the assignment particularly difficult.

19. _____

E. Purpose (9 points)

20. The author's *chief* purpose is
    (a) to awaken the public to the dangers of a nuclear war.

20. _____

(b) to give some facts about the workings of a nuclear missile launch crew.

(c) to expose the public to the problems faced by
the launch crew members.

(d) to explain that an accidental launch of a nuclear missile is almost impossible.

Total Retention and Comprehension Score: _____

QUESTIONS FOR DISCUSSION (MEANING AND TECHNIQUE)

1. Look up the word "Armageddon." How is it pronounced? What does
it mean? What language is it from? What book is it from originally?
What does it have to do with the subject of this article?

2. In the fifth paragraph the author says the theory behind the missiles is
"that their readiness guarantees that the order to fire the missiles
never need be given." What do you think of this theory? Is it valid?

3. Some people think the more of these missiles we (and others) have,
the greater the chance there is they'll be used. What do you think of
this theory?

4. Why do some people think these one-megaton nuclear missiles (that
can go 6000 miles at 15,000 miles per hour and land within a few
yards of their targets) need to be replaced by an MX? Do you agree?
Why or why not?

5. Could you (would you) turn the key to fire these missiles? Why or
why not?

6. Where does the introduction to this article end and the body begin?
Does the introduction give interesting background that whets your
appetite for more information? How?

7. Name some of the details given in the body of the article that make it
not only informative but interesting.

8. The last sentence of the article is "He wasn't smiling." Is that a good
concluding sentence? What does it mean in a broad sense? What does
it make you think about?

9. Most people know about our missiles, but do most people have a
concrete image or picture of how and where they're placed and who
mans them and how they can (or can't) be fired? Does it affect your
feelings about them when you find out these details about them?
How? Why?

10. Do you think an exchange of nuclear missiles is winnable or survivable? In what sense? Would you want to survive one?

11. What is a "nuclear freeze"? Are you for it or against it? Why?

12. Is it possible to disarm or cutback arms? Why or why not?

13. Are the safeguards against accidental or unwarranted firings "failsafe"? Why or why not?

SUGGESTIONS FOR WRITING

1. Write an "argument" essay for or against nuclear disarmament or a nuclear freeze. Give good reasons. Look up important facts.

2. Write a composition (based on some research) describing the effects of a one-megaton nuclear explosion.

3. Write an essay (based on some research) for or against the MX. Give good reasons.

4. Imagine yourself a Minuteman crewmember inside an "Oscar." What are your thoughts and feelings—describe them.

5. Imagine yourself as a crewmember emerging from your "Oscar" (assuming you can) several days after a nuclear war: describe your thoughts/feelings/experiences.

6. Write an essay explaining why you think you would (or wouldn't) turn the firing key if the order came.

7. Write a description (after some research) of our total nuclear capability (what is the "triad concept"?) and what it could do to any targeted nation and/or the world.

8. Write an essay explaining why you think a nuclear war is or isn't winnable and/or survivable. Give good reasons.

9. Write an essay explaining why the safeguards against accidental or unwarranted firings are or aren't "failsafe." Deal with anticipated counterarguments.

Selection 29

Overall Reading Performance

Your overall reading performance is a combination of how fast you read and how much you comprehend and retain. The chart below allows you to find out quickly your "overall reading performance."

First enter your "reading time" and your "retention and comprehension" score in the two blanks at the bottom of the page. Then simply lay a straightedge of any kind (the edge of a sheet of paper or a pencil will do) across the chart, placing the left side of the straightedge at the appropriate point on the "Reading Rate" scale, and the right side at the appropriate point on the "Retention and Comprehension" scale. The point at which the paper or pencil intersects the scale in the middle of the page will indicate your overall performance.

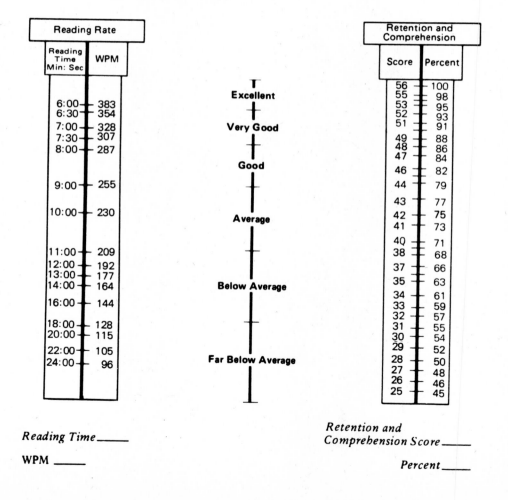

Reading Time_____

WPM _____

Retention and
Comprehension Score_____

Percent_____

Selection 30

Joshua Slocum's Magnificent Voyage

PIERRE BERTON

One of the most experienced saltwater men of his age, a master mariner who refused to accommodate himself to steam, he stubbornly set sail on his greatest adventure: a three-year journey, alone, around the world

May 6, 1896. The sun burnishes the South Pacific sky. In all the vast circle of the ocean, there is only a single moving speck, a sloop barely 36 feet long, aptly named the *Spray,* sliding westward on the hot breath of a tropic breeze. Her decks are empty. No one is at the helm. She will remain alone in the immensity of the southern sea for 72 days, until she reaches Samoa, nearly 7000 miles as the gull flies. And this is only a small part of a remarkable odyssey.

Aboard the *Spray,* Joshua Slocum sits in his book-lined cabin, totally alone, as he has been since he departed Yarmouth, Nova Scotia, the previous July. He is reading his way through his library, especially the stories of his favorite authors, Robert Louis Stevenson and Mark Twain. Occasionally he pokes about in his galley, or digs out his sextant to check his longitude.

At 52, he is one of the most experienced saltwater men of his age, but also an anachronism—a committed sailor in a world that has done with sail. But Slocum, the out-of-work sea captain, doesn't care. Too old to learn new tricks, he has embarked on an adventure no one else has dared, sailing by himself around the world. Forty-six thousand miles. Three full years. Another lifetime.

For what else is left for Slocum? He has stacked salt cod out of Kamchatka, gunpowder from Shanghai to Taiwan, sugar from the Philippines, timber out of Brazil. He has broken three mutinies, survived storms, hidden reefs and the explosion of Krakatoa in the East Indies, which killed 36,000 persons in August 1883—but not Joshua Slocum, who sailed past

Source: The Reader's Digest, Feb. 1977. Reprinted from "My Country" by permission of McClelland and Stewart, Ltd.

the volcanic island while it was in full eruption.

He has made fortunes. His race to catch the crack mail schooner out of Honolulu brought him a $5000 sack of gold. But he has also lost everything. The lovely barque *Aquidneck* was battered to pieces off Brazil with a full cargo of timber, leaving him a pauper.

Since the age of 16, Slocum's whole existence has revolved around saltwater. All seven of his children were born at sea or in foreign ports. The wife who bore them, the marvelous Virginia, sailed with him on every voyage, from their honeymoon trip out of Sydney, Australia, to that last voyage aboard the *Aquidneck*. When a mutineer stabbed Slocum's first officer aboard the *Northern Light* in 1882, Virginia had covered her husband, a revolver in each hand, as he subdued the crew. Her death at 34 was a terrible blow. His 24-year-old cousin, Hettie, whom he married 19 months later, could not take her place. After one remarkable 5500-mile voyage together, from Brazil to the Carolinas, they usually lived apart.

So here he is, alone as he now prefers to be—Joshua Slocum, born in 1844 in Nova Scotia into the age of clipper ships: a seaman at 16, second mate at 18, master of his own ship at 25, king of the ocean at 37, washed up at 50. Joshua Slocum, master mariner, stubbornly refusing to come to any accommodation with steam power or iron hulls, instead picking up odd jobs on Boston harbor boats and dreaming of the great days of canvas, hating his work, until one day a load of coal half-buries him. He can stand it no more: he determines to return to the sea.

Spring 1893. In a pasture at Fairhaven, Mass., the hulk of a rotting oyster sloop lies propped in a field. Slocum can have her; her owner is a friend. Like a sculptor gazing on a lump of Carrara marble, Slocum sees a new ship hidden somewhere in the old. He will keep her name, *Spray,* but little else. He cuts new timbers to replace the old, and the new ship takes form: 36 feet, nine inches overall; nine tons net; rigged as a sloop—a big craft for a lone man to handle. She has no engine, no power windlass, few navigational aids save a compass, some charts, a sextant. But there's a secret to her, which even Slocum doesn't yet know. He has hit upon a perfectly balanced vessel that, ballasted with cement, will be almost impossible to capsize. He has worked on her for 13 months, supporting himself with odd jobs, and she has cost him exactly $553.62.

Though the *Spray* claims Boston as her home port, Slocum's voyage will really begin at Yarmouth. He has come back to Nova Scotia to spend six weeks in the hometown he ran away from a generation before. He decides he'll sail eastward, through the Mediterranean, the Suez Canal and the Red Sea. He has two barrels of ship's bread soldered up in tin cans. He has flour and baking powder. He has salt beef, salt pork, ham and slabs of dried codfish. He has condensed milk in tins, butter in brine and muslin, eggs hermetically sealed, potatoes that he will roast in their jackets, sugar and tea, and coffee beans that he will grind himself. He is without a chronometer—he cannot afford the $15 it will cost to have his old one cleaned and reset. So he buys a tin clock in Yarmouth for a dollar; its face is smashed—no matter.

July 2, 1895. Slocum and the *Spray* clear Yarmouth harbor at a fast eight knots, scurrying past Sable Island to get clear of the track of the ocean liners which might run them down at night. He has designed a self-steer-ing mechanism and discovers that it is successful beyond his wildest dreams. He can lash the helm and sleep while the sloop holds her course. But he cannot shake off the realization that he is totally alone. He shouts commands, fearful that in the long days ahead he may lose his ability to speak.

He reaches the Azores in just 18 days. He has some letters to mail and he takes on a cargo of fruit, the gift of the islanders. Later he harpoons and roasts a turtle, with fried potatoes on the side. When he reaches Gibraltar on August 4, he finds that he has crossed the Atlantic in near-record time. And here he learns that he must turn back. The British officers who wine and dine him urge him to avoid the Red Sea. This narrow waterway is infested with pirates for whom he would be an easy victim. So Slocum sets the *Spray's* course westward for Brazil.

Irony of ironies: He is scarcely back in the Atlantic before he encoun-ters pirates in a Spanish felucca. He changes course but the felucca, a swift and slender sailboat, continues to close. Quickly, he reefs the mainsail and prepares for an unequal fight; and then a monstrous wave strikes both ships. Slocum snatches up a rifle to ward off his attackers—only to find that the wave has destroyed the felucca's rigging. Exhausted but safe, he sets the sloop back on course.

It takes 40 uneventful days to recross the Atlantic. Later, the dauntless Nova Scotian runs into furious seas along the Argentine coast. A towering wave roars down, swamping the *Spray*. She reels, rights herself and sails on. In the Strait of Magellan, he sails into a southwest gale. "I had only a moment to douse sail and lash all solid when it struck like a shot from a cannon . . . For 30 hours it kept on blowing hard." Finally he puts into Punta Arenas.

February 19, 1896. Back in the fury of the strait, he has encountered the dreaded williwaws, "compressed gales" of wind that strike vertically down the mountain slopes. He reaches Froward Cape, the southernmost point of the South American mainland; and here he meets a group of pirates led by one Black Pedro, notorious as the worst murderer on the bleak islands of Tierra del Fuego. Shrieking, they attack the *Spray* in canoes, but Slocum fires a shot across the bow of the nearest boat and aims another close to Black Pedro himself. They turn tail.

The *Spray* clears Cape Pilar and enters the Pacific. But a violent storm drives her down the coast of Tierra del Fuego toward Cape Horn. She runs for four days before the gale, her mainsail in rags. Slocum rigs up a square sail to replace it. The seas are mountainous and in the distance he can hear the deafening roar of tremendous breakers. As dawn lightens the sky, in a remarkable display of seamanship he somehow guides the *Spray* through a foaming labyrinth of hidden rocks and tiny channels to the comparative safety of some small islands near the Strait of Magellan. "Jaded and worn," he feeds himself a meal of venison stew; then, after sprinkling his deck with tacks, he turns in. At midnight he is awakened by shrieks. Some natives have boarded the *Spray;* startled by the tacks, they leap into their canoes, and flee into the night. Slocum goes back to sleep.

Two days later, when the gales abate, he sets sail again. He salvages a barrel of wine and an entire cargo of tallow from the wreckage of a doomed ship. The tallow comes in 800-pound casks which he must winch aboard. But the old sea trader knows its value. He tries several times to reach the Pacific but is driven back by new gales. An Argentine cruiser offers to tow him east to safety; but he will not give up. On his seventh attempt he succeeds.

April 14, 1896. As the *Spray* sails out into the Pacific, a giant roller washes over her. Slocum has been at the helm for 30 hours. But soon the sloop is under full sail. Next stop: the Juan Fernández islands, where Alexander Selkirk, the real-life castaway who was Defoe's model for Robinson Crusoe, was marooned.

On this "blessed island," a boatload of natives greets the mariner, who treats them to a breakfast of coffee and doughnuts cooked in the salvaged tallow. They are delighted. He shows them how to make doughnuts and then sells them the tallow; they reward him with a pile of gold coins salvaged from a sunken galleon. He scampers about the hills with their children, picking ripe quinces that he will preserve as he sails out again across the empty Pacific on a 72-day leg to Samoa.

July 16, 1896. The *Spray* casts anchor in Samoa. Three lissome women approach in a canoe. But Slocum is far more interested in the widow of his hero, Robert Louis Stevenson. She comes down to greet him personally and presents him with her husband's sailing directories, which he accepts with "reverential awe."

After an idyllic month in Samoa he sails for Australia, where enthusiastic welcomes await him. There he recoups his finances, moving from Sydney to Melbourne to Tasmania, lecturing as he goes to paying audiences. Then he swings north again.

May 24, 1897. The *Spray* moves gingerly through the Great Barrier Reef opposite New Guinea. The newspapers report that Slocum is lost at sea. Not until he arrives at Mauritius, in the Indian Ocean, in September can they correct the error.

Meantime, he has been the chief actor in a comic-opera scene on the remote island of Rodrigues, some thousand miles east of Madagascar. The local abbé has been filling the islanders' heads with tales of the approaching Antichrist, a piece of sermonizing calculated to keep them on the narrowest of pathways. Suddenly, into the harbor, scudding before a heavy gale, her sails all feather-white and her single gaunt occupant holding down the deck like a bearded prophet, comes the *Spray*. To the jetty flock the faithful, fearfully crying that the Antichrist has truly arrived. The islanders soon recover, however, and entertain him royally. On he sails to Durban in South Africa, where he is introduced to the explorer Henry Stanley. Livingstone's savior is fascinated that the ship has traveled through treacherous waters without any built-in buoyancy compartments. What would happen, he asks, if the *Spray* should strike a rock? Slocum's reply: "She must be kept away from the rocks."

March 26, 1898. Slocum sails from South Africa for St. Helena, the island of Napoleon's exile in the south Atlantic. A celebrity by now, he dines with the governor and, unhappily, allows a goat put on board by a friend to remain. The goat begins to eat his way through the ship. No rope can hold him; he devours everything, including the charts of the Caribbean. Finally he munches Slocum's straw hat. Slocum suffers the presence of the ravenous goat for nearly a thousand miles until, at Ascension Island, he sets him ashore.

Off the coast of Brazil, the U.S. battleship *Oregon* speeds up behind him and hoists a puzzling signal: *Are there any men-of-war about?* Slocum is baffled. He doesn't know that war has broken out between the United States and Spain. *Let us keep together for mutual protection,* he signals back. The *Oregon* ignores this badinage and steams away.

Chartless and cursing his late passenger, the goat, he racks his memory of wind and water as he approaches Trinidad. He moves from island to island, packing lecture halls with accounts of his adventures. He is becalmed for eight days north of the Bahamas, in seas so smooth that each evening he can read by candlelight. A three-day gale follows the calm, and he begins to weary of the ocean—"tired, tired, tired, of baffling squalls and fretful cobble-seas."

June 26, 1898. Slocum reaches Newport, R.I., and journey's end. Because of the war, the harbor is mined and he must hug the rocks as he brings his sloop into port. At one the following morning he casts anchor. He cannot suppress a sense of triumph: the *Spray* is sound as a nut and hasn't leaked a drop. But no bands greet him. No civic dignitaries clamber aboard. No reporters seek him out. People's minds are on the war, not the *Spray*.

Slowly, the extraordinary character of his feat sinks in. He writes an account of his adventures, which the *Century Illustrated Monthly* publishes in seven installments. Later, as a book, *Sailing Alone Around the World* is translated into six languages and becomes one of the classic stories of the sea.

But for Joshua Slocum, life begins to go slightly sour. There are no more seas to sail. With his earnings he buys a farm on Martha's Vineyard and plants fruit trees. But the years pass, and Slocum is running down, like a leaky schooner, his personality increasingly waspish, his appearance more and more slovenly, his sloop, once so trim and shipshape, filthier and filthier. He is withering away, an old salt clinging to the past.

At 65, he must have one more adventure. Together he and the *Spray* will penetrate the mysteries of the Amazon. He will sail his sloop to Venezuela, follow the Orinoco and the Rio Negro to the headwaters of the great river and then set his course downstream into the unknown sponge of the jungle.

November 14, 1909. Joshua Slocum sets sail from Vineyard Haven, Mass., driving the *Spray* into the very teeth of an easterly gale. The little sloop scuds along as always, white sails billowing in the wind, until she vanishes beyond the horizon. And that is the last that anyone sees of her. She and her master vanish without a trace. His ship—his faithful and sole companion—is with him to the end.

No. of Words: __2540__

Reading Time: _____

Selection 30

Joshua Slocum's Magnificent Voyage

VOCABULARY BUILDING

Below are several words used in this article. They are presented in the context of the sentences or phrases in which they occur. If you are unsure of their meanings and cannot define them from the context, look them up in the dictionary. Spaces are provided for additional unfamiliar words from the article to add to your vocabulary.

1. "And this is only a small part of a remarkable *odyssey*."

    *odyssey:*_____

2. "...one of the most experienced saltwater men of his age, but also an *anachronism*—a committed sailor in a world that has done with sail."

    *anachronism:*_____

3. "...he somehow guides the *Spray* through a foaming *labyrinth* of hidden rocks and tiny channels..."

    *labyrinth:*_____

4. "Three *lissome* women approach in a canoe."

    *lissome:*_____

5. "After an *idyllic* month in Samoa he sails for Australia..."

    *idyllic:*_____

6. "Slocum suffers the presence of the *ravenous* goat for nearly a thousand miles..."

    *ravenous:*_____

7. '...the U.S. battleship *Oregon*... hoists a puzzling signal... Slocum is *baffled*.

    *baffled:*_____

8. " . . . his personality increasingly *waspish*, his appearance more and more *slovenly* . . . "

*waspish:*_____

*slovenly:*_____

9. _____:_____

10. _____:_____

11. _____:_____

12. _____:_____

RETENTION AND COMPREHENSION

A. True/False (1 point each)

1. Slocum's favorite authors for onboard reading were Melville and Conrad.

   1. T _____ F _____

2. Slocum was 65 years old when he left for his trip around the world.

   2. T _____ F _____

3. When Slocum reached the end of his long voyage, he was greeted by cheering crowds and much publicity.

   3. T _____ F _____

4. At one point the newspapers reported Slocum as lost at sea.

   4. T _____ F _____

5. On Samoa Slocum met the famous writer of adventure stories, Robert Louis Stevenson.

   5. T _____ F _____

B. Completion (3 points each)

6. In August, 1883, in the East Indies, Slocum survived the explosion of _____.

   6. _____

7. Before his trip, Slocum was supporting himself by _____.

   7. _____

8. Once, Slocum discouraged a native boarding party by sprinkling his deck with _____.

   8. _____

9. Slocum's trip took him _____ years to complete.

   9. _____

10. With Virginia, his first wife, Slocum had_____
_____ children.

10. _____

C. Multiple Choice (2 points each)

11. Slocum's adventure takes place (a) in the 1890s, (b) in the 1940s, (c) only in the mind of the narrator, (d) in the 1780s.

11. _____

12. Leaving Yarmouth, Slocum started his trip by going (a) north to Greenland; (b) south and west, toward the Pacific; (c) east, across the Atlantic; (d) south and east, to South Africa.

12. _____

13. After his first successful ocean crossing, Slocum was warned to change his course because (a) there were gale warnings in his path, (b) there were pirates in the Red Sea, (c) his ship was not seaworthy, (d) the Spanish-American war was on.

13. _____

14. Virginia, his first wife, helped him put down a mutiny by (a) hitting the mutinous leader on the head from behind, (b) waking him just in time, (c) "covering" her husband with two guns, (d) warning him of the coming rebellion.

14. _____

15. The goat Slocum took on board (a) provided him with milk, (b) amused him with its antics, (c) ate his navigational charts, (d) provided him with companionship.

15. _____

16. Slocum was the first man (a) to sail around the world accompanied only by his wife, (b) to sail around the world with only a goat for company, (c) to use a small vessel to sail around the world, (d) to sail around the world unaccompanied.

16. _____

17. Slocum's vessel, the sloop *Spray,* was (a) specially built by a yacht designer, (b) an old vessel that Slocum had sailed with his wife, (c) an oyster boat that he bought for $553.62, (d) given to him by a friend.

17. _____

18. Slocum's adventurous life (a) ceased when he retired on a farm on Martha's Vineyard, (b) included one more successful trip to Venezuela, (c) was not

18. _____

publicly recognized until just recently, (d) ended
with his disappearance aboard the *Spray* at sea.

D. Thematic (11 points)

19. Which statement *best* expresses the theme (*main*
    idea) of the article?
    (a) Slocum sailed around the world to avoid living
        with his second wife.
    (b) Slocum's voyage was a remarkable feat.
    (c) Slocum was driven by a need to prove his sea-
        manship by sailing around the world.
    (d) Slocum, despite his sailing ability, took unnec-
        essary chances in accomplishing his voyage.

19. _____

E. Purpose (9 points)

20. The author's *chief* purpose is
    (a) to show why old sailors must continue to face
        the dangers of the sea.
    (b) to indicate that seamen of the past were tough-
        er than modern sailors.
    (c) to present the story of an amazing, but rela-
        tively unknown, true sailor.
    (d) to show that any man with enough motivation
        can sail around the world in a small boat.

20. _____

Total Retention and Comprehension Score: _____

QUESTIONS FOR DISCUSSION (MEANING AND TECHNIQUE)

1. What is "Antichrist"? Look it up. Why did the natives of the island of
   Rodrigues think Slocum was "Antichrist"?

2. What made Slocum want to sail around the world? Why wasn't he
   satisfied to stay where he was? Do you sometimes have similar feelings? What are they?

3. What do you think happened to Slocum at the end of the story?

4. How effective is it to tell the story as if it were an abridged journal?

5. The story is told in the "historical present." Look this up. What does it
   mean? Is it a good way to tell a story?

SUGGESTIONS FOR WRITING

1. Continue the narrative (story) of Joshua Slocum in the same diarylike style, using the "historical present," from the point at the end of the story where it says,

> *November 14, 1909.* Joshua Slocum sets sail from Vineyard Haven, Mass., driving the *Spray* into the very teeth of an easterly gale. The little sloop scuds along as always, white sails billowing in the wind, until she vanishes beyond the horizon.

2. Write an adventure story about yourself—or about someone else—in the style of this one.

3. Write about some small, exciting thing that actually happened to you—or that you make up, pretending it really did happen.

Selection 30

Overall Reading Performance

Your overall reading performance is a combination of how fast you read and how much you comprehend and retain. The chart below allows you to find out quickly your "overall reading performance."

First enter your "reading time" and your "retention and comprehension" score in the two blanks at the bottom of the page. Then simply lay a straightedge of any kind (the edge of a sheet of paper or a pencil will do) across the chart, placing the left side of the straightedge at the appropriate point on the "Reading Rate" scale, and the right side at the appropriate point on the "Retention and Comprehension" scale. The point at which the paper or pencil intersects the scale in the middle of the page will indicate your overall performance.

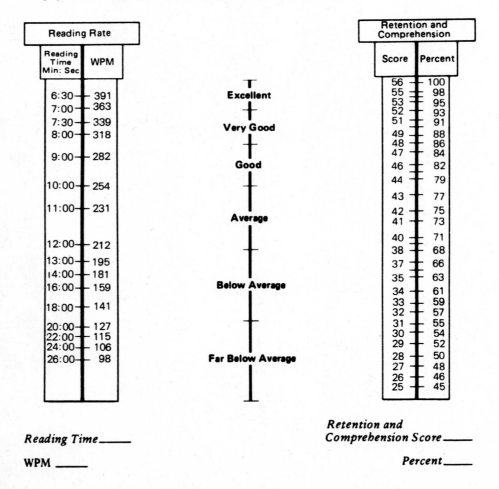

Reading Time_____

WPM _____

Retention and
Comprehension Score_____

Percent_____

Reading Rate Progress Chart

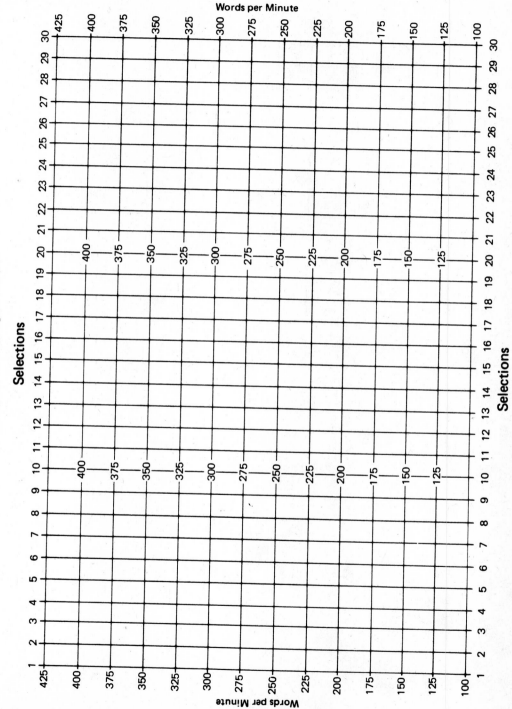

Retention and Comprehension Progress Chart

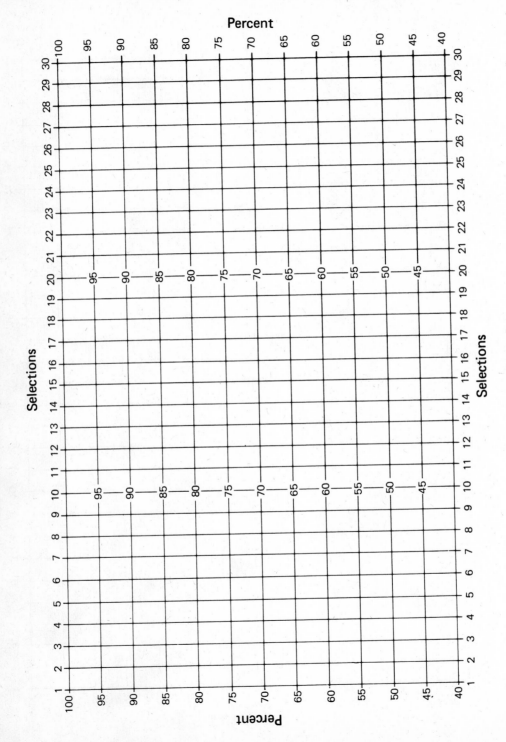

Overall Reading Performance Progress Chart

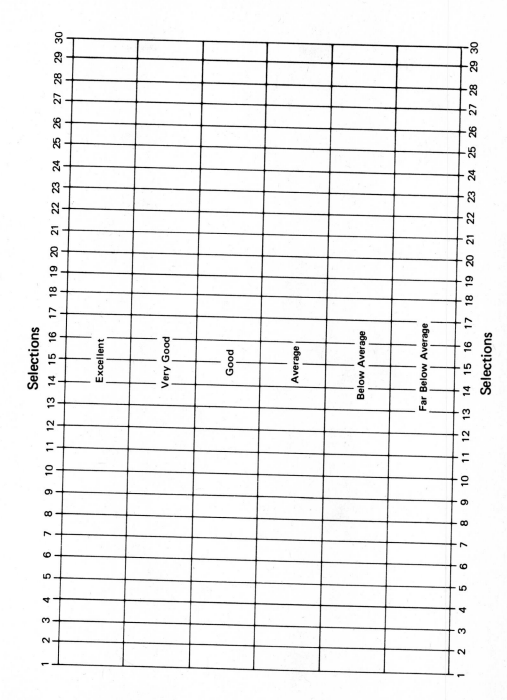

Vocabulary Index

The numbers following each word refer to the selection in which the word is introduced.